BENJAMIN FRANKLIN AND THE INVENTION OF MICROFINANCE

FINANCIAL HISTORY

Series Editor: Robert E. Wright

TITLES IN THIS SERIES

10 Financial Markets and the Banking Sector: Roles and Responsibilities in a Global World
Elisabeth Paulet (ed.)

11 Argentina's Parallel Currency: The Economy of the Poor
Georgina M. Gómez

12 The Rise and Fall of the American System: Nationalism and the Development of the American Economy, 1790–1837
Songho Ha

13 Convergence and Divergence of National Financial Systems: Evidence from the Gold Standards, 1871–1971
Patrice Baubeau and Anders Ögren (eds)

Forthcoming Titles

The Development of International Insurance
Robin Pearson (ed.)

Federal Banking in Brazil: Policies and Competitive Advantages
Kurt E. von Mettenheim

The Development of the Art Market in England: Money as Muse, 1730–1900
Thomas M. Bayer and John R. Page

Camille Gutt and Postwar International Finance
Jean F. Crombois

BENJAMIN FRANKLIN AND THE INVENTION OF MICROFINANCE

BY
Bruce H. Yenawine

EDITED BY
Michele R. Costello

Routledge
Taylor & Francis Group
LONDON AND NEW YORK

First published 2010 by Pickering & Chatto (Publishers) Limited

Published 2016 by Routledge
2 Park Square, Milton Park, Abingdon, Oxon OX14 4RN
711 Third Avenue, New York, NY 10017, USA

Routledge is an imprint of the Taylor & Francis Group, an informa business

British Library Cataloguing in Publication Data

Yenawine, Bruce H., 1949–
Benjamin Franklin and the invention of microfinance. – (Financial history)
1. Microfinance – United States – History. 2. Small business – United States
Finance – History. 3. Franklin, Benjamin, 1706–1790 – Will.
I. Title II. Series III. Costello, Michele.
332.7'0973-dc22

ISBN-13: 978-1-84893-034-6 (hbk)

Typeset by Pickering & Chatto (Publishers) Limited

CONTENTS

ACKNOWLEDGEMENTS

I am pleased to have the opportunity to acknowledge the intellectual contributions made to me during the course of my studies at the Maxwell School of Citizenship. I express my gratitude to Professors Stephen Saunders Webb, James Roger Sharp, David Bennett, Joseph Levine, Joan Burstyn and most especially, my dissertation director, Ralph Ketcham. Professor Ketcham, as a former editor of *The Papers of Benjamin Franklin*, helped guide my study of Franklin and, subtly, nudge me back on track from time to time. The History Department of the Maxwell School and the Graduate School of Syracuse University have provided me with financial support throughout my programme, without which my enrolment would have been impossible.

Peter Dobkin Hall, Bradford Gray and Yale University's Program on Nonprofit Organizations have provided support for my research by including me in an ambitious project supported by the Lilly Endowment, 'The Project on the Changing Dimensions of Trusteeship'. It is an unprecedented (in scale and scope) study of trusteeship and board governance involving many capable researchers. My examination of the Franklin Trusts is the only historical case study supported by the project. It is my hope that this comparative history of the trusts will illuminate the changing dimensions of trusteeship in the course of American philanthropy. I am appreciative of my designation as a research affiliate of Yale University allowing me access to the William Smith Mason collection of Franklin materials and to *The Papers of Benjamin Franklin* published by the Yale University Press, the supporting archive, and the expertise of their editors. I wish to acknowledge the assistance of the *Papers* editorial staff, Barbara Oberg, Claude-Anne Lopez, Ellen Cohn, Jonathan Dull and Kate Ohno and their collegiality.

The vast collection of Franklin manuscripts as well as the microfilm archive that supports *The Papers of Benjamin Franklin* co-published by American Philosophical Society, assisted me as an Andrew W. Mellon Research Fellow at the APS in Philadelphia. The single most important collection of the APS for my research was *Philadelphia, Dr. Franklin's Legacy*. These ledgers and account books of the Franklin Trust for the years 1791–1870 formed the base of the Philadelphia history. I give special thanks to Elizabeth Carroll-Hurrock, Martin

Leavitt, Roy Goodman and Whitfield Bell for their invaluable assistance and encouragement during my research trips to Philadelphia. David Weinberg and the archivists at Philadelphia City Archives were also most helpful.

I am very grateful to the Massachusetts Historical Society for awarding me an Andrew W. Mellow fellowship which supported my research expenses in Boston. My sincerest appreciation should be extended to the library staff, particularly Peter Drummey, Virginia Smith and Brenda Lawson for their enthusiastic and capable assistance. Their advice and guidance not only promoted more effective use of the MHS collections but also helped identify other Boston-based holdings which might provide additional support. This lack of scholastic chauvinism demonstrated a substantial interest in the success of my research wherever it led me, a quality of support not always forthcoming from research library administrators.

The MHS had a huge collection of un-catalogued manuscript material from the Minot family. I found in the MHS collection *William Minot's General Ledgers, Cash Receipts and Disbursement Journals*, a surprising discovery. The Minot financial records provide an unimpeachable primary source for documenting the relative successes and failures of the Franklin Fund's loan programme for married artisans.

Thank you to Phil Bergen at the Bostonian Society and to Roberta Zonghi at the Boston Public Library who provided important documents and several valuable research leads. The City of Boston Archives in Readville with the able administration of archivist Elizabeth Cousins and David Nathan located the indispensable early nineteenth century records of the Franklin Fund in Boston, having conducted a search for the veritable needle in the haystack.

I began my research in Boston at the Franklin Institute with the gracious assistance of President Richard D'Onofrio and faculty member, Alan Siegel. The Institute's records (mostly minutes, some correspondence and manuscript material) were excellent in documenting the progress of the Franklin Fund from 1908 (when the Franklin Union was founded) to the present. Alan Siegel's history, subsequently published as *Living Legacy: A History of the Franklin Institute of Boston*, is a most worthwhile piece of scholarship.

Finally, I dedicate the dissertation to my late father, Dr Wayne S. Yenawine, a gentle and wise academician, my late mother, Marjorie G. Yenawine, who pestered my father through his dissertation in 1956 and helped me in the same way, and to my two children, Heather and Philip, who adapted to the harsh winters of Syracuse with enthusiasm and joie de vivre. Most of all I dedicate this work to my wife, Neisja, whose love, trust and encouragement sustained me in my moments of doubt.

Bruce Yenawine

BIOGRAPHY

The late Bruce H. Yenawine was an Andrew W. Mellon Research Fellow at the American Philosophical Society in Philadelphia while authoring his dissertation entitled 'Benjamin Franklin's Legacy of Virtue: The Franklin Trusts of Boston and Philadelphia' from which this monograph was adapted. Prior to his death in 1997, Mr Yenawine had a distinguished career in academia and in philanthropic endeavours.

He served as Director of the Connecticut River Museum in Essex, CT from 1993–7. He was also a visiting faculty member in the Graduate Liberal Studies Program of Wesleyan University from 1995–7. He served as Dean of the Corcoran School of Art in Washington, DC from 1987–90. In Washington, Mr Yenawine served on the board of the DC Preservation League, the National Assembly for Visual Arts Education, and the Alliance of Independent Colleges of Art. While President of the Swain School of Design in New Bedford, MA from 1982–7, Mr Yenawine also served as President of the Southeastern Massachusetts Pop Orchestra, on the board of the New Bedford Glass Museum, on the Waterfront Historic Area League and as corporator of New Bedford Five Cents Savings Bank. Prior to that, he directed the Louisville School of Art from 1977–82.

From 1974–91, Mr Yenawine was very active on behalf of the National Association of Schools of Art and Design, having served in several capacities on the Board of Directors as well as the Commission on Accreditation. He was a very experienced accreditation visitor in higher education, having visited twenty-eight colleges and universities throughout his career.

Mr Yenawine received two to degrees from the University of Louisville: a Bachelor of Arts in English (1972) and a Master of Arts in Higher Education (1980). He also received a Master of Philosophy in History (1993) from Syracuse University. He was born in Urbana, IL on 30 December 1949.

INTRODUCTION

Benjamin Franklin and his Founding Father contemporaries sought to sustain the liberty of the young American nation through promotion of virtues such as 'thrift, industry, prudence, self-reliance, independence, and civic concern'.[1] Franklin exemplified such virtues in his own life, through his publications and through his efforts to manage debt, organize credit, and build capital. In this regard, he created self-sustaining trusts that would produce ever-increasing capital to be used by the industrious to live virtuously and improve the quality of their cities and communities.

Specifically, in 1789, Benjamin Franklin added a codicil to his last will and testament. He bequeathed £2,000 sterling ($4,444) to Boston and Philadelphia and to the commonwealths of Massachusetts and Pennsylvania with explicit instructions as to how they should utilize and dispose of the sum over the course of two hundred years. The Franklin codicil funds were intended for loans to young married artisans (the class of manual workers who performed skilled trades)[2] in order to help establish small businesses. In addition, when certain milestones were obtained, funds reverted to the cities of Boston and Philadelphia for public works.

While many loans were successfully made with the codicil funding, the managers of the Franklin Funds in both Boston and Philadelphia failed to continuously make loans to individuals as intended by Franklin for a variety of reasons. In this sense, they failed to continuously promote the value of industry as Franklin had envisioned. Courts were forced to intercede in order to command adherence to Franklin's original intent.

As a result of departures from Franklin's clear instructions regarding use of the funds over time, the trusts failed to generate the $36 million forecast by Franklin in the codicil. The 1991 combined value of the two Franklin Trusts was $6.5 million of compounded capital. The impressive growth of the original funding, despite departure from the codicil's instructions, successfully demonstrates the virtue of frugality in the way that Franklin had envisaged. However, the Franklin Funds did not inspire politicians and leaders to retire large public debts in the manner Franklin had hoped. In the words of the late Bruce Yenawine, '...

the nation is still struggling with the management of capital and the economic, social, and political consequences of large public debt. The promise and prosperity of a saving people and a saving nation remains elusive.'[3]

While the Franklin Funds touch on a wide universe of topics (politics, sinking funds, historical context, etc.), the programme also bears much in common with the contemporary microfinance and micro-lending movement. The term 'microfinance' refers to the provision of financial services (including credit products known as 'microloans', savings, insurance, fund transfers, and related services) to low-income clients who would not otherwise have access to financial services. Organizations that provide such services are referred to as microfinance institutions (MFIs) in the industry.

The modern microfinance movement gathered momentum in the 1960s and 70s through formation and growth of organizations such as Accion International, Opportunity International and Grameen Bank.[4] Microfinance was popularized when Grameen Bank and founder Muhammad Yunus were awarded the Nobel Peace Prize in 2006. 'Yunus is recognized as a visionary in a movement that has spread globally...', and his microfinance institutions are '... providing small loans without collateral, collecting deposits, and, increasingly selling insurance, all to customers who have been written off by commercial banks as being unprofitable...'[5] Typical microfinance clients include street vendors, service providers (hairdresser, rickshaw driver), artisans, blacksmiths and seamstresses.[6] In addition to financial services, many microfinance institutions provide '...social intermediation services such as group formation, development of self-confidence, and training in financial literacy and management capabilities among members of a group.'[7]

Loans made with the Franklin codicil funds can be considered 'microloans' in the broad sense because they provided capital to entrepreneurs who did not otherwise have access to the financial system. His programme targeted trained labourers, rather than the largely unskilled population targeted by modern microfinance, and therefore also bears resemblance to small or medium enterprise lending (sometimes referred to as the 'missing middle' in modern microfinance).[8] Franklin was truly a pioneer with regard to use of small loans as a poverty alleviation and economic advancement strategy.

He also took his mission a step further by proclaiming that such advancement of the economically disadvantaged was important to the success of democracy. As Yenawine states in the Conclusion of this monograph, '... artisans without access to financial capital would be an "empty bag" and nothing less than America's unprecedented aspirations to be politically and economically free hung in the balance ... Franklin offered the cities [of Boston and Philadelphia] a formula for building a strong democracy based on individual empowerment, broad enfranchisement and collective responsibility.' There has also been recent dialogue amongst microfinance industry practitioners with regard to the potential links between micro-loans and advancement of democracy. The Nobel Peace Prize awarded to Grameen Bank was partially predicated on the ability of micro-loans to sustain democracy and lasting peace through poverty alleviation.[9]

Themes raised in disbursement and monitoring of Franklin's 'micro-credit' programme are also relevant for practitioners today. The modern microfinance industry continues to grapple with issues such as appropriate interest rates, client risk evaluation and credit scoring in the absence of borrower credit history, collateral requirements, training or skill enhancement of borrowers, realization and measurement of desired social impact, and loan programme administration.

In the case of the codicil loans, predatory interest rate concerns were addressed by Franklin's clearly established fixed rate of 5 per cent. [10] Microfinance organizations formed in the last 30 years have dealt with interest rates in a divergent manner. One segment of the industry has steadfastly maintained that interest rates should be below market or "subsidized" relative to rates dictated by traditional risk management theory. Such microfinance groups are organized under a non-profit or philanthropic type of management profile (for example, Grameen Bank and BRAC). Yunus has been particularly vocal in his criticism of MFIs which charge relatively high rates, arguing that the industry should avoid charging rates greater than 15 per cent above long-term operating costs.[11] Other MFIs have adopted a market-based philosophy, whereby higher interest rates are charged to reflect the full risk of the programme and thereby generate a profitable MFI enterprise.[12] Examples include Compartamos[13] and SKS India.[14] Some MFIs are also constrained by government imposed interest rate ceilings in their countries. Franklin's programme shows both benefits and limitations caused by interest rate caps (at least in a micro-loan enterprise with a very focused mission and finite goals). The fixed rate made the loans interesting to borrowers, but also limited the return on funds to be redeployed in new loans. However, there is insufficient data to draw any broader conclusion. Furthermore, many modern microfinance institutions do not have fixed interest rate caps in order to reach poorer segment of the population (outside of Franklin's intent) while covering operating costs.

Stewards of the Franklin programme addressed lack of borrower credit history through the codicil's borrower screening criteria and guarantors to reduce repayment risk[15] (including age, gender, marital status, ability to obtain character witnesses, and apprenticeship training requirement to ensure relevant skills for entrepreneurial venture).[16] Contemporary microfinance institutions use similar screening criteria, such as gender, age, and number of family members, to achieve appropriate client selection in the absence of formal credit history.[17] Both Franklin codicil fund administrators and modern MFIs have achieved successful risk mitigation through appropriate screening criteria for clients.

The Franklin Funds also mitigated risk through collateral from guarantors.[18] However, the modern microfinance movement aims to enhance financial access by removing collateral requirements. In order to target the poor, most microloan programmes recognize that collateral is simply not feasible amongst borrowers. Instead, these organizations rely solely on appropriate borrower screening. In some cases, microfinance organizations also use cross-guarantor structures amongst groups of borrowers (called 'group' or 'solidarity' loans)[19] and education and support programmes to enhance the potential of loan repayment.

The Franklin programme did not offer skills enhancement or training as part of their loan programme, contrary to certain modern MFIs, due to the borrower requirement of acceptable apprenticeship or technical training. Today, some MFIs also require a baseline level of skills to access the programme as a way to enhance probability of a successful borrower experience and loan repayment.[20] For example, Fonkoze, a well known microfinance institution in Haiti, requires borrowers to graduate from basic literacy and assistance programmes before becoming eligible as potential borrowers.[21] In other cases, entrepreneurs can access training relevant to their venture. For example, Actuar of Columbia offers borrowers a screening and consultation program for their venture as well as ongoing support in the form of computer workshops or technical training.[22]

Regarding social impact, the Franklin codicil specified a very clear target cohort and desired social impact goals for the loans. Despite explicit instructions from the founder, the codicil loan programme suffered from 'mission drift', or deviation from its stated purpose, throughout the years. Microloan programmes today also grapple with 'mission drift.'[23] Some MFIs have drafted clear social impact goals and policies, such as Grameen's Sixteen Principles[24] and Progress out of Poverty Index,[25] to ensure consistent application of goals and mission. However, systematic enforcement and measurement of mission amongst MFIs remains elusive due to cost and infrastructure challenges. The Franklin Funds experience highlights the need for clearly outlined social impact goals and a mechanism for enforcement beyond the tenure of a visionary founder or leader.

In a related topic, the Franklin Funds experience also highlights concerns regarding administration of philanthropic loan funds which can be instructive for practitioners today. Deviation from Franklin's intent was exacerbated by the absence of a professional full time management team and by individual volunteers whose goals were not always aligned with the social mission of the fund. Examples include the temporary shift in fund usage to medical student loans[26] or to investments in the Massachusetts Hospital Life Insurance Company.[27] At the time, such investments were justified as a way to ensure safety of the funds or to address a need that was unforeseen by the founder. Such usages were clearly outside of the original mandate of the codicil and failed to generate Franklin's intended social impact. Modern MFIs with philanthropic funding also aim to keep overhead as low as possible in order to deploy maximum funding and social benefit to the target client audience. There is limited research on modern MFI staffing impact, but it is clear from observation that many MFIs rely on significant volunteer forces which can have a high turnover. Leadership positions amongst MFIs tend to be filled by visionary founders or are paid positions sought out by applicants who are committed to the vision and mission of the organization. In this way, issues of conflicting interests or departure from mission as seen in the Franklin funds are muted. As MFIs mature and original founders and leadership move on, we may begin to see some of the same problems faced in the Franklin Funds due to leadership with divergent visions or agendas for the microloan capital.

The topics mentioned are only a few of the interesting facets of the Franklin codicil legacy. Without fully realizing it, Franklin invented an idea that would come to fruition some two centuries later in the global microfinance movement. This monograph aims to trace the development of Franklin's important programme, which is absent from the existing scholarship. Both the significant achievements of the Franklin Funds and their shortcomings are explored, and key themes which remain relevant today are drawn out.

I am honoured as editor of the monograph to help bring this important body of work to the public forum, and thereby share the meaningful contribution Bruce Yenwaine made to the existing Franklin scholarship during his life. I would also like to thank organizations such as Women Advancing Microfinance (where I serve as a board member), the Microfinance Club of New York (member), Accion USA (member, microfinance council), the NYU Microfinance Initiative, the UN Year of Microfinance training programme and staff (2005 trainee), and professional contacts in the industry for developing my knowledge of microfinance and forwarding the mission of poverty alleviation through financial access.

As an administrative matter, please note that quotations are transcribed verbatim from the original manuscript. In addition, general historical background information and use of related material which is not specific to the codicil were retained from the original manuscript in this edited version of the monograph.

1 FRANKLIN'S INTENT: THE AUTOBIOGRAPHICAL ORIGINS OF THE CODICIL

In 1789, Benjamin Franklin added a codicil to his *Last Will and Testament*.[1] He bequeathed a total of £2,000 sterling to the cities of Boston and Philadelphia and to the Commonwealths of Massachusetts and Pennsylvania with explicit instructions as to how they should utilize and dispose of the sum over a span of 200 years. Conscious of the vicissitudes of human nature, Franklin anticipated problems in execution of these provisions: 'Considering the accidents to which all human Affairs and Projects are subject in such a length of Time, I have, perhaps, too much flattered myself with a vain Fancy, that these Dispositions, if carried into execution, will be continued without interruption and have the Effects proposed'.[2] Franklin's recognition that his testamentary instructions might not be honoured or remain effective, conveyed a quality of humility and vulnerability that he frequently feigned but rarely internalized.[3]

The Founding Fathers of America, including Franklin, held strong opinions about civic virtue forged by the trials and triumphs of their illustrious lives. They believed that good citizens, whether tradesmen in the cities or farmers in the country, exemplified such virtues as 'thrift, industry, prudence, self-reliance, independence, and civic concern'.[4] Franklin, however, stood alone in his extraordinary ability to personify and command public attention for these virtues. He utilized his extensive printing business and his literary skill to profoundly influence his generation. Franklin was not content with eminence in his own age. He expressly designed his codicil to actively promote his views on civic virtue for at least 200 years after his death in 1790. It has done so to some degree.[5]

The language of Franklin's codicil is clear and direct. Its terms are precise, and its provisions are carefully drawn. Throughout his life, Franklin advocated certain personal and societal paradigmatic virtues, especially industry and frugality. These virtues, he believed would produce an enlightened citizenry, the prerequisite for a vital republic. They also informed his personal code of conduct. In his 'Advice to a young Tradesman, written by an old One', Franklin says:

> In short the Way to Wealth, if you desire it, is as plain as the Way to Market. It depends on the two Words, INDUSTRY and FRUGALITY; i.e. Waste neither Time nor Money, but make the best Use of both.[6]

The attainment of wealth for Franklin was of little value unless it allowed the wealthy to serve a higher public purpose. Franklin had an instrumentalist view of property, i.e. he saw material gain as a means to an end. Moreover, Franklin believed that with citizenship came responsibility to improve living conditions and promote opportunities for gainful employment.[7]

Foreshadowing his codicil, in 1748, Franklin had advised: 'Remember that Money is of a prolific generating Nature. Money can beget Money, and its Offspring, can beget more, and so on'.[8] The ethos of thrift and the stewardship of money was consistently evident in Franklin's thoughts and actions throughout his life: in a callow youth's juvenilia,[9] in a contending young printer's work ethic,[10] in a recurrent theme in *Poor Richard's Almanack*,[11] and especially in advice in his essay 'Rules Proper to be Observed in Trade'.[12] The prescription within the codicil was Franklin's prophetic version of long considered opinion.

Franklin intended the codicil to his last will and testament to serve as a vehicle, delivering his beliefs to generations of Americans. He perpetuated the structure of his own success by institutionalizing the virtues of industry, frugality and the value of civic involvement. Franklin's scheme required the creation of two strategically designed philanthropic trusts whose executors and beneficiaries would be carefully constrained to fulfil his explicit instructions.

In the codicil, Franklin established these elaborate trusts in Boston and Philadelphia. Franklin described the purpose of the Boston Franklin Trust first. Later in the codicil Franklin placed the same constraints on the mangers of the Philadelphia based Franklin Trust with the instruction: 'All the directions herein given respecting the Disposition and Management of the Donation to the Inhabitants of Boston, I would observe respecting that to the Inhabitants of Philadelphia ...'[13] Franklin set forth his philanthropic purpose as follows:

> The said Sum of One thousand Pounds Sterling, if accepted by the Inhabitants of the Town of Boston, shall be managed under the direction of the Select Men, united with the Ministers of the oldest Episcopalian, Congregational, and Presbyterian Churches in that Town, who are to let out the same upon Interest at five per Cent per Annum to such young married Artificers, under the Age of twenty-five Years, as have served an Apprenticeship in the said Town; and faithfully fulfilled the Duties of their Indentures so as to obtain a good moral Character from at least two respectable Citizens, who are willing to become their Sureties, in a Bond with the Applicants, for the Repayment of moneys so lent, with Interest, according to the Terms herein after prescribed ... And as these Loans are intended to assist young married Artificers in settling up their Business ...[14]

The primary beneficiaries of the Franklin Trusts, between creation in 1790 and distributions in 1890 and 1990, were married artificers. In the codicil, the term 'artificers' was used synonymously with 'artisans'. Franklin used these terms to refer to a class of manual workers who practised skilled trades.[15] Other popular synonyms for 'artificer' used in the eighteenth and nineteenth century included craftsman, tradesman, mechanic or leather apron man. Although 'artificers' described a type of occupational group, it also referred to a middling class of citizens with social status inferior to the merchants, clergy and professionals but superior to the unskilled labourers, apprentices, slaves and servants. Skilled craftsmen, builders, small scale manufacturers and other producers were considered artificers.[16] Considering this variety of occupations, the artificers that Franklin sought to assist in the codicil constituted a large segment of the population. According to Boston and Philadelphia Inventories from 1685–1775, artificers (in the Retail Crafts, Building Crafts and Industrial Crafts occupational categories), represented 29 per cent and 38 per cent, respectively, of the urban populations. In the Philadelphia tax list of 1772, artificers in the same categories constituted 47 per cent of the population.[17]

The original principal of the bequest was to be loaned to married artificers who had completed their apprenticeships in amounts 'not to exceed Sixty Pounds Sterling to one Person'[18] and 'upon Interest at five per cent per Annum'.[19] Although the principal was to be loaned out, Franklin established additional restrictions that virtually assured the full repayment. He expected that the requirement of two prominent guarantors for each loan would prevent default and enable the trustees to return the appreciated principal (i.e. aggregated repaid principal with interest) to the corpus of the trust.[20] Having written a policy position regarding paper currency and its inflationary effects and having admonished Congress about the dangers of printing too much paper money,[21] Franklin also insulated the principal by requiring that the surety bonds were to be '...taken for Spanish milled Dollars, or the value thereof in current Gold Coin'. Ever the careful businessman, in his codicil, Franklin detailed the types of records that should be maintained and limited the maximum and minimum amounts of the individual loans. Perhaps fearing misapplication of the funds by misfeasance, he specified that the 'Managers shall keep a bound Book or Books wherein shall be entered the Names of those who shall apply for and receive the benefit of this Institution and of their sureties together with the Sums lent, the Dates, and other necessary and proper Records ...'[22]

Franklin planned a powerful demonstration of magnanimity made possible by the careful stewardship of money on the first centennial anniversary of the Franklin Trusts. He estimated that 'the Sum will then be one hundred and thirty-one thousand Pounds ...'[23] The enlarged principal after the first one hundred years was to be divided. A 3/13th portion was to be held in trust for another hundred years and loaned to married artisans on the same basis as it had been during the first term. The balance of principal, a 10/13th portion,[24] was to be distributed to two cities for civic improvements. The codicil describes this plan as follows:

> ... I would have the Managers of the Donation to the Town of Boston, then lay out at their discretion one hundred thousand Pounds in Public Works which may be judged of most general utility to the Inhabitants, such as Fortifications, Bridges, Aqueducts, Public Buildings, Baths, Pavements or whatever may make living in the Town more convenient to its People and render it more agreeable to Strangers, resorting thither for Health or a temporary residence. The remaining thirty-one thousand Pounds, I would have continued to be let out on Interest in the manner above directed for another hundred Years, as I hope it will have been found that the Institution has had a good effect on the conduct of Youth, and been of Service to many worthy Characters and useful Citizens.[25]

Embodied in this prescription is the essence of civic republicanism. Franklin believed that thrift and industry would yield profits which could and should be employed to improve the community and promote the good 'conduct of Youth' as well as help the 'worthy' and the 'useful'. Just as the collective good was served by the achievement and prosperity of each individual citizen, so also was each individual invigorated and supported by the benevolent spirit of the socially and politically engaged citizenry. Franklin was firmly committed to the marvellous reciprocity of rights and obligations.[26]

In the codicil Franklin explicitly provided for loans rather than gifts. By this method, he underscored the need for young citizens to establish credit and earn self reliance through timely repayment. The loans were to be provided to married artificers in establishing their own business. Franklin believed that marriage stabilized the young tradesman and contributed to sound business practices.[27] He wrote that:

> A Man does not act contrary to his Interest by Marrying; for I and Thousands more know very well that we could never thrive till we were married; and have known well ever since; What we get, the Women save; a Man being fixt in Life minds his business better and more steadily; and he that cannot thrive married, could never have throve better single; for the Idleness and Negligence of Men is more frequently fatal to Families, than the Extravagance of Women.[28]

Franklin also promoted young marriages for the sake of the country as well. In his essay on population growth, Franklin predicted rapidly expanding economic strength would result from the settlement of America's vast tracts of arable land.[29] Franklin's forecast of the population of America doubling every twenty years turned out to be very accurate.[30] The matrix of growth depended on early marriages and large families. Franklin also believed that urban artificers would be better served by young marriages while acknowledging the higher cost of living in the city. Early marriage was especially virtuous for urban dwellers as it would tend to discourage luxury, profligacy and undercut the demand for servile domestics.

Paralleling his own life, Franklin also thought that early marriage set up the proper chronology for a 'useful' life. He explains: 'Marriages are generally in the Morning of Life, our Children are therefore educated and settled in the World by Noon, and thus our Business being done, we have an Afternoon and Evening of cheerful Leisure to ourselves ...'[31] So convinced of the efficacy of marriage, Franklin states in the same letter 'An odd Volume of a Set of Books, you know is not worth its proportion of the set; and what think you of the Usefulness of an odd Half of a Pair of Scissors? It cannot well cut anything'.[32]

As for his own marriage, Franklin sustained a long partnership with his wife Deborah. For the first twenty-seven years of their marriage, Franklin's businesses thrived and his family grew in dynamic Philadelphia thanks in large measure to Deborah's careful stewardship and keen management ability.[33] Franklin described his soul mate, Deborah, in his autobiography as follows:

> ... it was lucky for me that I had [a wife] as much dispos'd to Industry & Frugality as my self. She assisted me chearfully in my Business, folding & stitching Pamphlets, tending shop, purchasing old Linen Rags for the Paper-makers, &c. &c.[34]

Women as wives constituted an important part of the formula for economic independence and consequently, marriage appears as a prerequisite in the language of the codicil.

Despite his reputation for infidelity, and, notwithstanding his florid and, on occasion, passionate love letters to other women, Franklin maintained the highest respect and gratitude for Deborah's dutiful affection. Although Franklin's correspondence with Deborah during his many years in England and France usually discussed practical matters, Franklin felt forever grateful to his wife for her assistance in maintaining his private affairs allowing him to lead a preeminent public life. Deborah's intellectual limitations, lack of sophistication and fear of travelling abroad prevented her from sharing more fully in her husband's extraordinary career.[35] After Deborah's death in 1774, he paid homage to his 'old and faithful Companion'.[36] As wives built the foundation for the success of artificers, so were artificers able to form the bedrock of urban character.

Franklin well understood the symbiotic relationship between the artisan class and the developing urban centres of America.[37] The codicil was constructed to reinforce their mutual interdependence. Franklin selected the leaders of the cities as trustees, demanding an active engagement with the industrious tradesmen within their community. The leadership's cooperation in executing Franklin's purposes was virtually assured; for, if they followed the instructions of the will, their cities would become beneficiaries of a considerable estate after decades of compounding interest. By appealing to the self interested side of government, Franklin exhibited a realistic view of human nature and the possibilities for short sighted actions. Franklin's Poor Richard said: 'He's a Fool that makes his doctor his Heir'.[38] It would seem to follow that it would be a wise man who would make his beneficiary his partner. Ever the wise man, Franklin established an economic incentive for proper stewardship. The codicil described Franklin's wishes for dissolution of the Franklin Trusts after the second period of one hundred years:

> At the end of this second Term, if no unfortunate accident has prevented the operation the Sum will be Four Millions and Sixty one Thousand Pounds Sterling; of which I leave one Million sixty one Thousand Pounds to the Disposition of the Inhabitants of the Town of Boston and Three Millions to the Disposition of the Government of the State, not presuming to carry my Views farther.[39]

Franklin, at last, left to his urban heirs a legacy to use at their discretion. Undoubtedly, he expected that the lessons taught over 200 years would impress upon his heirs in Boston and Philadelphia the value of thoughtful investment.

In the main 1788 *Last Will and Testament*, Franklin also bequeathed immediate legacies to both cities. To Boston, he left £100 Sterling to 'the free Grammar schools' for awarding Silver Medals 'for the encouragement of Scholarship'.[40] Franklin had attended the Boston Latin School, the first public school in America, which by the time of Franklin's bequest, had celebrated its sesquicentennial anniversary. In supporting the Boston public schools, Franklin joined the distinguished company of John Cotton, John Winthrop and Cotton Mather.[41]

To Philadelphia, Franklin bequeathed in the 1788 will £2,000 Sterling '... to be employed for making the River Schuylkill navigable'. Thomas Jefferson's mention of the Schuylkill River in correspondence may offer some insight into what might have motivated Franklin. According to Jefferson, with the construction of a bridge and the rendering of the Schuylkill River navigable: ' ... what a copious resource will be added, of wood and provisions, to warm and feed the poor of that city ...'[42] Franklin's intent to accomplish this engineering feat as expressed in 1788 will was abandoned in the subsequent codicil.[43]

These provisions of the main will, and still more those of the codicil, constitute Franklin's legacy of virtue. His testamentary vision is an extrapolation from his life experience; a transformation of an individual's code of conduct into economic imperatives in two urban polities. Franklin's personal developments in Boston and Philadelphia explains his loyalty to the two cities and his appreciation of apprenticeship and marriage. The struggle of artificers without financial resources to establish their own business and become 'useful' citizens was Franklin's own struggle.

Franklin was born in 1706 and lived for the first seventeen years of his life in Boston, the spiritual spring of New England Puritanism. Franklin was exposed to the Calvinist doctrine of 'the calling' which stressed above all 'diligence, moderation, sobriety, thrift'.[44] Franklin accepted the Puritan translation of these virtues, as espoused in the sermons of Boston religious elite and by the practice of his father, Josiah, into the language of business as prudence and industry. Franklin gave explicit credit to Cotton Mather and his *Essays to do Good* for having enlightened him as to the utility of charity and virtue.[45] As a result of their medieval inheritance and as a logical extension of their Puritanism, the people of Massachusetts Bay were imbued with a profound sense of community. In *Essays to Do Good* Mather urges that:

> ... You must accept of any public service, of which you are capable, when you are called to it ... The fault of not employing our talent for the public good is justly styled, "a great sacrilege in the Temple of the God of Nature". It was a sad age of which Tacitus said, "indolent retirement was wisdom".[46]

Mather, like most Boston intellectuals, did not place constraints on the potential of common citizens like Franklin to serve their community as they served God and themselves. Although Franklin was considered by his contemporaries to be a secular humanist, he respected the religious beliefs and intellectual abilities of many clergymen during his life. This respect is echoed in the selection of high ranking clergy in Boston as Trustees of the Franklin Trust created by the codicil. Although Franklin declined to profess a faith in the denominational sense, religious principles may have been a more substantial force in his life than even Franklin recognized. The Puritan faith of his father, Josiah, was profound and stabilizing for all members of the Franklin family.[47]

Benjamin Franklin first served as a child apprentice to his father, Josiah Franklin (1657–1745), a dyer and tallow chandler. At the age of twelve Benjamin was indentured to his brother James, who had established a small printing business in Boston. James Franklin (1697–1735) not only instructed young Benjamin in the technical aspects of printing but also gave him the opportunity to write the famous Mrs. Silence Dogood letters for their weekly newspaper, *The New England Courant*.[48] In Silence Dogood letter, No. 4, Benjamin, at the tender age of fourteen years, took on the Boston intelligentsia by satirizing Harvard College. Having fallen asleep after dinner, Silence Dogood dreamed of a 'Temple of LEARNING' with a throne that was attained only by an arduous effort. Mrs Dogood's dream unflatteringly characterized the students of the temple with the following: ' ... the work proving troublesome and difficult to most of them, they withdrew their Hands from the Plow and contended themselves to sit at the Foot, with Madam *Idleness* and her Maid *Ignorance*, until those who were assisted by Diligence and docile Temper, had nigh got up the first Step ...' Franklin, articulating the rational pragmatism that would become his hallmark, coupled idleness with ignorance and, conversely, knowledge with industry.[49]

Benjamin had already begun advocating the virtues that he would later reflect in the language of his codicil.

The trade of printing inextricably bound as it was with journalism provided young Benjamin more intellectual and political engagement than any other trade could have possibly provided. It was this combination of creative writing and reportage with the technical tasks of typesetting and press work that held Franklin's interests and nourished his intellect.[50] Franklin aggressively pursued his own personal education, purchased or borrowed from various collections and read not only Mather but Bunyan, Plutarch, Defoe, Addison, Locke and Xenophon.[51]

Although Franklin's apprenticeship followed the conventional indenture contract, his prodigious journalistic ability distinguished him from the usual artificer's apprentice. Franklin simply could not assume the conventional apprentice's role. Although obedience to the master was one of the terms of his indenture, relations with his brother were frequently acrimonious.[52] Benjamin was not the only person who found fault with James Franklin. From the earliest editions of the *Courant*, the content of the newspaper aggravated the formidable Cotton Mather.[53] James Franklin's anti-establishment editorial policy ultimately landed him in jail in 1722 and gave brother Benjamin the opportunity to act as temporary chief publisher.[54]

In order to answer the demands of the Governor's Council to shut down the newspaper, an alternative strategy to change management was proposed by James. Benjamin was to temporarily replace his brother as Publisher.[55] When James Franklin received the edict from the Assembly to suspend publication,[56] Benjamin recalled that:

> There was a Consultation held in our Printing House among his [James's] Friends, what he should do in this Case. Some propos'd to evade the Order by changing the Name of the Paper; but my Brother, seeing Inconveniences in that, it was finally concluded on as a better Way, to let it be printed for the future under the name of Benjamin Franklin. And to avoid the Censure of the Assembly, that might fall on him, as sill printing it by his Apprentice, the Contrivance was that my old Indenture should be return'd to me with a full Discharge on the Back of it, to be shown on Occasion, but to secure to him the Benefit of my Service I was to sign new Indentures for the Remainder of the Term, wch were to be kept private.[57]

The 'promotion' of Benjamin, and the consequent abbreviation of his indenture, was supposed to be a ploy. 'A very flimsy Scheme it was, however it was immediately executed, and the Paper went on accordingly, under my Name for several months'.[58] By publicly declaring the primary indenture satisfied, James unwittingly allowed Benjamin to escape his original contract fully four years short of the nine year term. Benjamin describes the denouement:

> At length a fresh Difference arising between my Brother and me, I took upon me to assert my Freedom, presuming that he would not venture to produce the new Indentures. It was not fair in me to take this Advantage, and this I therefore reckon one of the first Errata of my Life ...[59]

Franklin broke the apprenticeship rules for tradesmen. By both defying his father's wishes and injuring his brother's business, Franklin was guilty of an ethical lapse of considerable proportion. Franklin's agreement, later in life and as a successful printer, to accept his nephew, James Franklin Jr, as his own apprentice, was a way of making amends and reaffirming the traditional economic institutions and moral strictures on which he would put so much stress in his codicil.[60]Despite his own connivance to escape indenture, Franklin considered the practice of taking apprentices into his Philadelphia printing business desirable and assisted several of his kinsmen and the children of friends in obtaining indentures.[61] He sought to reinforce the vocational educational system by which children from the middling sort acquired a skill and concomitant vocation. The dual accomplishments of a fulfilled American apprenticeship indenture, i.e. learning a competence and becoming literate, were prerequisites to a gainful, virtuous and rewarding life. Apprenticeship was of particularly exaggerated importance in Franklin's age given the scarcity of skilled labour and the lack of public education in America. Not only was apprenticeship virtually the only way to entering a trade, it was a matter of civic responsibility for senior skilled labourers to pass on their knowledge to the younger generation. Economic necessity as well as the pride of handed down craft tradition sustained the system of apprenticeship. In the codicil, Franklin affirmed the apprenticeship system of the artificers. Prospective loans to artificers were contingent on successful completion of their indenture. He declared in the codicil:

> I have considered that among Artisans good Apprentices are most likely to make good Citizens; and having myself been bred to the Manual Art Printing, in my native Town, and afterwards assisted to set up my business in Philadelphia by kind Loan of Money from two Friends there, which was the foundation of my Fortune, and of all the utility in life that may be ascribed to me, I wish to be useful even after my Death, if possible, in forming and advancing other young men that may be serviceable to their Country in both those Towns.[62]

For Franklin the promotion from apprentice status to that of master craftsman and the opportunity to establish a new business was contingent upon his relocation from Boston to Philadelphia. James Franklin, angered by his brother's betrayal, successfully blocked his brother from working with any of the other Boston printers and forced him to move away.[63]

After several years of searching for employment opportunities in New York City and England, Franklin settled in Philadelphia in 1726, and with a partner,

Hugh Meredith, established his own printing press.[64] Franklin's calculated and public declaration of a work ethic is one of the earliest precedents for the language of the codicil: 'In order to secure my Credit and Character as a Tradesman, I took care not only to be in *Reality* Industrious & frugal, but to avoid all *Appearances* of the Contrary'.[65] When Franklin juxtaposed 'Credit and Character' he expressed for the tradesman the connection between access to the economic means to prosperity and the virtuous quality of the individual. The codicil links credit, character, industry and frugality.[66] The reference to the importance of 'appearances' also establishes Franklin's conception that leading citizens kept a look out for aspiring, hard-working youth and would reward those they recognized with greater opportunity.

The diligence with which he pursued his own printing business was only equalled by Franklin's energy as he searched for remedies to Philadelphia's urban problems. These problems were caused by shifts in trade, rapid population expansion, disease epidemics, currency depreciation and the intense concentration of ethnically diverse colonists.[67] Powerfully influenced by the idea of 'Friendly Societies', prominently featured in Defoe's *Essay on Projects*, and by the 'Young Men Associated', proposed in Mather's *Essays to do Good*, in 1727, Franklin eagerly organized a fraternity or academy of Philadelphia artificers who could help each other even as they improved the quality of urban life. Franklin and his fellow tradesmen or 'Leather Apron Men' called their club: 'The Junto'.[68]

Franklin and the young men of the Junto utilized volunteer organizations, new scientific inventions, and improved management systems to promote better health care, roads, fire protection, insurance, education, law enforcement and sanitation for the people of Philadelphia. The codicil's references to 'worthy Characters and useful Citizens' and to the 'young men that may be serviceable to their Country'[69] are Franklin's idealization of the class of artisans which created, powered and profited from these civic benevolent societies and of the Junto, in particular.

The mutual assistance aspect of the Junto took on personal and pecuniary meaning for Franklin in 1728 when Robert Grace and William Coleman, original founding members of the Junto, loaned Franklin the money to buy out his partner and become the sole proprietor.[70] Robert Grace (1709–79) practised the trade of iron casting and, later, assisted by Franklin's gift of the iron stove design, was the proprietor of the Warwick Iron Works.[71] William Coleman (1704–69) was a young Philadelphia businessman and one of the first of the class of leather apron men to enter political life. He served as 'common councilor, clerk of the city court, justice of the peace, and, in 1758, a justice of the Supreme Court'.[72] Franklin's warm reference in the codicil, was to these generous loans from his fellow tradesmen, Grace and Coleman.

The significant accomplishments of Junto reinforced Franklin's native belief in the virtue of civic stewardship and leadership regardless of social station or wealth. He expected that, by increasing their involvement in the affairs of the cities, the artificers would help politically shape the new governments of the United States.[73] Franklin presided over the 1776 Pennsylvania Constitutional Convention which developed a document that was considered 'ultra-democratic' and eliminated all property holding prerequisites for election to public office.[74] Certainly in Philadelphia the class of artisans was ultimately very successful in achieving political prominence.[75] Unlike most men who became politicians in or diplomats from the United States in the second half of the eighteenth century, Franklin did not come from the landed gentry or the professional classes. Franklin inherited no property and became a freeholder through his success as a printer. He had no formal education beyond 'not quite one Year' at the Boston Latin School.[76] Yet he became one of the most influential writers and creative scientists of the age by taking advantage of association and intellectual camaraderie that he institutionalized in the Junto. His pride in being a self-made man is reflected in the language of the codicil:

> It has been an opinion that he who receives an Estate from his Ancestors, is under some kind of obligation to transmit the same to their Posterity: This obligation does not lie on me, who never inherited a Shilling from any Ancestor or Relation ...[77]

He demonstrated that a tradesman can achieve the status of freeholder and substantially improve his economic, social and political status. With the high demand for skilled labour in Franklin's Philadelphia, artisans were economically successful, politically powerful and fully employed.[78] In Boston and, particularly, in Philadelphia, the American Revolution was powered by the political perspective, organization and fighting force of urban artisans.

The relationship between the ambitious middling artisans class and the progress of the cities was expressed in the codicil's designation of the two city governments as agents for the Franklin Trusts. In the codicil, Franklin sought to involve the Boston Selectmen and the local religious leadership[79] as stewards of his plan to assist artisans:

> And it is presumed that there will always be found in Boston virtuous and benevolent Citizens, willing to bestow a part of their Time in doing good to the rising Generation by Superintending and managing this Institution gratis, it is hoped that no part of the Money will at any time lie dead or be diverted to other purposes, but be continually augmenting by the Interest ...[80]

This instruction accomplished two things. First, it kept the major leaders of the city continually aware of the needs of the artificers. Presumably the activity of reviewing the qualifications of applicants for the loan would continuously inform the Selectmen and the religious leaders of the economic status of the artisan class and serve to introduce 'the young married Artificers' to the politically powerful whom they might someday join. Second, the Franklin Trusts also avoided high administrative overhead costs by utilizing the free service of the trustees pro bono publico. To Franklin, the privilege of success was the ability to serve mankind and he expected that of other prosperous citizens.

The virtue of utility, reflected in Franklin's earliest utterances and his last testament, was to him the predominant American ethic. In his essay entitled 'Information to Those Who Would Remove to America', Franklin described the circumstances that any immigrant would encounter in America:

> ... people do not inquire concerning a Stranger, "What is he?" but "What can he do?" If he has any useful Art, he is welcome; and if he exercises it and behaves well, he will be respected by all that who him ...[81]

A competence in life could be earned by diligence and useful industry and would form the foundation for prosperity measured by material gain, virtuous action and social esteem.

Franklin had unshakable faith in the faculty of human rationality and the ability of fair-minded and hard working men to squarely face the trials of their lives and times and devise inventive, effective and compassionate responses. Franklin was less concerned with the miscarriages and mistakes of the majority, believing that the poor, short sighted and self interested actions of government, which were inevitable no matter how the government was structured, could usually be corrected by reflection, compromise, and subsequent reversing actions. Two years before writing the codicil's provisions for municipal government management of his two trusts, Franklin expressed his belief in the wisdom of representative government (despite its bicameral legislature) with all of its frailty while supporting the proposed 1787 US Constitution:

> In these sentiments, Sir, I agree to this Constitution with all its faults, if they are such; because I think a general Government necessary for us, and there is no form of Government but what may be a blessing to the people if well administered ... I doubt too whether any other Convention we can obtain, may be able to make a better Constitution. For when you assemble a number of men to have the advantage of their joint wisdom, you inevitably assemble with those men, all their prejudices, their passions, their errors of opinions, their local interest, and their selfish views. From such an assembly can a perfect production be expected? ... Thus I consent, Sir, to this Constitution because I expect no better, and because I am not sure, that it is not the best.[82]

Franklin was comfortable with the foibles as well as accomplishments of republican government. His extensive experience of watching governments operating at all levels (local councils to world empires), gave him a unique perspective. He believed that the risks of faction associated with active consent of the governed and broad citizen engagement were not so destructive as to be avoided. Franklin, as reflected in his codicil, sought to cultivate a benevolent citizenry, capable of disagreement and consensus. Government based on pragmatic economic principles and the informed consent of the governed would make possible liberty for all.

Franklin wrote a plethora of essays, short stories and epistles that articulated his philosophy. Most noteworthy, *Poor Richard's Almanack* shaped the thinking of many economists and social thinkers in America and abroad. French economists in their enthusiasm for the moral teachings of *Poor Richard's Almanack* recommended that it be used as a primer in the schools. Franklin's almanac was so popular that it was frequently imitated.[83]

A French economist, Charles Joseph Mathon de la Cour, reacting to the significant impact and popularity of *Poor Richard's Almanack* in France, was inspired to write a derivative work in 1785, entitled *Téstament de Fortuné Ricard, maître d'arithmétique à D*** (hereafter referred to as *Téstament*). Mathon's creation had special significance for the conception of Franklin's codicil.[84] With a curious circularity of ideas common to Franklin's intellectual milieu, Franklin attributed the concept of the 200 year trust to Mathon de la Cour in a letter dated 18 November 1785.[85] Given this exchange, it is difficult to discern original sources and inspirations.

Insofar as the *Téstament*, written in the style of a fantasy, was the acknowledged model, Franklin's codicil might also be considered an implausible dream or a sophisticated mathematical parlour game. Franklin even admitted that the idea advanced in the codicil might be regarded as a 'vain Fancy'.[86] However, taken at its face value, the will and the codicil reflect the ordinary expressions of gratitude of an extraordinary man who hoped that some part of his wealth would continue to contribute to society. The language of the codicil implies the modest side of Franklin expectations:

> I hope however that if the Inhabitants of the two Cities should not think fit to undertake the execution, they will at least accept the offer of these Donations, as a Mark of my good-Will, a token of my Gratitude, Testimony of my earnest desire to be useful to them even after my departure.[87]

As if, while writing this sentiment, Franklin became suddenly aware that he might have left too much opportunity for the abrogation of the codicil's terms, he added:

> I wish indeed that they [Cities of Boston and Philadelphia] both undertake to endeavour the Execution of the Project: because I think that tho' unforeseen Difficulties may arise, expedients will be found to remove them, and the Scheme be found practicable ...[88]

This passage demanded due diligence and a sustained systematic effort to execute the project. Franklin was prudent to offer this admonition, given the vulnerability of philanthropic trusts of the seventeenth and eighteenth century.

Throughout the history of testamentary trusts in British and American common law, the testators' intent had been frequently compromised by inept, inefficient or corrupt management.[89] Franklin's use of responsible public officials as managers of the trusts was clever and provident. The early laws that governed charitable trusts varied from colony to colony and laws of Massachusetts were substantially different from Pennsylvania's, but vesting the Franklin Trusts with the City of Boston and the City of Philadelphia as agents rendered the will and codicil less vulnerable to legal challenge or abridgement by constructing a complex network of interested heirs. Such a system of bulwarks also tended to ward off court challenges under the *cy pres* doctrine.[90] The use of the municipalities as trustees not only stabilized the administration of his trusts, but more importantly, it kept the Franklin Trust Funds before the public.[91] According to an 1881 history of Boston, Franklin's gift created the largest municipal charitable trust to date.[92] Public notice meant that the Franklin Trust, as it benefited by the significant effect of compounding interest, would be disposed of only after a review of his intent.

His purpose in drafting the codicil is clear. In perpetuity, or at least for two centuries, Franklin sought to promote the economic strength of the artisan class and support its economic partnership with the two American cities he considered homes. The codicil is a recipe specifying the following ingredients: self help, social and political mobility through interdependence, good will, urban civic benevolence and creative economic planning and thrift. The work of the two Franklin Trusts would promote an industrious, intelligent, humane and inspired society through the conservation of economic resources and careful investment in working class people and public works. This picture of the future directly reflected Franklin's philosophy and his life. It was his formula for success and his concept of purpose.

Benjamin Franklin far surpassed the customary limits of his middling-class background during his lifetime. Not unexpectedly, he was not content to accept the customary limits of his own mortality. A student of irony and master of wit, Franklin would write six months after preparing his highly prescriptive *Last Will and Testament with Codicil*: 'In this world nothing can be said to be certain, except death and taxes'.[93]

2 FRANKLIN'S INTENT: THE SOURCES OF POLITICAL AND ECONOMIC CONCEPTS

Beyond the explicit instructions in the words of the 1789 codicil, the broader intent of Franklin's testamentary trusts can be determined from his correspondence, especially in the years 1783 through 1787, and in his lifelong consideration of economic theory and governmental monetary policy. Franklin's writings, while addressing narrow technical points, inextricably bind the consideration of money with issues of prosperity, morality, political independence and civil order. Influenced by English mathematician Sir William Petty (1623–1687), mathematician and philosopher Richard Price (1723–91), French Controller-General of Finance Anne Robert Jacques Turgot (1727–81), Director of the Treasury Jacques Necker (1732–1804) and mathematician/philanthropist Mathon de la Cour (1738–93), Franklin assimilated the currency of eighteenth-century European ideas and, then, synthesized them for application in the emergent United States of America. Several of these same figures, along with Franklin, provided the inspiration for Alexander Hamilton, the first great American finance minister and Secretary of the Treasury under President Washington, as Hamilton organized America's war debts and established the first national system of banking and controlled currency.[1]

General themes and specific features of Franklin's 1789 plan for the two municipal trusts in Boston and Philadelphia, i.e., (1) the ethos of saving and the specific phenomenon of the sinking fund,[2] (2) the industrious (as individual and as nation) and their need for working capital, (3) the value of labour and the basis for national credit and currency, (4) the concept of loans to individuals to stimulate the growth of business enterprise, (5) the length of the term of loans and the repayment plan, (6) the interest rate for the loans and the consequent rate of compounding principal with interest, are variations on ideas Franklin explored with his contemporaries. The trust scheme laid out in the 1789 codicil follows the same Franklin recipe for progress and prosperity that he designed for the new nation, based on his study of colonial American, English and French government.

Franklin lived in France from 1778 until 1785 as the Minister Plenipotentiary of the United States. His primary diplomatic mission was to convince the French to provide covert financial and military aid to help America win its independence. After the astounding American victory in the Battle of Saratoga in 1777, Franklin was able to secure direct and overt assistance from the government of Louis XVI and what remained of the *Ancien Regime*.[3] It was Franklin's growing rapport with Robert Gravier, Comte de Vergennes, wily Minister of Foreign Affairs, and chief French political strategist, that made possible the Franco-American alliance. Although this diplomatic alliance was of great international importance, Vergennes's judicious restraint prevented him from warmly embracing the intellectually ubiquitous and socially lionized Franklin. Their cautious and formal compatriotism and their subtle and reserved diplomacy facilitated the torturously complex negotiation that enabled the Americans to finance the war and maintained the delicate balance of power between the French and the English.[4]

It was Turgot, Controller-General of France from 1774 to 1776, capable economist and humanist, who most influenced Franklin's thinking and who openly admired Franklin for his potential and scientific contributions.[5] Turgot, in 1777 wrote a treatise on Physiocratic philosophy entitled *Memoire sur l'impôt*, considered one of the best articulations of this school's tenets of belief, expressly for Franklin's use.[6] Franklin, as reflected in his codicil, shared with Turgot a concern for cultivating a benevolent citizenry and good government for the people based on conservative economic principles. Ironically, Turgot was the most vociferous critic of the French loans to help fund the American Revolution, based on the exacerbating effect on the large French debt.[7] However, the appeal of Turgot's conservative economic policies for Franklin can be easily seen:

> No bankruptcy; no increase of impositions; no borrowing ... There is only one way of fulfilling these three aims: that of reducing expenditure below receipts, and sufficiently below to ensure each year a saving of twenty millions (*livres*) with a view to the redemption of long-standing debts. Failing this, the first gunshot will drive the State to bankruptcy.[8]

Reciprocally, the simple virtues of Poor Richard found resonance in Turgot's prescription for an economically distressed France. Turgot was the first of the French physiocrats to see in the author of *Poor Richard's Almanack*, a kindred spirit.

While Turgot imposed strict economics on France's overblown finances, he also was a keen observer of the progress of American independence. In a letter to Richard Price in 1778, Turgot expressed his concerns that even if a military victory over Britain were achieved, the American colonies could not overcome their sectional interests and idiosyncratic ways and form a just and equitable nation.

Despite his reservation about America's fractious character, he recognized the potential for political and social innovation and renovation, not likely in inveterate European systems of government.[9]

In 1784, as Benjamin Franklin and his contemporaries on both sides of the Atlantic Ocean considered what to do about the huge war debts that threatened the economic and political stability of Great Britain, France and the United States, a number of letters passed to and from Franklin that reveal his thoughts on the redemption of national debt as well as fascination with public credit, sinking funds and the power of compounded savings. The most important exchange was between Richard Price, the eminent English intellectual, and Franklin. The letters reveal a shared interest in political freedom and representative government, 'political arithmetic' - which is the mathematical analysis of national economies (particularly the calculation of the interest on debt), and the development of systems of credit and debt that promote international peace, free trade and domestic prosperity. Many of the features found in Franklin's 1789 codicil can be traced to this exchange of ideas and theories.

Price, in his successful effort to influence William Pitt's financial reforms and British policy, and Franklin, in his effort to encourage the American Congress and the American people to honour and discharge war debt, sought to present their ideas to the general public. They both utilized widely distributed/reprinted pamphlets, broadsides and treatises to share their views. For Franklin and Price, political liberty and economic independence were inextricably bound together. Considered a matter of moral obligation and national virtuousness, Franklin in 1787 said 'that our independence is not quite complete, till we have discharged our public debt ...'[10] and that '... only a virtuous people are capable of freedom'.[11] Likewise according to Franklin's plan, a frugal and industrious citizenry in Boston and Philadelphia worthy of political freedom and economic prosperity would be assisted by the Franklin Trusts which compounded capital available to launch many young artisans in new independent business.

Franklin enthusiastically welcomed the publication of Price's pamphlet *The Importance of the American Revolution* in 1785.[12] While expressing the importance of the American Revolution to other nations, particularly his fellow British countrymen, Price emphatically described the problem of American war debt and suggested an especially designated fund to retire the debt.[13] At this time the credibility of the American nation depended upon its credibility, i.e. its ability to create a dependable and expandable currency, honour its foreign and domestic debt, support economic expansion, defend itself and establish a sufficient and politically sustainable base of taxation and other revenue production. The creation of an energetic national government capable of taxing its people, enforcing its decisions, and directing economic growth through a national banking system and an expandable currency was required, in Price's view, as it simultaneously occurred to Robert Morris and Alexander Hamilton, the principal authors of America's financial system.

As a result of having served the disparate colonial interests of Pennsylvania, Massachusetts and Georgia, as European agent before the Revolution, Franklin recognized that America required a strong central national government to restrain the divisive and particular interests of states and regions. Well before American independence, Franklin had been the first advocate of an American intercolonial organization with the Albany Plan of Union in 1754 and an early champion of a single, strong centralized government.[14] He joined Price in acknowledging that American independence would not only depend on a successful military triumph but on an economic revolution which severed America from the retarding effect of British colonialism and mercantilism and established a laissez faire international trade climate from which American's natural agricultural, demographic and maritime advantages could promote prosperity. Franklin also thought that inventions in government and disciplined financial management which he referred to as frugality and industry would also be required. Franklin's economic policies, articulated in essays and correspondences, were inspired by his long experience in public life as well as a comradeship with Price and other financial experts in France, England and America.

Franklin had written about the critical need for capital to expand the economy and the nature of interest as early as 1729 in his pamphlet, 'The Nature and Necessity of a Paper-Currency'.[15] Drawing heavily on the economic theory of Sir William Petty, Franklin made the case for a paper currency necessary to provide sufficient money supply to enable growth in foreign and domestic trade. Franklin wrote the pamphlet in order to build popular support for legislation that authorized Pennsylvania to issue £30,000 in new bills of credit, similar to two currency acts passed by the Assembly in 1723, to provide loans to private individuals, collateralized by mortgages on property, at 5 per cent interest for sixteen years. Governor Gordon of Pennsylvania recommended a ten year term rather than the sixteen years approved by the Assembly. The loans to private individuals for development of their business over a ten year term for repayment and at 5 per cent interest established the exact pattern that Franklin used in his 1789 codicil.

The purpose of the loans was to provide capital required by industrious American settlers who sought to develop their communities or expand their farms. The structure and intent of this 1723 Pennsylvania initiative was similar to those prescribed in Franklin's 1789 codicil. In this pamphlet, Franklin first articulated a life-long held view that want of capital thwarts economic growth, daunts the human spirit and promotes idleness, indolence, waste and prodigality. Contrarily, access to capital for people who work in earnest as artisans or farmers allows them to sustain their family and produce surplus goods to trade in the market. Integrity and independence are the fruits of labour combined with sufficient capital.

Also in this pamphlet, Franklin made the point that land security is the most reliable form of security in a country with expanding population. He recommended a currency system that stands on the security of land because he believed that land value was less volatile than money security. Without a natural source of specie, gold and silver, colonial America could not base its currency and its economic system on precious metals with intrinsic value. Land (valued by Franklin on the basis of the value of labour to make it productive) was the next best thing to secure the money supply.

However, Franklin must have reconsidered the stability of land value as security for loans to private individuals between 1729 and 1789 when he specified the terms of the Franklin legacy. In the codicil Franklin required that each artificer produce two sureties that would post bond in 'Spanish milled gold'. Franklin's emphasis on personal sureties and gold rather than physical equity may have been the result of his recognition that the urban artificer frequently had little or no land. If they were fortunate, artificers had acquired tools and equipment that gave them a means of living, social standing and the political franchise. However, tools were insufficient equity to secure business loans borrowed over a ten year period.

Given the endless debate during the nineteenth century, after Franklin's death, over the best base for the money supply, the old standard, bimetallism or promissory paper currency, it is not surprising that the Trustees of the Franklin Funds in Boston and Philadelphia ran into trouble with requirement of gold backed sureties for the loans of the artificers. In fact, the Philadelphia Franklin Fund managers claimed that by 1837 the loans had become unpopular, in part, because artificers could not secure the necessary sureties willing to guarantee with gold.[16] Eight years earlier the City Council passed a resolution that allowed 'one of the sureties in each bond for the said loans shall be the owner of real estate situate in the city or county of Philadelphia, sufficient to secure the payment of the principal and interest of such loan'.[17] With a *cy pres* adjustment of the Orphans' Court in 1917, Philadelphia's Board of City Trusts started accepting first mortgages on real estate as sufficient security for the Franklin loans. It seems that the managers of the Philadelphia Franklin Funds, while departing from Franklin's 1789 instructions, completed the thought cycle when it returned to wisdom of Franklin's 1729 belief that, in America, property was the most available and reliable security.

In the aftermath of the Restraining Act of 1764, Franklin, with former Massachusetts Bay Colonial Governor and Member of Parliament, Thomas Pownall, proposed to the King in Parliament a system to expand the colonial currency that resembled the earlier currency plan in colonial Pennsylvania. Pownall issued this plan in a slightly altered version, as a pamphlet in 1768 entitled *The Administration of the Colonies*. The plan called for the issuance in each colony through a colonial loan-office of legal tender notes loaned for ten years with an interest rate of 5 per cent with a year's interest and 1/10th of the principal due annually (the exact format for the Franklin Trust loans.) The interest generated from the loans were paid to the Crown in lieu of the tax revenue. As Franklin explained 'It will operate as a General Tax on the Colonies, and yet not an unpleasing one; as he who *actually* pays the Interest has an Equivalent or more in the use of the principal'.[18] The plan thus served as a source for revenue while providing a more adequate supply of money to foster colonial economic growth, avoiding the regressive effects of the Stamp Act.[19] Variations of this basic plan were submitted in 1764, 1765 and 1766 before the effort was abandoned by Franklin and Pownall.

In his analysis of the design and actual experience of Pennsylvania regarding authorization of paper money in the 1720s, Franklin utilized language and concepts of accountability that he would repeat in the 1789 codicil.[20] For Franklin, the idea of re-loaning the repaid principal and interest in loans to 'fresh borrowers' conjured up an impressive magnification effect. The purpose of both the public currency plan of colonial Pennsylvania and Franklin's 1789 trust plan was to create a pool of funds that would cycle through many worthy citizens. Industry would beget industry, new citizens would be able to build on the accomplishment of other citizens. As a recent historian put it, Franklin's design was predicted on 'the mobilization of mutuality'.[21]

Franklin also cites the dual purpose of the currency scheme as serving to provide income for 'public services'. The codicil plan required a compounding period before any funds could be used for 'public works'. Both plans call for money to act as catalytic in stimulation of the private sector, i.e. private individuals, while serving the public good. Franklin saw these interests as ones that could be served simultaneously and with synergistic effect. While Franklin acknowledged the power of enlightened self interest as a motivation for industry, the true test of progress and the merit of civilization was the degree to which the broad public interest was ultimately served.[22]

In the 1765 proposed colonial currency plan, Franklin drew out in some detail the management of the loan offices which required the creation of Trustees in each colony who maintained the integrity of the loan funds. The Trustees of the loan offices (freeholders appointed by the act of the Assembly) were to maintain a book of applications, book of allowances and day book which recorded the particulars of individual loans, especially the details of the borrower's surety, the amounts loaned, the payments received and calculation of interest and principal. These instructions are similar to the management provisions in the 1789 codicil.[23]

It should not be overlooked that Franklin subscribed to the view that the basis of all value in society is labour. Franklin again turned to Sir William Petty's *A Treatise of Taxes and Contributions* (1662) as a source for his economic views. In wording paraphrased from Petty's, Franklin explains:

> By Labour may the value of Silver be measured as well as other things. As, Suppose one Man employed to raise Corn, while another is digging and refining Silver; at Year's End, or at any other Period of Time, the compleat Produce of Corn, and that of Silver are the natural Price of each other; and if one be twenty Bushels, and the other twenty Ounces, then an Ounce of that Silver is worth the Labour of raising a Bushel of that Corn.[24]

The implications of Franklin's views in 1729 can be seen no only in the specific grounding of the currency on America's rich resource of arable land, but in the fundamental notion that the value of land, and thus the ultimate basis of the economy, is the industriousness of the people, i.e. their productivity. The expansion of the collective value of America would derive from its population growth and its vast lands available for settlement. At the heart of national strength and vitality is the productive man. As Franklin says in *Information to Those Who Would Remove to America* in 1784, in America 'People do not enquire concerning a Stranger, *What is he?* but *What can he DO?*'[25] Unlike the physiocrats, Franklin did not devalue the labour of the artificer while he acknowledged the value of the farmer. All industrious settlers contributed to the prosperity of America.

Franklin, not surprisingly, believed that, although America and Americans lacked specie, and thus credit, they had a corpus of virtuous citizens, who working together and assisting each other, could stimulate growth and increase prosperity. Notwithstanding the requirement of gold bond, from the 1729 pamphlet to the 1789 codicil, Franklin adjusted his proscription for the basis of credit from 'coined land' to the strength and benevolence of its virtuous citizenry.

Poor Richard's Almanack also expressed much of Franklin's optimism about the sturdy and virtuous American. Attesting to the popularity of its message, the almanac was seriously considered by French intellectuals (notably French Physiocrat, Dupont de Nemours and the Abbé Morellet) for use as a grade school primer with the right mix of practical advice and moral instruction.[26] Franklin, in turn, reacted to the French responses to his work. In his 1789 codicil, Franklin copied the idea of creating a public trust that was constructed upon the notion of one hundred year terms from a French economist named Charles Joseph Mathon de la Cour.

Mathon de la Cour (1738–93) was a native of Lyons, resident of Paris, and a second generation mathematician.[27] Known for his philanthropy as well as his writing about French economic conditions, Mathon bridged the worlds of the *American Regime* and the Enlightenment. Clearly caught up in the intellectual stirrings that resulted in the French Revolution, Mathon wrote on political matters in *Discours sur les meilleurs moyens de faire naître et d'encourager le patriotisme dans une monarchie* (1787), an essay that Franklin read (apparently in pre-publication draft form) and felt 'must have a great effect on the minds of both princes and people'.[28] In this work Mathon explored the themes of political and economic independence that were part of the currency of the times while dancing around the edge of Louis XVI's absolute monarchy. Mathon, in his writings, commented on the value of compounded savings, benevolent government, peace and domestic abundance contrasted with vain despotism, corrupt bureaucracies operating the church and court, large national debts, world wars, famine and oppressive taxation.

On 9 July 1785, Franklin wrote to Mathon de la Cour thanking him for sending a copy of Mathon's *Téstament de Fortuné Ricard, maître d'arithmétique à D***. In another letter dated 18 November 1785 Franklin acknowledges the *Téstament* as his inspiration for what was to become the terms of his codicil:

> It is right to be sowing good seed whenever we have an opportunity, since some of it may be productive. An instance of this you should be acquainted with, as it may afford you pleasure. The reading of *Fortuné Ricard's Testament*, has put it into the head and heart of a citizen to leave two thousand pounds sterling to two American cities, who are to lend it in small sums at five percent to young beginners in business; and the accumulation, after a hundred years, to be laid out in public works of benefit to those cities.[29]

As his 1785 correspondence with Mathon de la Cour attests, Franklin had fully developed the idea articulated in the 1789 codicil before he executed his main will drawn in 1788. While Franklin is silent on the reason he withheld his plan from the main will, his disposable estate was increased between 1788 and 1789 by the long delayed payment of his salary as President of Pennsylvania. Disapproving of salaries for elected executives in government, it is logical that he would assign that part of his estate that came from public office to create two public trusts that would inure to the benefit of the public.[30] Mathon's imaginative work, coupled with the payment from Pennsylvania, must have provoked him to draft the revision.

Mathon's *Téstament* is the elaborate Last Will and Testament of a fictional 'Teacher of Arithmetic', M. Fortuné Ricard. In this imaginary will, M. Richard bequeaths 500 livres in trust for 500 years. At each century one fifth of the trust along with its accumulated interest must be applied to certain, specified charitable uses.[31]

At the first one hundred year mark, the proceeds must be used as a prize to the best dissertation on the subject of the value of saving money, allowing it to compound with interest, along with supporting the costs of publication and distribution of the dissertation. M. Fortuné Ricard's *Téstament* went on to specify that with the first century's proceeds:

> Copies [of the prize dissertation] shall be sent, *gratis*, to all bishops, clergy, consellors of the kingdom. I had intended to have sent them also into foreign countries; but I observe that all the universities of the Christian world, excepting those of France, have solemnly recognized the lawfullness of putting money on interest, and that it continues necessary only in this kingdom to explain a question in morals so interesting to the welfare of the State.[32]

Here Mathon criticizes Catholic France for holding on to outmoded beliefs that lending money at interest (usury) is unlawful and immoral. In the *Téstament* the coupling of university study with considerations of public economic policy describes the kind of academic interest that Franklin, Price and Mathon shared in 'political arithmetic'.

After the second hundred years, the second fifth must be used to establish an endowment fund that would distribute prizes for virtuous acts and distinguished scientific, literary, mathematical, agricultural, artistic and athletics accomplishments. Mathon predicates the enlightenment of civilization (described as virtuous acts and accomplishments) upon a perpetual source of economic support. Franklin agreed that freedom and peace depended on intellectual, political and economic independence. After 300 years, the third fifth would be sufficient value to do much good work. M. Fortuné Ricard's bequest would create '500 patriotic banks for lending money without interest ... to succour the unfortunate, or ... towards promoting agriculture, trade and industry'.[33] The underlying premise is that the banking system widely distributes capital where it is required for expansion of the nation's economy. The fund would establish twelve endowed museums in the major cities of France each with a common library, concert hall and theatre, laboratories with literati and artists in residence each of whom will not be admitted '... till he has previously given proof, not of his rank, descent, or nobility, but of his morals ... [and] that he will prefer virtue, truth, his country to every thing; and the general good of literature to his own fame'.[34] With this commitment to create large cultural institutions in major cities, Mathon identifies and affirms urban centres as citadels of enlightened civilization and sources of economic power, not the loci of corruption, social disintegration and the unproductive concentration of capital. This hope and belief is clearly echoed in the language of Franklin's 1789 codicil.

After 400 years the proceeds from the fourth division would be an enormous sum enabling the trust to build one hundred new towns, and offering a formula for population expansion through planned procreation. The towns would eventually add fifteen million inhabitants to France effectively doubling the population. M. Fortuné Ricard acknowledged that this would require more currency than would exist in all of Europe, by his calculations, so the executors would have to exchange cash for land and other real property. In this provision of the *Téstament*, Mathon invokes the importance of population growth to the prosperity of the nation. Franklin's speculations on American demography written in 1751, *Observations Concerning the Increase of Mankind*, sets forth Franklin's views that America's economic development will be based on its ability, due to the availability of land and related patterns of procreation, to double its population every twenty years. Whether Mathon wrote with the knowledge of Franklin's pioneering work in demography or from his own experience in France, the two men shared the view that the future would depend on managed exponential population growth.

Five hundred years after the death of M. Fortuné Ricard the last portion of his bequest would allow for paying off the national debt of France and England. For this favour M. Ricard desires that ' ... the English nation will consent to call the French their neighbors and not their natural enemies; that they be assured that nature never made man an enemy to man; and that national hatreds, commercial prohibitions, and above all, wars, constantly produce a monstrous error in calculations'.[35] Mathon's view that extreme nationalism, mercantilism and constant warfare are unnatural was shared by Franklin. They both subscribed to the concept that through credit building and debt retiring policies, laissez-fair trade policies and managed peace, nations would grow economically interdependent and their peoples would prosper in the light of liberty. The elimination of debt in the *Téstament,* is the vehicle to ultimate peace and prosperity.

Showing Mathon's skill at political satire, Fortuné Ricard's bequest would purchase a special domain for the French crown as well as provide a personal pension and gratuities slush fund for the King, thus, alleviating the need of levying taxes on the people to support the corrupt habits of the monarchy. Mathon recognized the potential for great calamity if a monarch fails to manage a nation's economy, contributes to a spiralling national debt and imposes an unbearable burden of taxation. Mathon must have feared the destructive forces at work during the last years of the *Ancien Régime*, that ultimately led to the French Revolution of 1789 and regicide.

The *Téstament* also considered solutions to other societal ills. Funds would be made available to the clergy to provide them sufficient income to relieve the imposition that they make on the people for their services. Franklin shared Mathon's concern that clerics, rather than providing comfort, succour and relief, only contributed to the impoverishment of the people. It is not surprising that Franklin, in 1789, when seeking proper custodians for his two trust funds, selected secular authority through municipal government rather than institutionalized religion.[36]

Additionally from the fifth division, M. Fortuné Ricard's executors would buy up land and provide small farms with cottages to 500,000 married peasants who with their heirs and assigns must live on the farms. Funds would be provided to buy up all of the manors and free the vassals from their bondage. Funds would be provided to establish 'houses of education' and 'public work houses'. Funds would be directed to assist women to find employment, achieve better pay, run more effective households, and create institutions to help avoid 'the snares which are laid by vice for women without fortune ...'[37] Funds would be used to create free hospitals as well as provide home based health care.

The rest of the Fortuné Ricard Trust Fund would be designated by the executors at their discretion for public improvements that 'cooperate in every possible method with nature, which seems to have designed France to be the most delightful country under heaven'.[38] This provision is similar in tone and feeling to the Franklin codicil's general instruction for civic improvements at the one hundred year and 200 year marks.

Moving from the heroic to the pragmatic, M. Ricard allowed that it was within his executors discretion 'to deepen the beds of rivers so as to render them navigable ...'[39] This idea was directly parroted by Franklin in his 1788 *Will* when he bequeathed £2,000 for his executors to hold ' ... In Trust to be employed for making the River Schuylkill Navigable'.[40] The 1789 codicil modifies the notion as follows: 'But understanding since, that such a Sum will do but little towards accomplishing such a Work and that the project is not likely to be undertaken for many Years to come; and having entertained another Idea, that I hope will be more extensively useful, I do hereby revoke and annul the Bequest ...'[41] Franklin willingly adjusted his plan to accommodate changed circumstances and the likelihood of measurable effect. The difference between Mathon de la Cour and Franklin is that the latter actually left a creative and compelling testament that not only dreamed of a constructive future but actually contributed to its achievement.

Following the narrative of his will, M. Fortuné Ricard added charts which support his calculations as to the value of the funds at each centennial distribution and his estimate of the costs of the good works that he directed. Although Franklin did not include charts to back up his calculations, he evidently developed a mathematical progression similar to *Téstament*'s which allowed him to determine the value of the appreciated principal at the first and second century marks.[42]

Franklin was instrumental in having the *Téstament* translated into English.[43] The translated text was printed as an appendix to a reprint edition of Price's important and serious treatise entitled *Observations on the importance of the American revolution and the means of making it a benefit to the world*.[44] This edition of Price's work also included, at Franklin's behest, another appendix that reprinted a work by Turgot.

The Téstament de Fortuné Ricard and Mathon de la Cour's advocacy of compounded savings was only a small part of tri-national debate on the condition of public credit, the impact of public debt and the desirability and practicality of sinking funds. Lenders of the debate for two decades were Franklin's fellow Whig Club member, Richard Price, the controversial Swiss born French Finance Minister, Jacque Necker and American Alexander Hamilton, America's first Secretary of the Treasury.

Best known for his political tract *Observations* ... which endorsed the necessity and vitality of the American Revolution as the birth of a great and prosperous new nation, Price's most significant contribution was as a financial impresario to William Pitt, the Chancellor of the Exchequer of Great Britain. Pitt's radical financial reforms. although based on precedents established by Walpole in 1716, were in direct response to Dr Price's mathematical analysis of Britain's national debt and Price's proposals restructuring the interest-bearing and term conditions of the government's annuities and bonds. Price contended that the preservation of national credit, necessary for economic growth and social prosperity, depended on the conscientious redemption of the war debts which were hobbling the current operating funds and eroded foreign financial capital's confidence in Britain's economic integrity.

Price's advocacy of the sinking fund as a device that utilized compounded savings to expand the money supply and to amortize and eventually eliminate the national debt, found an enthusiastic supporter in Franklin. The idea of a sinking fund is based on a simple economic principle of thrift: capital is lent at interest and reserved in an inviolable form. The interest returned on investment is automatically added to the original principal providing for the rapid compounding of the capital in the fund.

Eighteenth-century national (French, English and American) sinking funds designated for the redemption of large war debts had three essential components: (1) the sinking fund must receive an annual appropriation from the surplus of revenue (tax and other) for the purchasing of the nation's own debt (in the form of bonds and annuities), (2) debt service must continue to be paid out of general funds to all creditors including the sinking fund (just as if it were held by a non-governmental creditor) and (3) the interest earned on the principal must be added to the principal in the fund. The compounding effect combined with the disciplined depositing of new appropriations into the sinking fund provided a fund sufficient to pay, or sink, virtually any size debt.

The early British versions of the sinking fund during Walpole's ministry had been applied to both the amortization of the national debt as well as to a fund underwriting extraordinary current expenses. The sinking fund concept was inextricably bound to the idea of sustaining the public credit. English legal authority Sir William Blackstone, and French political philosopher Montesquieu expressed the belief that a viable national sinking fund would build public confidence and, thus, assure the public credit.[45] In 1786, William Pitt with the material advice of Richard Price, recommitted to a national sinking fund for the retirement of the large British war debt.

Like Price, Franklin equated political independence with economic independence. With the Treaty of Paris in 1783, Franklin understood that the most serious challenge facing the nascent United States of American was the lack of public credit and, more importantly, the conficence of foreign investors in the credit worthiness of the new nation. Without a ready source of investment capital, the new nation, despite its natural resources and swelling population, would not be able to sustain itself. From Price's analysis, Franklin was aware of the horrendous burden the war debt had placed on post-war England and knew that the highly vulnerable America would be corrupted in infancy or crushed by debt. Benjamin Vaughan, Franklin's friend and fellow printer in London, recognized Franklin's enthusiasm for Price's programmes and welcomed Franklin's efforts to have Mathon's *Téstament* (believed by Franklin, Price and Vaughan to be based on serious principles while expressed in a satirical form that would be understandable to the general public) published as an addenda to Price's 1785 edition of '*Observations* ...' Vaughan expressed this belief in a letter addressed to Franklin in 1785:

> Dr. Price has done well to publish an abridged translation of the Testament da M. Fortuné Richard, though not of your writing. Both of us had supposed you *concerned* in it, though parts of it certainly did not bear marks of you. It is tolerably well veined with humor, and though not perfect in its matter, yet I doubt not will be of use, because it will convey political arithmetic into the way of laughers & men of wit. It has for some time been in the hands of serious men, but it was not for that reason much the nearer to being brought into practice by statesmen.[46]

Franklin was also influenced by another French contemporary, Jacques Necker and Necker's efforts to avoid the cataclysmic financial collapse of the *Ancien Régime* in France. Necker, worried about the social and political effect of heavy taxation required to pay the high interest requirements of the French national debt, imposed reforms that distributed the burden of interest payments on the debt over the long term, by renegotiating the terms and interest rates of the debt. He also emphasized the need for operating surpluses, general savings, and a sinking fund with especially designated and reserved revenues to amortize the debt, the latter set forth in the King of France's *Edict on the Sinking Fund* (1784). Mathon de la Cour was a serious student of the national finances of France and published a collection of French financial reports in 1788.[47] Franklin and several of Franklin's correspondents (Price and Vaughan) felt that Mathon's *Téstament* represented Necker's financial reform policies in a popularized form. Necker wrote his own *magnum opus*, the *Administration de Finances*, in 1784, a work which Franklin much admired. In a letter to Richard Price dated 1 February 1785, Franklin juxtaposes Mathon's *Téstament* and Necker's *Administrations of Finance* as expressions of the same concern for what money saved by avoiding calamitous wars and eliminating the national debt can do for the betterment of the nation.

> I sent you sometime since a little Piece entitled, *Testament de M. Fortuné Ricard*, which exemplifies strongly and pleasantly your Doctrine of the immense Powers of compound Interest ... I send herewith a new Work of Mr. Necker's on the Finances of France. You will find good Things in it, particularly his Chapter on War ... I think I sent you formerly his *Conterendu* [sic]. This Work makes more Talk here than that, tho' that made abundance. I will not say that the Writer thinks higher of himself and his Abilities that they deserve, but I wish for his own sake that he kept such Sentiments more out of sight.[48]

In the Chapter on War, Necker lists prospective expenditures for a stronger military establishment, public improvements, support for industry, assistance to the poor, improved prison conditions and better funded charities, all made possible if the 'fifty to sixty Millions of its annual revenue' was not diverted to cover the cost of war. Reflecting Franklin's similar interests in the investment of the nation's resources toward the commonweal, Necker drives the point home in the following passage:

> It is not war, but a prudent and peaceful administration alone, that can procure to France, all that it still wants ... The population of the kingdom is immense; but the excess and the nature of the taxes render the country inhabitants poor, and discourage them: the human species is weakened from too great wretchedness; and the number of children who die before the age at which strength is displayed, surpasses the natural proportion. The sovereign's revenue is immense; but the public debt consumes two-fifths of it; and it is only with the produce of a prudent economy, and by lowering the rate of interest, that the charge can be lessened.[49]

For Necker and Franklin debt not only sapped the sovereign of strength but rendered the citizens of the nation indigent functioning under an oppressive tax burden. Prosperity and peace depended on changing the national course from crushing debt to enabling savings.

Americans had experimented with debt retirement schemes that had the characteristics of sinking funds in colonial Massachusetts. The idea of a national sinking fund emerged during the confederal period by proposals from Americans Governeur Morris (1778), Alexander Hamilton (1781) and Tench Coxe (1787). Price and Necker and the idea of a sinking fund especially influenced the financial genius, Alexander Hamilton. In 1781, at an astoundingly young age of twenty-four, Alexander Hamilton wrote a lengthy and highly technical letter to Robert Morris who had been appointed by the Congress under the authority of the Articles of Confederation as Superintendent of Finance.

Hamilton, reacting to European solutions as well as drawing together the ideas of earlier American financial planners including Franklin, offered a detailed analysis of the financial condition of the nation and elaborated a plan for the creation of a national bank, a controlled currency and war debt redemption with an overall goal of establishing America's public credit, promoting economic growth by creating a steady supply of investment capital, and political liberty. According to Article 13 of Hamilton's plan, the new national bank would loan money to Congress for the purpose of creating a sinking fund in order to pay off the national debt of '£1,200,000 at eight per Cent interest for the payment of which with its interest a certain unalienable fund of £110,400 per annum to be established for twenty years'.[50]

In the preparation of this 1781 letter to Morris, Hamilton relied on the mathematical calculations and economic theories on currency and debt of Richard Price.[51] In 1782 with fellow committeemen James Madison and Thomas Fitzsimons, Hamilton recommended to Congress that a sinking fund be created from any surplus funds provided by the states for debt redemption, an idea whose popularity was largely attributed to Price.

While the precedent for the later eighteenth-century sinking fund was creating of the Sinking Fund in England in 1716, Walpole's experiment also demonstrated the fundamental flaw in the concept. The rapid compounding were only possible if the principal was increased by the addition of the earned interest. Any withdrawals of capital defeated the compounding effect. Price was critical of the early version because it did not provide sufficient property of alienation, safeguarding the fund. He also recognized that the English government during Walpole's administration had lacked the discipline necessary to provide tax revenue sufficient to service the Sinking Fund.[52]

For both Price and Hamilton the lesson to be learned, especially in light of the burgeoning war debt on both sides of the Atlantic, was that no debt should be contracted without identifying a means to extinguish it.[53] The sinking fund, independent, undisturbed and appropriately funded from specially designated funds or surplus general tax revenue could provide for the responsible redemption of practically any size debt. The result would be the maintenance of the public credit, a condition essential to economic growth and prosperity. Franklin had no less of a positive expectation from the compounding testamentary trusts he created in 1789 for Boston and Philadelphia.

Throughout the American Revolution, Richard Price criticized Lord North's strategy of financing the British war debt and called for the reestablishment of the Sinking Fund. Price, in *Observations on Reversionary Payments*, first published in 1771 and *An Appeal to the Public on the National Debt of 1772*, called for a policy that would put the British national debt on a reliable and fixed course of redemption. Price's advocacy won a convert in Prime Minister Shelburne but it took the administration of William Pitt, Chancellor the Exchequer and later First Lord of the Treasury, to recreated the sinking fund. Dr Price sent Pitt several schemes for reducing the national debt. While Hamilton, with Price as his inspiration, was investigating means to establish public credit in America, Pitt was introducing financial reforms, derived from Price's proposals, in England. Hamilton in a letter dated 25 November 1789 to William Bingham admired Pitt's achievements:

> By a Variety of Skillful Operations in Finance, he not only Secured a Sufficient revenue to pay the regular Interest of the Debt, but obtained a considerable Surplus, which constituted a Sinking fund of a Million P% Annum. which by Act of Parliament was put out of the Power of Administration, & was vested in Commissioners, in Trust for the purpose of being invariably applied to the gradual Extinction of the National Debt ...[54]

Hamilton also acknowledged the economic writing of Jacques Necker as a source for his proposed system of finance.[55] Perhaps the most significant belief that Hamilton and Franklin gained from Necker was the positive impact of managing the nation's debt, while not necessarily eliminating it. Thomas Jefferson held the opinion that debt should not exceed that which can be retired completely in thirty-four years and that debt and its inter-related system of government with a creditor class was pernicious. In contrast, Hamilton felt that debt had the effect of binding diverse interests together.[56] Franklin saw borrowing not only as a means to self-sufficiency but as a process of mutual assistance and community building consistent with a virtuous people.

When Hamilton said that debt is a blessing, he meant that the ability to manage debt would demonstrate the energy, maturity and stability of America and it would have a galvanizing effect on the young nation. Like Franklin, Hamilton recognized the exigency of incurring debts in order to conduct the war for independence and also saw that an expansion of the post-war economy beyond America's limited amount of specie was required. But debt must be managed creatively within the economic and political limitations of taxation. Both Franklin and Hamilton as self-made men understood the value of credit to the frugal and the industrious. They shared the belief that the new American nation must behave as virtuously as aspiring individual Americans must. Necker's financial reforms showed similar acceptance of enabling capacity of debt while attempting to reform the character and system of French debt.

While Necker was criticized for his lack of theoretical consistency compared with his predecessor and penultimate Physiocrat, Turgot, Necker was credited with financial ingenuity and political pragmatism. As Franklin's subtle and opportunistic style of diplomacy confused the doctrinaire John Adams, Necker's business acuity, and political adeptness in dealing with the complex forces at work in the final years of the *Ancien Regime* seemed sullied when compared to Turgot's pure and theoretical reformism. Products of the Enlightenment, Franklin, Necker and Hamilton, with the theoretical and intellectual contributions of Price and Turgot, rationalized the economic chaos of their times. These men also had a sophisticated understanding of the importance of the 'appearance' of stability and integrity to support of the public credit, conjuring up Franklin's formula for success as a young man in Philadelphia.

Far from 'a vain fancy' (Franklin's feigned modesty in the codicil), the idea of the compounding trust found its genesis in significant economic theory, particularly that of the sinking fund, and in practical initiatives that Franklin witnessed or experienced through his long life. The explicit features of the trusts, including the designation of industrious artisans, the system of sureties, the interest rate, the terms of repayment, the management of the trusts and the public benefits, all have antecedents in the correspondence and writings of Franklin, Price, Necker, Mathon and Hamilton. In life, Franklin sought to manage debt, organize credit, build capital and promote virtue in order to sustain liberty in the young American nation. After death, Franklin sought to create self-sustaining trusts that would produce ever-increasing capital which could be used by the industrious to live virtuous lives and improve the quality of their cities.

3 BOSTON: THE FIRST CENTURY

Boston's status as the birthplace of Benjamin Franklin and its first citation as beneficiary in the language of the codicil of his will makes the first one hundred years of the Franklin Trust there the beginning of the 200-year story of his bequest to the two cities. The history of the Boston based trust is informed by the social, political and economic trends from 1791 until 1891 with important contributions from the record keeping Franklin required of the trust as specified in the codicil and the recorded actions of its board of managers.

The first public acknowledgement of the bequest from Dr Franklin was recorded in the minutes of the Boston Town Meeting of 25 May 1790 when the town officially accepted the gift. Given his omnipresence in American colonial affairs and international prominence during the revolution, Franklin's remembrance flattered the townsmen. Seizing the opportunity for reciprocal tribute, the following laudatory expressions were sent on 1 June 1790 to Franklin's executors:

> ... The many useful designs projected by that great man, during A Long and Valuable Life. perhaps even more than his exalted Talents as A Patriot, Statesman and Philosopher, must endear his Memory To Americans, While they in A More Particular manner, reflect Honor upon the Town of Boston, which gave him Birth and Education--
>
> Every Step to Carry into full Effect his Benevolent plan, will be Cheerfully Pursued by those Who he was Pleased to Constitute his Trustees, – And rising Generations will for ages. Bless the Name of their illustrious Friend & Benefactor ...[1]

In March of 1791, the Treasurer of the Town received a draft for $4,444.44, the converted value of £1,000 Sterling. Buoyed by the promising economic development of the new American constitutional government and the after glow of Franklin's optimism about 'the rising Generations', the managers of the Franklin Fund met and were successful in lending the entire fund balance to married artificers who had completed their apprenticeships and who could provide two guarantors (pledging Spanish Milled dollars or the gold equivalent) to back each loan. For the 'first few years' the Franklin Fund was completely loaned and the accumulations of interest at 5 per cent per annum began to increase the principal balance of the Fund, per Franklin's expectations.[2]

The board of managers was initially composed of the nine selectmen of the Town of Boston according to the codicil. Also per Franklin's instruction the board of managers was to include three ministers, those leading the oldest Episcopalian, Congregational and Presbyterian churches. Insofar as there was no Presbyterian church in Boston until the establishment of the First United Presbyterian Church in 1847, initially only two rector/ministers representing the oldest Congregational church (First Church) and Episcopal church (Christ Church) in Boston served on the board of managers. Although Franklin expected that the elected public officials would continuously change, the composition of the managers including the ministers provided continuity. However, contrary to Franklin's explicit instructions, the public officials ignored the ministers and excluded them from management decisions from 1822 to 1866.[3]

The selectmen served until 1822, when the town of Boston incorporated as the enlarged city of Boston with a new governmental structure. The act of incorporation created an eight member board of aldermen and a thirty member city council, who with the mayor of the city acted as the elected representatives of the citizens to govern the municipality. The new mayor and the board of aldermen presumed that they automatically served, ex officio, as members of the board of managers of the Franklin Fund along with two of the three ministers provided by the language of the codicil. They served until 1854, when the city charter was revised to provide a twelve member board of aldermen. The twelve aldermen then presumed that they inherited seats on the Franklin Fund board, now expanded to twelve seats along with the three ministers. The Mayor of Boston was excluded from the reconstituted board of managers because he was no longer a member of the board of aldermen. All of these changes the managers accomplished by fiat and without the concurrence of any court of equity.[4]

The official account and bond books along with a set of private accounting ledgers maintained by William Minot (1783–1873), Treasurer and Manager of the Franklin Fund from 1811 to 1866, provide information for all of the loans to married artificers from the Franklin Fund for the first one hundred years. (No loans were made between 1886 and 1891, the centennial of the trust). According to these records, 291 bondholders borrowed Franklin Fund money through 1886 in the following decades:

1791–1800	89
1801–10	67
1811–20	65
1821–30	27
1831–40	13
1841–50	7
1851–60	10
1861–70	2
1871–80	9
1881–90	2
Total	291

Of these borrowers 267 individuals (92 per cent) satisfied their bond in full using an average of just under the prescribed ten year term (9.96 years) to pay in full. Of the twenty-four defaulted loans eleven bondsmen made substantial payments (at least $120 of the $200 original amount borrowed). A remaining nine (3 per cent) made some payment and only four (1 per cent) absconded with the money. Of interest is the fact there is no record of a suit being filed on fifteen of the twenty-four defaulted accounts. The total forfeited capital (loan payments less original face of the loan) for all accounts reached only $2,344 over the entire first hundred years of the Franklin Fund in Boston.[5]

Housewrights represented the largest artisanal category among the Franklin Fund bondholders at fifty-six bonds or 19 per cent of the total. The second largest group were the seventeen bakers at 6 per cent. Coopers constituted the next largest trade at sixteen bonds or 5 per cent. Other trades with significant presence were, in descending order, tailors, printers, cabinet makers, brick layers, hatters, painters, blacksmiths and bookbinders. While large numbers of coopers, tailors and printers found themselves facing extraordinary changes (mostly adverse from an employment standpoint due to technological improvements), Boston housewrights, brick layers and painters found that the rate of new buildings starts and relatively stable building types throughout the nineteenth century created considerable employment opportunity. Craft specialties like hatters, bookbinders and cabinet makers sustained themselves in the market supported by the expensive and sophisticated taste of Boston urban elites and the expanding Middling Interest.

The general success of the loan programme based on the audit of the accounts contradicts Minot's early characterizations of it as failing to meet 'the benevolent intentions of the donor'. The fund had more than doubled in value in its first twenty years to $9,000 when the town first retained Minot as Treasurer. The fund doubled again by 1831 worth $18,010, notwithstanding the unstable economy of this period. The people assisted by the fund also prospered. Franklin's grand scheme was made manifest in the example of one particular artisan assisted by the Franklin loan fund. Charles Wells, listed on bond #142 as a bricklayer, borrowed $100 on 14 February 1808. Harris Leach, caulker by trade, and Seth Lathrop, a housewright, provided the surety and, consequently, co-signed the bond note. The ledgers record a satisfied account with the final payment received in the tenth year from origination and recorded on 2 February 1818.[6] Besides paying his loan back on time and in full, Charles Wells rose to an elevated station in the political life of Boston.

Charles Wells, born in Boston on 30 December 1786, became a successful 'master builder' in the town and entered the race for Mayor in 1831 as the National Republican Party candidate. The National Republican Party, led in Massachusetts by Governor Levi Lincoln and former US President John Quincy

Adams, stood for a conservative platform, especially supporting protectionist legislation that assisted the nascent textile industry. Wells, in contrast to most of the Mayors of Boston before and after his election, was a self-made man who, through his own industry and frugality, earned the confidence and support of the people of Boston. Described as 'a man of simple character' and 'not ill-qualified', in Justin Winsor's *Memorial History of Boston*, written with a decidedly condescending tone, Wells had served as a member of the Common Council and the Board of Aldermen prior to his election as Mayor. Interestingly, he was elected on a platform that objected to the amount of debt build up by the extravagant and aristocratic former Mayors Josiah Quincy and Harrison Gray Otis.[7] Certainly his electoral triumph over Theodore Lyman, former Mayor Otis's son-in-law, startled many of Boston's Old Guard. During his term, Wells, with other prominent National Republicans, actively denounced the State of South Carolina and its defiant act of nullification, vocalizing the united interests of mechanics, merchants and manufacturers in the industrializing Northeast.

Notwithstanding Mr Wells's personal success story, Treasurer Minot in 1836 concluded that 'it is not advantageous to married mechanics under the age of twenty-four years, to borrow money to be repaid in easy instalments, at a low rate of interest; and the improvidence of early marriages may be inferred'.[8] Despite the general contention of the time that men tended to marry later as a result of industrialization and urbanization (an impression shared by Minot and repeated by other nineteenth century observers of the Franklin Fund), twentieth century studies of demographic trends claim that there were 'neither rapid nor sustained long-term changes in median age at marriage until the 1940's'.[9] For the years covered in recent research, the median age for marriage of males generally stayed around twenty-five to twenty-six years of age. Although the age and marriage provisions of Franklin's codicil likely reduced the number of eligible applicants, it is statistically impossible, given the size of Boston's mechanic class, that the pool diminished below the capacity of the fund to make loans on that basis, as alleged.

After the first decade of lending, the managers reported that the loans were becoming progressively more difficult to make, as artificers failed to meet the Fund's requirements.[10] Despite complaints about its viability the Fund did make 255 loans between the years 1791 and 1836. Only a small percentage of bonds were not satisfactorily paid in full. The Franklin Fund board of managers was 'unable' to loan out more than 6 per cent of the appreciated principal after 1836.[11] The three reasons given for the erosion of the artificers's loan programme were the abolition of the apprenticeship system, the change in economic conditions (explained in one place as changes in the interest rates) and the difficulty in finding sureties.[12] While the first two aforementioned reasons are explanations offered much later in the century, the last reason regarding sureties was plainly stated in 1836 by William Minot.[13]

Although the apprenticeship system, as Franklin knew it, virtually disappeared, the rapid industrialization of Boston and surrounding towns continued to demand skilled workers to manage the new technology that supported manufacturing. Some of the trades, for example, the machinists, continued to prepare apprentices throughout the nineteenth century.[14] Where specific industries did not have training programmes, they relied on mechanics and tradesmen schools. The Boston Mechanics Institution, a mutual assistance membership organization with a major educational mission, existed and had received $6,119 in gifts before 1830.[15] The colleges in Boston also offered applied scientific and technical instruction at the Lawrence Scientific School of Harvard University (1846–7) and the Massachusetts Institute of Technology (1861).[16] It is curious that the managers would not have sought out mechanics societies, trade schools and specialized institutes for the successor to the apprenticeship system when contemporary voices widely acknowledged that apprenticeship was being supplanted by formal school programmes. Nevertheless, the Franklin Fund managers failed to consider modifying the apprenticeship requirement in order to attract a larger field of applicants.

The dwindling number of Franklin Fund borrowers inverted the trend established by the overall population growth of the city, and, in particular the size of the artisan class. During the antebellum period Boston grew from 43,300 inhabitants in 1820, to 61,400 inhabitants in 1830, to 84,400 inhabitants in 1840, to 136,900 inhabitants in 1850, to 177,800 inhabitants in 1860. National and state census records, cross checked through Boston city directories and other local records, reveal substantial growth in the artisan population and persistent residence patterns for artisans within the core wards and neighbourhoods of Boston. The number of skilled artisans as heads of households grew from 1,875 heads of households in 1830, to 2,560 in 1840, to 6,260 in 1850 to 6,820 in 1860. The skilled worker category in this survey included carpenters, stonecutters, metalsmiths, printers, engravers, machinists, milliners, inventors and tallow chandlers; all tradesmen that Franklin would have felt occupationally qualified for the loans.[17] Certainly the gross number of potential artificers and those who could stand as sureties increased substantially.

The definition of artificer, artisan, mechanic or tradesmen, was, however, undergoing significant revision. The word 'artificer' fell out of use in the early nineteenth century. The historiography of the antebellum period favours the term 'mechanic' for the occupational designation and the term 'Middling class' or 'Middling Interest' for the socio-economic category of people who Franklin referred to as artificers. Some confusion could have been caused by the term 'mechanic' which sometimes referred to wage earning or unemployed journeymen who would be considered from the 'lower class'. The term 'Middling Class' also included merchants, traders and shop keepers, and others who were not skilled craft workers and would not be covered by Franklin's definition of artificer.[18] Nowhere in the record was there evidence of an effort to updated Franklin's terms or interpret them in light of changing definitions in or out of the Massachusetts courts of law.

Many mechanics were able to ride the tide of industrialization and become part of Boston's aggressive aspiring Middling Interest. The Middling Interest figured prominently in Boston politics and gradually won some concessions from Boston's merchant capitalists, reshaping the economy and government to extend privilege with great equity. In 1822–3, the mechanics and middle class businessmen demonstrated their new political muscle by convincing the Boston town meeting to repeal an unfavourable building code that limited the size of wooden buildings (hence, limiting the amount of construction available for skilled carpenters) and to approve ward voting which increased the voting strength of the Middling Interest. Such political movements in Massachusetts as the Free Bridge Party (1827), the Anti-Masonry Party (1830–4), the Workingmen's Party (1832–4) and the Jacksonian Democratic Party (from 1827) all were propelled by a significant force of mechanics.[19]

Yet from 1822 to 1834, Franklin Fund Treasurer Minot could only find twenty-nine young married mechanics in all of Boston who sought and qualified for Franklin loans. The mechanics who shaped Boston's law making and political structure also shared Franklin's precept that upward social and economic mobility would be the natural result of a frugal and industrious life.[20] Given the size and self assertive nature of Boston's Middling Interest, it is unlikely that their need for capital to invest in small independent operations was completely satisfied by early commercial banking or emerging thrift institutions as Franklin records contend.

During these same decades some master craftsmen were squeezed out of the skilled labour force, leaving them unemployed or compelled to work as wage labourers in jobs requiring little or no skill. This was particularly true for cordwainers, shoemakers, tailors, weavers, printers, metal workers and some classifications of wood workers where the factory system of manufacturing and new machinery replaced hand work. The surplus of workers spun off by industrialization coupled with the daily arrival of more immigrating workers created a log jam of people looking for employment. Contemporary social critic Joseph Tuckerman, in an 1830 essay, describes the plight of unemployed Boston mechanics '... who have no capital but time and industry; who have no resource for self-support, but their daily labour; and who, in a failure of demand for their services, are at once brought to great, and perhaps, to utter want...'. Reverend Tuckerman continues:

> But I believe that I may state with confidence, that in consequence [sic] of the improved machinery, which is now used in printing, and by the substitution of boys and girls, for men, in the work of printing offices, there are at this time, or within the

> past summer there have been, in our city, *between two hundred and three hundred journeymen printers, who have been able at best, to obtain but occasional employment in the occupation, in which they have been educated.* I am assured, too, that *there are as many as two hundred journeymen carpenters, and in all, not less than a thousand journeymen mechanics, in the same condition.*[21]

Despite the staggering numbers of artisans who needed help in gaining a living, the Franklin Fund during the same period languished. The managers of the fund considered no alternatives for investment in the large population of unemployed and underemployed artisans of the city.

Although the prevailing interest rates varied throughout the nineteenth century in response to radical shifts in the condition of the economy, the fund managers proposed no changes to the interest rate in council or in the courts to keep it attractive. Franklin's clear intent in setting the rate at 5 per cent per annum, one percentage point below the fixed lending rate at the time of his death, was to offer favourable, below-market rates. The Fund managers could have remained true to the testator's intent and simply indexed the interest rate on Franklin Fund bonds just below prevailing rates in order to always be discounted and, thus, highly competitive.[22]

Artificers required capital to expand their small manufacturing operations into larger, more competitive enterprises. Mechanics felt intense pressure to compete with merchant capitalists who increasingly ventured into manufacturing. Although some types of artisans were slow to embrace new manufacturing technologies, many skilled craft masters eagerly sought to expand their output to meet the growing market. The effort in Boston to organize mechanics associations and banking institutions responsive to mechanics needs vigorously responded to the growth associated with mechanization, and expansion of the market economy.[23] Writing about New York City artisans, a historian explains the situation:

> The most suitable source of capital were the city's commercial banks. Unfortunately, bankers seldom made direct loans to independent artisan manufacturers; they preferred to invest in mercantile-controlled enterprises. Furthermore, merchant bankers, many of whom were Federalist, were disinclined to deal with the predominantly Republican mechanics. Finally, merchants' pervasive bias against treating mechanics as business equals made direct credit transactions rare. The unfortunate consequence was, as the Evening Post noted, that all too often 'the application of the laborious mechanic is treated with contempt and rejected disdain'.[24]

The problem, most assuredly, was the same in Boston. It is practically inconceivable that there was a vanishing market for loans to artificers after 1811 because of better credit alternatives, as claimed by the board of managers.

The problem of the two sureties mush have been the overriding difficulty. Treasurer Minot in 1836 claimed:

> The great number of instances in which sureties have been obliged to pay the loans, has rendered it not so easy, as formerly, for applicants to obtain the required security. This proved by the small number of loans from the fund, averaging for the last five years, not more than one a year.[25]

It is not evident from the review of Minot's financial records that the mechanics who had borrowed from the fund had abused the good faith of their respective sureties. The records implied that kinsmen (people with the same surname) served as sureties and, occasionally, made regular payments on behalf of their son, nephew, or brother. The records failed to specifically identify the source of payment in many cases but for those records which noted the identity of the payee, only twenty-five bonds recorded at least one payment by a surety. It cannot be determined whether the sureties willingly or obligingly paid on some accounts. Given the long-term, simple interest conditions of the Franklin loan, family members or even close associates interested in assisting a young man start-up his own business would have preferred to stand as surety than make a similar loan using their own capital.

The strict collection policies of the Managers and tough examination of proposed sureties made the prospect less attractive. The Managers established swift and aggressive pursuit of delinquency as early as 1791 when then authorized that bonds to be 'immediately put in suit' for recovery of late payment.[26] Minot, on behalf of the Fund, doggedly pursued timely and complete repayment. There is one notation that the Selectmen in 1819 directed the Treasurer to take a charitable Christmas break from collection, explaining that 'compulsive measures at this season would be attended with distressing consequences to their families'.[27] Apparently default on loans due to the premature decease of the bondsmen or sureties occurred sufficiently often to warrant an adjustment to the requirements of the loan programme as follows:

> ... whenever by the decease of either of the obliges, or by reason of any other cause, the [managers] shall deem it expedient to require additional security, the same shall be given to their satisfaction, or the amount due on his bond, both principal and interest, be paid upon demand ...[28]

Minot charged 6 per cent for late payments rather than the 5 per cent prescribed by Franklin, an invention that did not comply with the letter of the codicil but made good business sense.[29] Notwithstanding Minot's fifty-five years of diligent performance as collections manager and fiduciary, the economic times were turbulent and money invested in small business by struggling artisans was implicitly risky.

While housewrights acted as the largest group of sureties for the Franklin Fund borrowers (seventy-four of 582 or 13 per cent), the other large groups represented have characteristics consistent with Franklin's expectations. Sixty-one merchants, thirty-eight gentlemen and twenty-eight traders (occupations/identities associated with the economic elite) stood as sureties for a wide variety of artificers, representing a total of 22 per cent. While the financial crises of 1815–20 and 1837–40 in Massachusetts caused economic stress for the merchant capitalists of Boston and made them more cautions, they were well represented in the surety group throughout the period.[30]

By 1850, a select group of the wealthiest capitalists, known as the Boston Associates, 'controlled 20 per cent of the national cotton spindleage, 30 per cent of Massachusetts railroad mileage, 39 percent of Massachusetts insurance capital, and 40 per cent of Boston banking resources'[31] The approximate eighty men who constituted the Boston Associates exercised tight control over the economic life of the city, including the availability of credit. The Associates were very careful about loaning their credit or joint venturing projects with unknown partners. The idea of acting as a surety for a young, married artificer starting his own business would have generally been considered a dubious business practice.[32] And yet, these were exactly the 'respectable Citizens' that Franklin counted on to support the 'rising Generation' by standing as their guarantors.[33] The virtuous and benevolent citizens who might have stood as 'Sureties in a Bond with the Applicants' may also have been wholly unwilling to extend their credit on behalf of political and economic rivals.[34] Franklin envisioned a more generous spirit and sense of civic responsibility from American capitalists than to be found in nineteenth century Boston. Franklin would have disdained the process of concentration of wealth in a narrow sector of urban society.

Concerned about the corruption associated with luxurious living, the natural progress of unbridled self-interested acquisitiveness, Franklin expected that broad access of common people to the political franchise would promote equality of economic opportunity. In a letter to Franklin regarding the pamphlet entitled *Observations concerning the Increase of Mankind*, Richard Jackson described from Franklin a circumstance that unfortunately foreshadowed the human condition dominating Boston's nineteenth century Franklin loan fund. Jackson commented: 'Steady virtue, and unbending integrity, are seldom to be found where a spirit of commerce pervades everything ...'[35]

The banking reserves of Boston were swollen with capital, so much so that the failure of the Second National Bank of the United States resulting from Andrew Jackson's withdrawal of federal deposits had little sustained effect on Boston financial institutions.[36] Reinforcing its regional pre-eminence, Boston banks held 67 per cent of banking capital in the region in 1830. Notwithstanding Boston's insulation from deep economic depression during the Jackson/Biddle bank war, William Minot offered his opinion in 1837 on the financial and political bad times:

> All the banks in Boston refuse specie for New Bills. It is an unexpected shock to most of our Citizens but is rendered necessary by the call for silver & gold to remit to England in payment of our debts ... We are indebted to the egregious folly of Gen Jackson for some part of our present distress. In his wisdom he has tried to force a specie currency in this country. Never since the Revol. War has the distress of the county equalled the present. The quantity of Bank paper forced into the Market since the expiration of the Charter of the US Bank has led people into extravagant speculations. Vast investments have been made in Wild land in the Western Country & in Maine & in lands in the vicinity of all our cities. Farms have been bot [*sic*] in Roxbury at $1000 and acre for building lots. Nearly the whole of East Boston & South Boston have been sold in house lots which will not be wanted for a Century. India Rubber manufacturers, malleable iron manufactories & various other stocks have been created which have proven to be of no value. In fact a universal rage for speculation & an avarice [sic] of growing suddenly rich had seized all classes of the community which produced great extravagance in living & the neglect of men's proper occupations. Cotton, the great staple of the country had attained an excessive price, & a sudden fall seemed to destroy all the reserves of the southern & western country. The people of these States are always in debt, continually anticipating next years crop & for the decline of the produce are unable to pay their Atlantic Creditors. New York has been a deplorable creditor. Hundreds of Merchants declared rich have stopped payments & had not the suspension of specie payments (which proceded even a few days) enable[d] the bank to discount there would have been an end of commerce in that City. There is great alarm & many failures & but for the suspension it is thought some of our first Merchants must have stopped. Debts are not collectable & merchandize cannot be sold for money & scarcely a Credit. Gov't does not pay cash & has had the impudence to require it of its debtors. This is resisted.[37]

Unlike the conditions in New York City which Minot deplored, the linkage between Boston's financiers who controlled the banks and capital reserves, and the manufacturing interests was so strong that resources to support the high cost of industrial expansion of the Associates, in the form of enormous private industrial, commercial and transportation corporations, was readily available and in large quantities.[38] There was no contraction of credit for the economic elite. Moreover, access to these funds generally excluded all but the elite – controlling risk, concentrating capital, while limiting development.

Minot, in the above quoted excerpt from his diary, also revealed his desire to hold people within inflexible occupational and social class definitions. His comments about reckless speculation, extravagant living and financial irresponsibility were directed at the political followers of President Jackson, a group in Boston virtually synonymous with the interests of the mechanics. Expanding class conflict in Boston was a likely explanation for the unwillingness of the wealthy citizens to assist 'the rising Generation' as Franklin intended.

Despite the effort of the National Republicans and the Whigs to sell the doctrine of the 'harmony of interests', most Boston workingmen felt that the distribution of wealth resulting from the rapidly expanding economy and the attendant concentration of political power was increasingly uneven and unjust.[39] Franklin recognized the potential for abuse of the people that resulted from 'profitable Preëminence'. In 1787, Franklin issued this warning:

> Sir there are two Passions which have a powerful Influence in the Affairs of Men. These are *Ambition* and *Avarice*; the Love of Power and the Love of Money. Separately, each of these has great Force in prompting Men to Action; but when united in View of the same Object, they have in many Minds the most violent Effects.[40]

Franklin's intent in the codicil to assist artificers in establishing their economic independence ran counter to the interest of Boston Brahmins who sought to establish and maintain their economic and political hegemony. Boston's affluent citizens left the artificers 'an empty Bag'.[41]

William Minot, serving as Treasurer of the Franklin Fund during virtually all of this turbulent period, had political views and economic ties that aligned him with the Boston Associates. Minot's young legal practice was greatly boosted in 1811 by the responsibility to manage the Franklin Fund, a privilege given him by the Board of Selectmen. Although Minot was not compensated for his services to the town (then city) of Boston, the management role that he played brought his practice to local pre-eminence for matters regarding trusts and estates. Minot served as Treasurer of the Boston Mill Company which developed the mill pond land for residential housing and operated a bridge to Charlestown. Minot was also a founder of the Massachusetts Historical Society, the Massachusetts Charitable Fire Society, and the Massachusetts Mutual Fire Insurance Company. As a graduate of Harvard College, distinguished class of 1802, Minot had a durable network of classmates including City Treasurer Richard Harris, Congressman Samuel Hoar, Governor Levi Lincoln and Leverett Saltonstall.[42] Minot like Governor Lincoln and his other classmates held strong anti-Jackson political opinions. Minot berated Jackson in his diary:

> Genl Jackson has exercised unlimited sway by the force of his popularity. So great has been his power that he has dismissed officers vetoed acts of Congress & committed many acts apparently against law with impunity. He is the idol of the lower classes but generally and particularly in N. E. detested by people of education. In the professions and many merchants of property & intelligence his supporters in Mass are scarcely two in ten. Posterity must settle his character. His enemies consider him passionate yet crafty & and hypocrite, & unforgiving in his resentment. A bold & daring man tho he is narrow minded & illiterate. His attempts to introduce a specie currency prove him to be wholly ignorant of political economy.[43]

Minot showed the customary disdain that the Boston elite had for the groundswell of urban democrats and their national champion. Correspondingly, Minot advised the Board of Managers to invest the Franklin Funds away from the interests of the mechanics.

According to Minot's reports (and *not* substantiated by the financial accounting record), the lack of demand of the Franklin Fund's loan programme for artificers during the first twenty-eight years of the fund provoked the managers to seek alternate means of investment. Beginning in 1819, the Fund began to invest in other types of short term (maturity within five years) obligations. In 1827, the Fund purchased certificates of deposit with the Massachusetts Hospital Life Insurance Company, and remained heavily invested in that company for over one hundred years.[44] Thus, the accumulations that successfully magnified the value of the Fund during half of its 200 year term were derived from conventional endowment investment strategies, rather than the plan specified by Franklin in the codicil. The Fund had taken a permanent shift toward placing a priority on accumulation (frugality) at the expense of loans to qualified artificers (industry).

There is great irony in this investment decision. The Massachusetts legislature granted a charter to Massachusetts Hospital Life Insurance Company in 1818, which gave the company a monopoly on life insurance in the Commonwealth in exchange for the payment of one-third of the net profits from the sale of life insurance to the Massachusetts General Hospital.[45] Of great significance was the Company's empowerment within the terms of the charter to conduct trust business as well as insurance business. Although they prevented any other insurance companies from organizing in Massachusetts until 1835, the Massachusetts Hospital Life Insurance Company wrote very little life insurance. As of 1830 its trust deposits stood at $5 million contrasted with insurance policies and annuities worth $67,000.[46]

The Massachusetts Hospital Life Insurance Company, characterized by Boston Associate, John Lowell, as 'eminently the Savings bank of the wealthy' held in a pooled investment trust fund huge amounts of capital.[47] The company's status allowed wealthy Bostonians to create trusts that would protect their assets for their heirs, subtly circumventing the prohibition in American courts of aristocratic entail. In the early years the insurance company invested heavily in mortgages with a collection policy that appeared heavy handed to at least one contemporary observer.[48] Harriet Martineau, in her famous 1837 travel journal entitled *Society in America*, unflatteringly described the Massachusetts Hospital Life Insurance Company in the following excerpt:

> In Massachusetts the farmers have so little property besides their land, that they are obliged to mortgage when they want to settle a son or daughter, or make up for a deficient crop. The great Insurance Company at Boston is the formidable creditor

to many. This Company will not wait a day for the interest. If it is not ready, loss or ruin ensues.[49]

After the charter was amended to remove some of the more limiting collateral requirements on loans to industrial corporations, Massachusetts Hospital Life Insurance Company invested heavily in the textile companies in Lowell, Lawrence and Holyoke owned by Boston Associates, who also constituted the majority of the insurance company Board of Directors. William Minot was a Vice President of the Board of Directors from 1840 to 1864. The Franklin Trust was among many of the major eleemosynary institutions to wholly invest their endowments through Massachusetts Hospital Life Insurance Company.[50] The strength and mettle of the insurance company was tested in the 1837 panic when it held more than $70 million in assets with liabilities of $26 million. Only $420,000 mortgages and loans fell in arrears and, through sale of collateral, $400,000 in securities were regained.[51]

Despite the explicit investment instructions of the trust's creator, the Committee of the Board of Mayor and Alderman appointed in 1852 to examine the Accounts of the Treasurer of the Franklin Fund endorsed Minot's report and recommended 'that the amount of funds deposited in the Massachusetts Hospital Life Insurance Company remain there as a permanent investment'.[52] With this action the board of managers of the Franklin Fund abandoned the artificers loan fund very early in the Fund's 200 year lifespan in favour of investments in the 'Savings bank of the wealthy'. Functionally the Franklin Fund was privatized, i.e. placed beyond the public's eye. The managers declined to invest in Boston's human stock, in those intended to form the foundation of a free and enlightened citizenry.

The Franklin Fund's co-optation into a private investment pool happened so subtly that nobody apparently noticed. Other Boston charities were drawn into a heated debate over the boundary between public responsibilities and private privileges in the management and delivery of the human services. Public relief to the indigent (with eleemosynary private help) had been long established through the work of Boston's Overseers of the Poor who were responsible for the almshouse, first built in 1738 and replaced with a new building in 1800. As early as 1824, during the Mayoral term of Josiah Quincy, the confusion of private charity and public accountability had caused serious trouble.[53]

The City Council, newly created in 1824, eagerly demonstrated its democratic ideals by demanding that the Overseers of the Poor, customarily drawn from the socially and politically elite, be held publicly accountable for the use of eleemosynary funds. The Overseers felt that the application of charitable funds was fundamentally a private matter which they administered on behalf of the public. Mayor Quincy described, in 1824, the House of Industry City Council Committee's reaction to the conflict in the following:

> The reluctance thus exhibited by the Overseers of the Poor to be subjected to the same principles of accountability which the city Council had established, with regard to all boards and individuals who had expenditures of public moneys, made a deep impression upon the minds of the Committee.[54]

The record provides no explanation as to the reason the Franklin Fund Board of Managers, which had a parallel status to the Overseers of the Poor, avoided a similar challenge of authority and accountability. At least one might expect a challenge of the Board of Alderman's control by the Common Council or the public-at-large. It would be 1890 with the prospect of the centennial bounty when the public would demand an accounting of the governance of Benjamin Franklin's trust.

The courts during this same period reacted strongly and conservatively against the invasive moves of the government by supporting the emergence of the private corporation as a favoured legal status, protected from legislative invasion.[55] The privatization of business and charity limited the ability of the new political forces within Boston to achieve social and economic control. As a recent historian characterized it:

> By the 1820's, the Standing Order had been thoroughly transformed. Its power was no longer based on public authority, formal or informal. The disestablishment of the churches, the abolition of the property qualifications for voting and office holding, and the disintegration of traditional patterns of deference voting, had broken the hold on religion and government ... Instead, its power now derived explicitly from its possession of wealthy [sic] and, more, importantly, its control on incorporated cultural, economic, and social welfare institutions ... The pattern of charitable benevolence in New England shows clearly the reorientation of the old Standing Order from an elite with public responsibilities to a group whose influences was mediated through private institutions.[56]

The renovation of older quasi-public charities through clarifying their corporate status or through court directed reincorporation as private philanthropic foundations occurred in many states and local jurisdictions.

Notwithstanding the pride the managers of the Franklin Fund took on the 'success' of compounding of the Franklin Fund by 1890 reaching a value of $432,000,[57] especially when they viewed the performance in light of Philadelphia's lackluster experience of the first hundred years, several dubious developments were noticeably uncelebrated. The increase in value of the principal of the Boston trust had occurred at the expense of making no loans to successive generations of Boston's skilled workers intent on establishing small businesses. The investment in the Massachusetts Hospital Life Insurance Company, a decision directed by Treasurer William Minot, profoundly defeated Franklin's second intent of the testamentary trust. The lack of judicial review throughout the nineteenth century, rump management by the Aldermen without the three ministers designated by Franklin, and the delegation of inordinate responsibility to a single Treasurer/Manager contributed to the maladministration of the Franklin Fund. The permanent shift toward accumulation at the expense of the loan fund, while ostensibly the result of lack of sureties and poor credit practices of the bondsmen during the opening decades of operation of the loan fund, was more likely the outcome of expanding class conflict in the city of Boston.

William Minot's claims about the conduct of bondsmen, prospective sureties, and potential borrowers, upon which most pivotal Franklin Fund investment decisions were predicated, are at odds with the documentary evidence. The contrary evidence about credit practices and mechanics interests cast doubt about the intellectual integrity of Minot's representations. Certainly, the evolution of Boston city government did not produce a climate of benevolence nor attract enlightened and publically spirited leaders who understood Franklin's intent in creating the Franklin Trust loan programme and consistently endeavoured to implement his plan.

In preparation for the centennial division of the trust, the board of managers, led by the very powerful lawyer and alderman Henry L. Higginson, recognized that the Board of Aldermen's status as successors to the town selectmen had never been formally confirmed by the courts. They sought and obtained a decree in March, 1887 from the Probate Court of the county of Suffolk, naming the Aldermen as the legitimate successors to the vacancy created by the elimination of the Town of Boston Selectmen of 1822. This was the first attempt since receiving the Franklin bequest in 1791 that the managers sought to have changes which, heretofore, had been accomplished simply by fiat, sanctioned by a legal authority. Thinking that he was clarifying the situation, the Probate Judge referred to the managers as the 'trustees' of the fund.[58] With this began a protracted process of discovery and litigation in the 1890s and the first decade of the twentieth century that critically evaluated the quality of the city's past performance as manager and as trustee and challenged the first century's assumptions regarding custody and trust policy. The result would be a radical change in the direction and structure of the Franklin Fund trust designed, implemented and enforced by the Supreme Judicial Court of Massachusetts.

4 PHILADELPHIA: THE FIRST CENTURY

Long before Franklin's death in 1790, the debate over the Bank of North America created by the Pennsylvania legislature in 1781 had stimulated widespread opposition from artisans who had been excluded from access to the bank's credit and who objected to the concentration of wealth and commensurate power in a small minority of citizens. Access to capital posed the greatest obstacle to economic development in Philadelphia and Franklin responded in the 1789 codicil to his great need with his self-styled 'bank' of capital for aspiring artificers. The tension between the exclusionary policies of the Federalists of the 1790s and the mechanics interest in Philadelphia continued to build, notwithstanding the artisans support for the new US Constitution and a Bill of Rights.[1]

The largest of forty-six Democratic-Republican Societies created from 1793 to 1798 nationwide, the Philadelphia-based Democratic Society of Pennsylvania, was considered the 'mother' chapter and consolidated the artisans's belief in popular sovereignty and egalitarianism. Thirty-three percent of the membership of the club was drawn from craft trades.[2] The Democratic Society expressed concern over issues such as the frequency of elections, the responsiveness of representation, the availability of credit, the education of the people, the management of debt, foreign relations, taxation and the dangers of a standing army. The artisans of Philadelphia found their political voice through the Democratic Society.

With the editorial support of Philadelphian William Duane's *Aurora* and the political advocacy of Governor Thomas McKean and Dr Michael Lieb, Thomas Jefferson's 'Revolution of 1800' took Philadelphia by storm with the enthusiastic support of the artisan interests. In this context of democratic fervour in the nation's largest city, Franklin's executors in 1791 conveyed $4,444 creating the Franklin Legacy (as it was called in Philadelphia) and the loan fund commenced operation. There could not have been a warmer welcome for the designs of Franklin or a more auspicious beginning.

Philadelphia, in contrast to the Town of Boston, was established as a municipal corporation by 1789, when Franklin penned his codicil. He acknowledged this difference in his instruction, by delegating the management of the Funds to the city corporators exclusively, reserving no position for clergymen as managers. The town, upon receipt of the trust from Franklin's executors in 1791, placed the responsibility for the administration of the trust on the Committee on Legacies and Trusts of the Select and Common Council. This committee, with shifts in membership, terms and appointment procedures, administered the Fund from 1791 until 1869.

The account books of 'Dr Franklin's Legacy' describe the first fifty years of the Franklin Fund as somewhat more successful than an 1837 report of the Common Council's Committee on Legacies and Trusts. According to the account ledgers and the bond books, 304 bondholders were loaned Franklin Fund money through 1850 in the following decades:[3]

1791–1800	44
1801–10	70
1811–20	78
1821–30	65
1831–1840	34
1841–50	13

Of these borrowers 222 (73 per cent) paid back their loan in full. Another twenty-two (7 per cent) made most payments (at least seven of ten annual payments). A remaining forty-seven (15 per cent) made some payments and only thirteen (4 per cent) absconded with the money.

A source in 1810 indicated that the city treasurer reported the original $4,444 had been 'regularly loaned and ... has increased to more than double the original sum [$9,547]'. This same source noted that the 5 per cent interest rate was 1 per cent below the interest established by law making it highly favourable.[4] Hence, the first twenty years of the Franklin loan programme seemed to have operated successfully serving a large number of deserving Philadelphia mechanics.

Liberty Browne, a Franklin Fund borrower in 1800 of $319, was just the type of individual Franklin sought to assist. Browne, in establishing himself in business as a silversmith, obtained sureties from kinsman Peter Browne, an ironmonger, and Joseph Lownes, a fellow silversmith, Like Boston, the Philadelphia artificers seemed to secure sureties from relatives or people with the same surnames. Philadelphia's loan fund also showed much crossover among trades in the sponsorship of bondsmen with sureties listing a wide variety of occupations and trades. Liberty Browne, who was civically active during the War of 1812 on a committee to 'tend to better security of the port' and as a member of the Committee of Defense, later stood as surety for another Franklin Fund bondsman, Caleb McKenzie, a fellow silversmith. Rising up just as Franklin intended, Liberty Browne was elected to the high office of President of the Select Council of the City of Philadelphia in October of 1813.[5] His example demonstrated the power of Franklin's concept of the compounding effect of investing in human capital.

Problems of collection generally did not occur from 1790 to 1820. Only after 1820 did the number of partial or full defaulted accounts begin to challenge the integrity of Franklin's system.[6] The books indicated that a major house cleaning on the accounts was done in 1853 where money from the Fund itself was used to pay sixty-one delinquent accounts, effectively writing off the unpaid balances.[7] While this straightened up the ledgers, the pass-through nature of the action contributed no value to the appreciation of the fund's net worth.

The largest occupational category represented among the artificer bondholders was that of carpenter at thirty-six or 12 per cent. The second largest group was the cordwainer (includes shoemaker and bootmaker) with thirty-two or 10.5 per cent. The third largest was the tailor totalling twenty or 6.5 per cent. Other trades well represented were painters, cabinet makers, bakers, brick layers and currier/tanners, clockmakers and chairmakers. While the shoe and textile industry were profoundly affected by technological invention and the introduction of the factory system of labour fundamentally reordering the world of the cordwainers, Philadelphia artisans who worked in the building trades (carpentry, bricklaying and painting) or in highly specialized craft (cabinet and clock makers, for example) maintained much independence in the face of massive industrialization and persisted as a vital part of the local economy. As evidence of their persistent power within the urban polity, building craftsmen were protected by the City of Philadelphia from ruthless speculators with the passage of legislation in 1809 that 'all dwellings, and other houses to be erected in Philadelphia, are subjected to the payment of debts contracted on the building the same; and where the house will not sell for sufficient to discharge all the demands, they are to be averaged and paid proportionately'.[8] This law helped carpenters and housewrights collect their accounts receivable promoting regular payments on their accounts payable.

By 1829 the Committee had experienced difficulty in collection of the loans. In response to increasing delinquency the City Council passed three resolutions intended to strengthen the Franklin Fund's capacity to secure repayment. The first change required that one of the two sureties on each bond be the owner of real estate in Philadelphia with sufficient value to secure the loan. The second resolution of council required 'that a warrant of attorney shall accompany each bond, containing an authority to enter judgement immediately, and to take out execution for each installment as it becomes due, and the Treasurer is directed to enter up judgement immediately, and keep the same revived from time to time according to law'.[9] The third change prohibited women from standing as sureties.[10]

In the nearly fifty years of operation of the loan fund, 193 artificers then known as mechanics, had received loans to start their businesses under the terms set forth by Franklin.[11] As a result of poor collection efforts on the part of the City (referred to as lack of 'proper continuity of stewardship')[12] and lack of due diligence on the part of the borrowers, the 1837 report declared that nearly 60 per cent (112 artificers) were delinquent. Nineteen Franklin Fund debtors had paid nothing back, neither interest nor principal.[13] Given the long period of inactivity, 'as long as thirty-four years', the Philadelphia managers had not aggressively sought repayment by seeking relief through law suit. Boston's strategy of quick and vigorous pursuit of delinquent borrowers and their sureties apparently was not Philadelphia's approach. The 1837 Report did include a declaration from the Committee that in the face of default and maladministration it had 'placed the debts in the hands of a proper person for collection'.[14] In addition to Committee sought payment from the sureties as well as the bondholders through legal means. They noted that 'Should all the debts be recovered, the amount of the Fund would be $23,627.09 ...' still considerably less than the $39,833.29 they estimated Franklin expected after forty-five years of compounding.[15]

The ledgers and account books of Dr Franklin's Legacy, while describing fully the amount repaid, did not record collection efforts on the part of the managers or distinguish who made payments (bondholder or surety). Late in the century, the heirs of Franklin claimed that the Trustees of the Franklin Fund exercised a lack of fiduciary control for the first hundred years of the fund accusing them of 'negligence and carelessness'.[16] While acknowledging poor past performance, the Committee on Legacies and Trusts in 1837 seemed attentive and echoed most eloquently Franklin's purpose:

> Had the requirements of the Will been, in former years, fully complied with, the operation of the Fund, at this day, would be sensibly felt by the mechanics of Philadelphia. Passing from one borrower to another, and increasing in a compound ratio, its effect would be to stimulate industry, which, without such capital, would have remained unproductive. It would have increased the number of those who do business on their own stock. It would be a standing lesson on the immutable connexion between capital and productive industry, thus constantly inciting to economy and prudence. It would be the reward of every faithful apprentice, who could look forward to a participation in its benefit ... These great advantages must not be blighted in the germ -- a fund capable of setting in motion an indefinite amount of labour, must be lost neither by negligence nor supineness.[17]

Although the Philadelphia Franklin Fund minutes and reports do not explain what specifically happened, it appears that the simple lack of effort of the city to collect the loans, particularly to enforce the Franklin Fund's right to collect directly from the two sureties on each loan, was a major factor in the poor performance of the trust. While Franklin had confidence in the perpetual nature and fundamental integrity of great cities, like Philadelphia, the lack of fiduciary responsibility in the administration of the Franklin Fund was only a small example of general collapse of city government from the 1790s to the 1850s.

Starting with William Penn's original charter, Philadelphia had established a form of municipal government common to English cities but distinctive among American colonial capitals. Philadelphia from Penn's act of creation in 1701 until the Legislative Act of 1789, was managed by a closed corporation, with life membership drawn from the freeholding social and economic elite. As Philadelphia became increasingly committed to the course of American independence and participatory democracy, the ethos of revolution bred local hostility to the corporate form of municipal government. An 1887 source describes the logical progression that created a corrupt and inept city government by the time of Franklin's death:

> There was an inevitable tension for the corporation to consider the public property as held by them as trustees for the community at large. From this idea the transition was not difficult to the idea that the property of the corporation was held for the benefit of the corporation as distinct from the community with which it was locally connected; and from this idea the final transition was also easy to the opinion that individual corporators must justifiably derive a personal benefit from that property.[18]

Philadelphia, the nation's capital, required a major governmental overhaul in 1789 with additional revision in 1796, 1803 and 1835 and consolidation of city and county government in 1854.

The revamped City government, while making provision for periodic election and delegation of powers, ultimately failed to construct a well balanced government, with clearly defined and assigned executive, legislative and judicial functions. Increasingly the longstanding practice of management through semi-autonomous elected and appointed commissions, committees and boards of wardens, assessors, and overseers represented government which lacked control, accountability and integrity. Not surprisingly, the management of the Franklin Fund in this era languished.

Unlike the Boston managers, the Philadelphia sources do not identify the poor credit practices of the mechanics class as the major reason for the lack of compounding principal and interest. What's more the Committee on Legacies and Trusts in its 1837 report to Common Council showed and understanding of Franklin's concern about obstacles facing a young married man seeking to establish himself in business. Given the changes in the early nineteenth-century industrial structure and the nature and scale of manufacturing, the Committee found that men without substantial capital to invest found establishing an independent enterprise even more difficult and were 'distanced in the race for wealth'.[19]

One of the constraints of Franklin's instructions, a loan limit of £30 ($200–60) per applicant, was overcome by the fortuitous gift of John Scott to the City of Philadelphia in 1816. Scott's bequest was also to be held in principal while invested in loans to married artificers, according to Franklin's prescription. Described by one source as a 'biographer's nightmare' relatively little is known about John Scott or the nature of his philanthropy.[20] Scott died in London in 1815 although for the preceding decade his residence is undeterminable. He wrote a codicil in 1813 to an earlier Will with the following provision:

> I, John Scott late Chemist in Edinburgh do leave to the Corporation of Philadelphia who are entrusted w[t] the management of Dr Franklin's Legacy the sum of Three thousand Dollars of my property in the American three percents to be applied to the same purposes as D[r.] Franklin's Legacy ...[21]

The specific rationale for the gift cannot be discerned. There is no evidence that Scott either visited Philadelphia, knew Franklin or had American friends in Europe. Scott's executor, Samuel Paterson, knew a prominent Scottish emigrant typefounder residing in Philadelphia from 1794, James Ronaldson, well enough to use his agency in the transfer of the bequeathed stock to the Corporation of Philadelphia. Ronaldson later became the first President of the Franklin Institute when it was founded in 1824.

The augmentation possible with the Scott loan allowed artificers to borrow a larger amount ($520), by qualifying for two loans (one from Scott funds and one from Franklin funds). The large amount of capital was warranted by the increased cost of buying equipment and tools, stocking raw materials, maintaining inventory and marketing products. One estimate held that as late as 1850 an enterprising and industrious artificer could open a shop with as little as $500.[22] In 1829, the City Councils resolved to accept Mr Scott's conditions and assigned the management of the legacy to the Committee on Legacies and Trusts following an identical course to the Franklin Fund.[23]

Despite the reform in administration following the 1837 assessment of the Fund and the positive effect of the Scott Legacy, the loan activity continued to deteriorate. The availability of alternative sources of credit for the aspiring mechanic, from local banks and trade associations, with less confining terms may have contributed to difficulty of attracting Franklin Fund borrowers. While Philadelphia credit practises most frequently took the form of individual to individual, the first American building and loan association was founded in the city as early as 1831.[24] An earlier organization, the Philadelphia Saving Fund Society, established in 1816 and chartered by the Pennsylvania Legislature in 1819 as a corporation, had a limitation of $300,000 worth of total deposits it could hold and made investments almost exclusively in government securities and mortgage loans on real estate. While the terms of these loans were for long periods (ten to sixty year repayment schedules), loans to individually-owned businesses, when available, were for very limited periods of time (one month to one year at the most) and intended to provide short-term capital for maintenance of inventory or to compensate for trade exchange lags.[25] By mid-century as many as 600 associations held the modest savings of prospective owners of Philadelphia real estate, representing a substantial amount of accumulated capital. Notwithstanding this Philadelphia resource, long term financing (ten year repayment plans) for initially establishing small, craft shops was rare in any form for much of the nineteenth century.[26] The want of capital persisted as a problem for enterprising, though property-less, young artisans.

Prior to the 1870s, the record is silent about what measures were taken to popularize the loan fund, while respecting all of Franklin's requirements. Franklin's imposed constraints of age, apprenticeship, the 5 per cent interest rate, two sureties requirement, $260 limit and married status clearly limited the pool of qualified applicants and thwarted the growth of the Fund. However, Franklin left open the possibility of adjusting the trust to the needs of future when he said in the codicil:

> I wish indeed that they [Cities of Boston and Philadelphia] both undertake to endeavour the Execution of the Project: because I think that tho' unforeseen Difficulties may arise, expedients will be found to remove them, and the Scheme be found practicable ...[27]

As early as 1837 the managers recognized some of the inhibiting features of the trust, particularly the problem of young married artificers reliably repaying in instalments. The 1838 report also noted that 'early marriages are less usual'.[28] Despite this recognition, the managers of the fund proposed no changes to the list of qualifications at that time.

During the first fifty years of the Franklin Fund, the mechanics of Philadelphia suffered through the Embargo Act of 1807, the War of 1812 (especially the British blockade of the Delaware River), the panic of 1814, the post-war depression of 1819–24 and the panic of 1837. While these economic trends forced failures of large and small business alike, Philadelphia still grew exponentially in population and industrial strength throughout the period. Contemporary observer John Bristed declared in 1818:

> There is no part of the world where, in proportion to its population, a greater number of ingenious mechanics may be found than in the City of Philadelphia or where, in proportion to the capital employed, manufacturers thrive better.[29]

Based on the large number of artificers and the expansion of small artisanal shops, and notwithstanding the emergence of large factory-type manufacturing, the demand for a long-term loan programme like the Franklin Fund did not diminish.[30] While a particularly industrious artisan might locate a source of capital to establish an independent operation, this type of assistance nearly always required real estate as collateral, effectively eliminating the option for many property-less individuals.[31] Specific trade associations attempted to compensate for the lack of capital available to sustain fledgling enterprise. These societies combined resources and extended small loans (usually short term) to manufacturers 'to encourage and stimulate the industry of persons of small means ...'[32]

In 1850 11.7 per cent of workers in Philadelphia (representing 6,779 businesses) worked in small, independent artisanal shops, similar in scale and format to those of Franklin's time. Despite the transforming effect of industrialization on modes of production, a substantial number of manufactories remained, throughout the nineteenth century, localized, single craft oriented enterprises with a small number of employees organized along traditional lines (master craftsmen-owner, journeymen wage earners and apprentices).

Although the year of the first investment of Franklin Funds in City of Philadelphia bonds cannot be absolutely established, by 1841, an investment course contrary to the instruction of Franklin had been chosen. Presumably, the outcome of the 1837 committee report to the Common Council was a certain resignation that the loan fund was obsolete and would never demand all of the funds available. In 1874, the Franklin Fund managers declared that 'restrictions in regard to age, residence, marriage, apprenticeship, and security appeared to be the principal reasons why this trust fund was not more fully utilized by the citizens of Philadelphia'.[33]

By 1870, the managers committed nearly all of the Franklin Fund to the purchase of long-term, interest bearing loans to the City of Philadelphia itself. City bonds were first created and sold in order to finance long-term capital investment in urban infrastructure, i.e. bridges, roads, water works, other utility systems (gas), etc. The scale of the accumulating municipal 'funded' debt grew exponentially as follows:[34]

1807	$50,000	@ 6 per cent
1827	$600,000	@ 6 per cent
"	$991,000	@ 5 per cent
1853	$7,886,511	@ 6 per cent
1866	$33,837,794	–
1878	$61,721,542	–

Borrowing rather than revenue production from increased taxation was used to cover the cost of providing Philadelphians basic urban services and improving their living conditions. As in Franklin's day, the Mayor and City Councils in 1807 created a Sinking Fund as a vehicle to pay off the debt.[35]

The Sinking Fund of Philadelphia was as much a failure as Pitt's Sinking Fund in England of the 1780s. Remembering Richard Price's prescription, a sinking fund, in order to accomplish great accumulations, must be invested with all interest being returned to the fund to compound the principal. If the sinking fund is invested in municipal bonds, as in Philadelphia, then each annual city budget must attract enough revenue to be balanced *after* covering current expenditures and making regular repayment of interest and principal to the sinking fund. Philadelphia made the mistake (whether the result of political chicanery, hoodwinking or ineptitude depends on the historical recorder) of borrowing each year afresh, to cover the deficit created after all payments. The differential between interest paid (higher rates for new loans) to interest earned (lower rates on older loans) in the sinking fund created a fiscal sinkhole.

The city also borrowed directly from the Sinking Fund while contending that the Sinking Fund could continue to compound. Municipal reformers of the 1880s bear witness:

> The country was new, the faith of the people in themselves and their future was rightly boundless, and they easily permitted any occasional qualm to be salved by high-sounding ordinances about transfers to the sinking fund, and a spendthrift and specious book-keeping, and the pleasant fiction that the sinking fund was an actual practical security for the public debt. The touchstone of the fallacy is seen in the facts of history; the sinking fund did not sink; the debt increased with gigantic strides; the real collateral was increased earning power of the city and the increased capacity for tax-bearing.[36]

Investment in public debt not only defeated the Franklin loan programme but also completely ignored Franklin's deeper message about the ethos of saving. While Boston's strategy of investing in the 'Savings Bank of the Wealthy' was loaded with irony, Philadelphia's investment of Franklin Funds in public debt constituted an even greater travesty.

The account ledger of the Franklin Legacy first recorded in 1841 the purchase of stock in Philadelphia Gas Works which matured after twenty years and paid 6 per cent interest. Not insignificantly, when the managers of the Franklin Legacy sought alternative investment, they chose to invest in a corrupt, self-dealing utility scam. The Philadelphia Gas Works, purchased from private owners in 1841, was run by twelve trustees whose corrupt practices gained them the title of the Gas Ring. As historian Dorothy Gondos Beers explains:

> The purchase agreement stipulated that the trustees should pay no part of the profits of the works into the city treasury until all of the gas company's loans were paid – but no provision was written into the agreement against the acceptance of further loans with the same priority claim against revenues. In consequence the trustees negotiated a seemingly endless succession of loans as a means of awarding favors and creating relationships of mutual dependence with various business interests.[37]

The Gas Ring captain, James McManes, also wielded power as the war-time political boss of the local Republican Party. The political and economic grip of the Gas Ring on Philadelphia power eventually loosened through the work of the Committee of 100, businessmen reformers who sought to root out corruption in municipal government. The Committee's greatest accomplishment, the Bullitt Bill reform legislation, reorganized Philadelphia's government but not until 1885.[38]

Typical of the last half of the nineteenth century, in 1872, of the $53,150 of Franklin Fund assets, $4,300 was invested in 5 per cent municipal loans, $47,900 was invested in 6 per cent municipal loans and $950 was loaned to young married artificers.[39] This policy of investment was a violation of the testator's explicit instructions and broader intent. Franklin could have directed that his legacy be invested in government bonds from the outset, given the popularity of public financing of this kind in the Early Republic period and Franklin's familiarity with debt management. Franklin, however, chose to require investment in young industrious individuals whose lives and businesses would strengthen the urban economy and stabilize the skilled labour base. He referred in the codicil to these young men as 'the Rising Generation', a portentous label full of Franklin's belief in Philadelphia's potential for growth and prosperity. The redirection of his trust funds away from providing credit and working capital for artificers and their new shops toward financing debtor government betrayed the testator's intent and failed to comprehend his larger message to posterity. Not until 1869 did the Franklin Fund managers attempt to counteract the unpopularity of Franklin Fund loans and seek legislation to amend and update the terms and conditions of the loan programme.[40] In 1874, the Court of Common Pleas in Philadelphia granted the first *cy pres* adjustment sought by the managers. This first adjustment responded to the under twenty-five years of age requirement which reduced the number of eligible applicants. While maintaining the marriage provision, a decree of the court raised the eligible age to thirty-five years.

Although popular opinion held that men delayed marriage in urban, highly industrialized areas due to their inability to financially sustain a family, demographic evidence reveals that the proportion of men who married before reaching twenty-five years of age remained relatively constant throughout the nineteenth century.[41] In Philadelphia, by 1890, the Board of City Trusts contended that the average age of marriage for males was twenty-seven years of age. By adjusting the age to thirty-five, the Board and the Court of Common Pleas alleviated one of the most confining requirements and greatly increased the potential of eligible artificers.

Applicants had trouble finding two sureties who would guarantee repayment over the decade as specified in the Franklin Fund bonds.[42] As early as 1829, the city managers had required real estate from one of the two sureties as equity rather than gold as Franklin had specified. This is the first time that the terms of the trust were simply modified by fiat. The record is silent as to why the managers felt empowered to make this modification and, yet, were unwilling to make other adjustments that might have also increased the viability of the trust. In any event, the decision to require real estate had a material effect on the Franklin Fund's future.

The legal system facilitated efforts to collect, through foreclosure, posted real estate in order to satisfy delinquent bonds. The legal course for the attachment or capture of pledged cash assets or intangible property required more time and attention. Periodic specie shortages and the related suspension and resumption of specie payments for public debts inhibited the commitment of gold-backed guarantees for the Franklin loans. While the use of real estate collateral strengthened the recourse of the managers of the Franklin Fund in the face of bondholder default, the gravity of placing substantial property at risk probably frightened would-be sureties.

The instability of the economic climate for prosperous Philadelphians who might have agreed to be signatories as a Franklin loan fund guarantors must be recognized as a significant factor. The ability, not to mention willingness, of wealthy citizens to act as sureties depended on their relationship to the bondholder, the character of their business, the economic cycles that affected their fortune, the nature of their fixed and liquid assets, their access to credit, their dependence on foreign commerce, their other familial and community commitments and their tolerance for risk. When financing for speculative business development (investment in new manufacturing enterprises, in particular) was readily available from commercial banks due to the rapid expansion of wartime money supplies, prices were also high, specie was scarce and prosperous men were likely to exercise greater caution. While land values in Philadelphia also fluctuated with the economic times, urban real estate persisted as one of the most durable investments.

The requirement of apprenticeship created another obstacle to finding acceptable applicants. While the later claims of the managers that 'indentures of apprenticeship have been practically abolished' had some truth to it, the system of education and training for most occupational trades during the nineteenth century underwent great transitions. Increasingly confused with underpaid and generally exploited child labour, the practice of apprenticeship varied widely among trades even within the City of Philadelphia and was the focus of much criticism of nascent labour organizations.

Indentured apprenticeship, while surviving in Philadelphia during most of the nineteenth century, underwent legal and conceptual redefinition. Apprenticeship at the beginning of the Franklin Fund's first centenary required signed consent by the minor, his parents and the master. While the teaching of a trade was paramount, the master also had to provide rudimentary education. The Master also took the apprentice into his own household and provided room and board. By 1845 the Orphans' Court changed the Philadelphia regulations regarding apprenticeship to allow the Master to compensate the apprentice or another purveyor with a cash payment in lieu of providing housing and food.[43] The requirement of teaching an apprentice a trade remained fundamental to the covenant.

By 1865 the Pennsylvania Legislature no longer required that the Master provide education as long as the apprentice had received sufficient instruction in reading, writing and arithmetic 'to render further schooling unnecessary'.[44] Beyond the basic literacy and computational skill component, apprenticeship training at this time underwent a fundamental change in the workshop. Technical innovation and improvements in the production process resulted in the increasing specialization of work tasks. Unlike earlier divisions of labour where employees contributed to a whole process or the production of a complete unit, most worker in highly industrialized trades learned only the operation of a single machine or a single repetitive task. Child labour adapted particularly well to this new type of employment and apprenticeship in some trades became the cover for large scale employment of low pay, unprotected child workers. In the Philadelphia labour newspaper as early as 1828 journeymen decried the corruption of the apprenticeship system and the use of 'berkshires', the pejorative term used for under-trained apprentices.[45] In the same year the Mechanics Union of Trade Associations, Philadelphia's first 'central labour union' was created and sought to regulate apprenticeship, recognizing the pattern of abuse associated with labour.[46]

Philadelphia's mechanics placed a premium on education as a prerequisite to informed political consent, the bedrock of America's republican form of government.[47] The early American master/apprentice indenture resembled those of familial rights and obligations. As American society's responsibility for the education of youth transferred from the private family to public government, the educational component of apprenticeship was redefined accordingly. The managers of the Franklin Fund apparently failed to recognize that Philadelphia's system of public education was fulfilling the role of apprenticeship in the preparation of children to become productive adults. Public education could have been acknowledged as the contemporary equivalent of apprenticeship, thus, opening up the possibility of Franklin loans to all graduates.

In 1834, when the Commonwealth of Pennsylvania passed legislation creating a state-wide system of tax supported public education, Philadelphia already supported twenty schools serving 6,769 students. Samuel Breck, a state senator and reformer associated with the 1827 Pennsylvania Society for the Promotion of Public Schools, eloquently expressed the Franklinian vision when he described the intent of the 1834 school legislation:

> ... your committee have taken care to exclude the word poor from the bill ... to make the system general, that is to say, to form an educational association between the rich, the comparatively rich, and the destitute. Let them all fare alike in the primary schools, receive the same elementary instruction, imbibe the republican spirit and be animated by a feeling of perfect equality. In after life, he who is diligent at school will take his station accordingly, whether born to wealth or not. Common schools universally established will multiply the chances of success, perhaps brilliant success, among those who may otherwise forever continue ignorant. It is the duty of the State to promote and foster such establishments. That done, the career of each youth will depend upon himself. The State will have given the first impulse; good conduct and suitable application must do the rest. Among the indigent 'some flashing of a mounting genius' may be found; and among the rich and poor, in the course of nature, many no doubt will sink into mediocrity or beneath it. You let them all start with equal advantage, leaving no discrimination, then or thereafter, but such as study shall produce.[48]

Industriousness was a value cultivated at an early age, for an apprentice in Franklin's day, and for a child in the Philadelphia public schools in 1834. With the development of a broad, decentralized and accessible system, Philadelphia no longer relied on apprenticeship as a means to provide basic education for children (particularly of those from poor and pauperized families).[49] The Franklin Fund was intended to be one more means available to equalize conditions and facilitate industrious youth of the city. The resignation expressed in the 1837 Committee Report pronouncing that the loan fund was Franklin's 'vain Fancy' seems incongruous with Mr Breck's nearly contemporaneous expression of youth's promise and need.

Most trade associations, realizing that the schools could not provide specific vocational skills, during the latter half of the nineteenth century pushed for reform of apprenticeship rules and regulations. While some trade unions saw apprenticeship in a narrow view as competing, low cost, under-skilled, alternative manpower to be thwarted at all costs, most unions accepted a leadership role in redefining the process for young artisans to gain access to quality vocational, on-the-job training. These reform interests focused mainly on the length of service (not less than five years), limitations on the number of apprentices by trade and by employer, and the breadth of vocational and moral education required. Gradually protective legislation and trade association self regulation discouraged exploitative child labour and, consequently, apprenticeship began to slowly rebound in popularity. Notwithstanding all of the modifications to the system of apprenticeship, a sufficient number of artisans successfully completed apprenticeships of one kind or another in Philadelphia throughout the nineteenth century to have fulfilled the technical requirements of the Franklin Trust.[50]

The claims of the Trust officers regarding the dissolution of the apprenticeship system are irreconcilable with their administrative responsibilities for Girard College. When Stephen Girard, highly successful merchant of Philadelphia, died in 1831, he left his estate of $7 million to the Philadelphia municipal corporation in trust to establish a school for white, orphan boys.[51] A lengthy document with more prescriptive detail than in Franklin's *Last Will and Testament*, Girard instructed the city of Philadelphia as his heir as follows:

> And whereas, I have been for a long time impressed with the importance of educating the poor, and placing them, by the early cultivation of their minds and the development of their moral principles, above the many temptations to which, through poverty and ignorance, they are exposed; and I am particularly desirous to provide for such a number of poor male white orphan children as can be trained in one institution, a better education, as well as a more comfortable maintenance that they usually receive from the application of public funds ...[52]

The administration of the endowment and the college fell on the same city authority as the Franklin Fund.

The white male orphans admitted to Girard College contracted for apprenticeships after completing their course of study '... to suitable occupations, as those of agriculture, navigation, arts, mechanical trades, and manufactures ...'[53] per Girard's testamentary instructions. While the college experienced initial difficulty in 1852 with finding proper 'bindings', the Trustees creatively adapted the education of Girard students to the changing needs of Master craftsmen and did not abandon apprenticeship placements until 1881. The college created a vocational education curriculum as a prerequisite to placement that prepared the boys with skills, especially general writing and computation skills, that the Masters tradesmen of Philadelphia were no longer willing to impart. The Girard College administrators understood the changes affecting apprenticeships in the city and compensated with formal in-school education.

These young graduates of Girard College, with their educations and their apprenticeships accomplished, were ideally suited candidates for the Franklin Fund's loan programme. Given the premium placed on the compounding aspect of the Franklin Fund and the problems with locating sureties, it seems odd that the city officials (managing both trust funds) never considered using some of the enormous income from the endowment provided by the Stephen Girard as a source of collateral for Franklin Fund loans for Girard College graduates. Perhaps the tortuous legal history of the Girard Trust discouraged any inventive uses of the endowment's income.

Stephen Girard's collateral heirs sued the city in an attempt to terminate the trust, arguing that Girard's intent failed to qualify as a charitable purpose in light of Girard's prohibition of any trespassing by ecclesiastic, missionary or minister of any religious order. While Girard directed that the young scholars be taught 'the purest principles of morality', he sought to protect these young charges from suffering 'clashing doctrines and sectarian controversy'.[54]

Considered by Girard's contemporaries as sacrilegious and 'uncharitable', this provision acted as a cultural incendiary in 1844 when litigation contesting Girard's will came before the Supreme Court of the United States. The secular, anti-clerical nature of the trust effectively severed the largest single charity ever established in the United States from the church which had historically dominated American charitable institutions.[55]

The religious community, ironically represented by Daniel Webster (the defender of the sanctity of the private corporation in the Dartmouth College Case), backed the heirs contending that America was fundamentally a Christian nation and, consequently, Girard's exclusive testamentary instructions failed to serve a broad public charitable purpose. In other words the interests of the church were characterized as synonymous with the interests of the public, specifically the citizens of Philadelphia. The US Supreme Court ruled that Girard's purpose was sufficiently broad and appropriately charitable citing ancient Anglo-Saxon jurisprudential precedent with its greater tolerances for the definition of charity.[56]

The judicial outcome of Girard Will Case reaffirmed the inviolable nature of the private philanthropic corporate trust. The Girard decision established the right of individual citizens to transfer private property to private corporations that have the same legal rights and privileges as the private person. While the outcome of the Girard case reinforced the corporate integrity of philanthropic trusts, it did not immunize trusts from reinterpretation and adjustment. The courts could still consider *cy pres* adjustments to the management of trusts that were apparently failing to withstand the vicissitudes of time.[57] Considerable discretion could be exercised by the judges of Philadelphia's Court of Common Pleas and, in the case of the Franklin Trust, the testator's directives were modified on *nine* occasions through the vehicle of manager-initiated litigation. Certainly, in the Philadelphia lower courts, the 'Dead Hand' of the idiosyncratic philanthropist while assured of some legal defence was not unaffected by the persuasions of changing judicial perspectives and priorities. Notwithstanding the Girard Case, the courts began to exert authority over the administration of municipally controlled trusts, like the Franklin Fund, through a retarded but steady evolution.

For nearly seven decades the Philadelphia municipal courts and Pennsylvania state courts provided virtually no protection to the Franklin Trust. The committee system of government had failed to consider even slight adjustments to the loans programme to keep it attractive to young married mechanics. The management failed to broadly market the availability of loans, and it failed to properly collect on the bonds that it did write. Despite the failures, there is no record of complaint from either the public-at-large or Court of Common Pleas during the entire first hundred years of Franklin Fund existence. The most dramatic improvements in the management of the Franklin Fund resulted from a broad legislative action intended to clean up the corrupt and inefficient Philadelphia city government that emerged from the American Civil War era.

As part of a municipal governmental reform movement and by an Assembly Act of 30 June 1869, the Commonwealth of Pennsylvania created a Board of Directors of City Trusts (BODCT), a virtually autonomous public entity who had the authority to manage the various charitable trusts owned and managed by the City. The court distinguished at this time the trusteeship of the Franklin Fund that remained with the City of Philadelphia and the management of the Franklin Fund which was under the exclusive control of the BODCT. The action of the city built on the earlier reforms embodied in the consolidation of the city and surrounding country into a single metropolitan government by Act of 2 February 1854. While the creation of the BODCT was intended to protect all of the major and minor trusts held by the City of Philadelphia, the reformers sought primarily to ensure the proper management of the Stephen Girard trust. The Franklin Trust benefited incidentally.

The Supreme Court of Pennsylvania, the District Court and the Court of Common Pleas appointed the members of the Board of Directors of City Trusts for lifelong terms. The Mayor and the Presidents of the Select and Common Councils joined the twelve judicially appointed trustees. This trustee appointment process tacitly acknowledged the protective role of the courts and effectively removed the trust management from misfeasance or political diversion. While the distinguished citizens appointed to the Board represented the highly educated, professional, affluent sector of Philadelphia society, the BODCT's court appointed constitution minimized the potential for conflicts of interest in the management of public trusts.

The value of the Franklin Fund in 1870, the date of the first annual report of the BODCT amounted to $40,018.70 (a considerably smaller sum than Franklin's forecast of $220,273 by the year 1870). The Second Annual Report of the BODCT reported that the artisan loan fund was moribund. With no loans even applied for since 1861, less than $1,000 was being invested according to Franklin's wishes. Despite the Board's scepticism about the efficacy of the loan fund, it made a concerted effort to advertise the availability of funds. The Board placed prominent notices and placards in artisanal businesses and factories in order to attract eligible applicants.[58]

After twelve years of administration of the foundered loan programme, in 1881, the BODCT revealed some animus toward the class of citizens seeking loans. A report in that year stated: 'There have been six applicants in 1881 for the benefit ... The applicants, however, not infrequently, prove to be more impelled by misfortune to seek relief, than to be governed by the desire to advance their ability to do good work'. This distinction between assistance for advancement and relief reflects the general disdain that many erstwhile reformers had for the unemployed (idle). The commentary revealed the degree to which the applicant's motive was suspect and demonstrated an unwillingness to loan the money strictly on the basis of meeting the eligibility criteria.

While the upward political and economic mobility of the industrious and frugal middle class in Philadelphia warranted Franklin's optimism, the place of mechanics with their complex and conflicting interests in this urban conundrum is difficult to isolate and describe. By the time of the nation's centennial celebration, the City of Philadelphia had experienced tremendous social upheaval, political unrest and several economic catastrophes which had divided the residents by neighbourhood, political party, ethnicity, race, religion and social status. Despite the divisions, Philadelphians had managed to fight a war to sustain the republic, reform their government and establish education and suffrage as fundamental civil rights.

The dynamic genealogical chain that Franklin had hoped to forge between 'a Rising Generation' and an enlightened and generous senior citizenry was broken after the first three decades of Franklin Fund operation, notwithstanding the positive impact of the augmenting John Scott loans after 1816. Prior to the creation of the Board of Directors of City Trusts, the Franklin Loan Fund, politically isolated from the protective vigilance of the courts, had suffered from a dangerous combination of benign neglect, limited insight and managerial incompetence. By the end of the first centenary the Board of Directors of City Trusts, out of touch with the needs of struggling skilled workers, had all but abandoned the loan fund and concentrated on simply compounding the money through investments in government bonds. The irony of investing Franklin's legacy in a bogus Sinking Fund, self-serving gas utility stock, or other public bonded indebtedness was missed on the Philadelphia managers.

After a century of uneven investment and saving, Philadelphia prepared to receive Franklin's appreciated gift of the first part. It is not surprising that the first claims to be made would be of the heirs of Franklin alleging gross mismanagement and seeking complete dissolution of the trust.

5 THE CENTENNIAL IN BOSTON AND PHILADELPHIA

Just as the two cities were poised, according to Benjamin Franklin's wishes, to reflect on the virtues of frugality and industry demonstrated by one hundred years of municipal stewardship, the nation debated the impact of industrial capitalism on labour and the public welfare. Reform politicians, advocates of the Social Gospel, labour leaders, philanthropists and other urban progressives launched a rhetorical and practical challenge to government-created corporate monopolies, wanton materialism, systems of human exploitation and moral depredation. They articulated the contrast between 'identity of interest', a view held by most capitalists, and 'conflict of interest', a view held by most labourers. Also at issue was the relative permanence of economic and social stratification by class in America, calling into question the viability of individuals moving 'upward' in power, status and wealth.

Significantly, the tortuous debate and conflict of opinion in the 1890s regarding the vitality of American democracy and the need for broad economic and political enfranchisement required consideration of the relationship among factors of power, liberty, labour and capital. The sustenance of a progressive dynamic of these factors was central to Franklin's message to posterity in creating the revolving loan funds in Boston and Philadelphia to support individual efforts of the artisans to establish economic strength and independence. In 1894, Washington Gladden, Massachusetts clergyman and Social Gospel reformer, echoed Franklin's optimistic prescription for a prosperous and free industrialized America in the following passage from *Working People and their Employers*:

> The subjugation of labor by capital is the first stage in the progress of industry; the second stage is the warfare between labor and capital; the third is the identification of labor and capital by some application of the principle of cooperation. This is what we are coming to by and by. The long struggle between these two conflicting interests promises to end by uniting them, and making the laborer his own capitalist.[1]

While Gladden and other visionaries could foresee solutions to the problems facing the age, the crushing reality of the economic depression of 1893 left three to four million people unemployed nationwide, including up to 62,500 Philadelphians.[2] Without question Franklin's two municipal beneficiaries were confronting large scale, unmet human need just as Franklin's centennial gift was distributable. Franklin stated his wishes as follows:

> ... I would have the Managers of the Donation to the Town of Boston [and, likewise, the Corporation of Philadelphia], then lay out at their discretion one hundred thousand Pounds in Public Works which may be judged of most general utility to the Inhabitants, such as Fortifications, Bridges, Aqueducts, Public Buildings, Baths, Pavements or whatever may make living in the Town more convenient to its People and render it more agreeable to Strangers, resorting thither for Health or a temporary residence.[3]

Franklin also expressed concern about the deteriorating quality of Philadelphia's well water and recommended that the Corporation tap the water of Wissahickon Creek, building a dam, if necessary. On the urban reform agenda in the 1890s in both cities was clean air and water, proper sanitation systems, general hygiene, urban parks and recreation, public facilities and better transportation and housing, a testimony to Franklin's remarkable prescience in 1789.

Boston

As the centenary division of 1891 approached, Boston's Franklin Fund increased in visibility and vulnerability. As a result of the combination of investments the Franklin Fund was valued at $431,756.18.[4] This total was to be divided on a ratio of one hundred to 131 with the largest portion of the accumulated principal to be distributed to the city of Boston for public improvements. The ratio came from the codicil's language, where Franklin projected the yield from compounding interest on the original £1,000 achieving an accumulation valued at £131,000.[5] £100,000 was designated as Franklin's centenary gift to the city of Boston. The actual yield converted to pounds equalled approximately £90,000, a little under 67 per cent of Franklin's estimate.[6] Thus, Boston divided the Franklin Fund into two parts, the first part totalling $329,300 for immediate outlay and the second part totalling $102,456 to be held in principal compounded by the earned interest until the bicentennial distribution in 1991. In the 1892–3 Annual Report of the City Auditors, just prior to the formal division, the Fund was invested as follows:[7]

Deposit in Massachusetts Hospital Life Insurance Company	$411,100
Deposits in Suffolk Savings Bank	$3,489
Cash	$13
Balance of bonds, for loans	$210

The predominant investment in the Massachusetts Hospital Life Insurance Company policies continued in the Franklin Fund (the portion reserved for the second hundred years referred to as Part II) after the funds were split in January, 1894 with only one bond for loan of $60 listed among the investments.

Mayor Samuel Abbott Green, in his inaugural address in 1882, advocated the application of the centennial Franklin legacy to the benefit of one of 'the new parks'. In an effort to respond to the language of the codicil, Mayor Green claimed that parks served as a 'convenience' of 'the whole people'. In too-eager anticipation of a Franklin Fund appropriation, the Park Commissioners, following the resolutions of the Board of Aldermen, renamed West Roxbury Park as Franklin Park (a large urban park that would come to include the municipal zoo) after its erstwhile benefactor. Predictably, the City of Boston had an ulterior reason, other than loyalty to Franklin's wishes, to apply the Franklin Funds to public parks. Samuel McCleary, Treasurer of the Franklin Funds, recalled the sequence of events in 1897:

> Upon the purchase by the city in 1881–2 of five hundred and twenty-seven acres of land in West Roxbury for a public park, the city issued bonds for the payment therefor. A large amount of these obligations matured in July, 1891, at the very time the city should have received its portion of the Franklin Fund ...
>
> But owing to the injunction by the heirs, the city share of the Fund was not available in July, 1891, and the city's bonds, which matured about that date, had to be met in some other way.[8]

The managers, having missed the bond maturation date, felt free to consider other options. By 1893, the board of managers, then synonymous with the Board of Alderman with the addition of the three ministers, invited the public to propose projects that the City of Boston might fund through the Franklin bequest. According to the codicil, Franklin suggested several possible public works projects 'such as Fortifications, Bridges, Aqueducts, Public Buildings, Baths, Pavements'.[9]

There were twenty-seven separate proposals considered, including the creation of a trade school, children's playgrounds, social centres, health institutes, a tuberculosis hospital, adult education programmes, public baths and a museum. The Board determined that only thirteen ideas appeared to be consonant with Franklin's wishes.[10] On 28 December 1893 the board of managers of the Franklin Fund adopted a plan to create the Franklin Trades School, believing that the decision was 'in keeping with Franklin's known philosophy of life to supply training in the trades that would be the greatest advantage to the community'.[11] Pursuant to this action of the board of managers, board Treasurer Samuel F. McCleary conveyed to city Treasurer Alfred T. Turner $322,490.20, the value of the Franklin directed division as of 1 July 1893. The managers explicitly retained the right to select the location of and plans for the new Franklin Trades School. The managers presumed, as they had since the incorporation of the city in 1822, that they were fully empowered in relation to the funds.[12]

Conceived as an educational alternative to high school on the one hand and 'mischief' and petty crime on the streets and wharves on the other, the Franklin Trades School's curriculum offered instruction in all 'branches of mechanical arts'. Treasurer McCleary explains: 'This school will take the place of the old apprenticeship system and a diploma upon the lad's graduation will furnish a complete proof of his competency to do faithful work, and will entitle him, if he be under the age of twenty-five and becomes married, to a loan of three hundred dollars with which to set up his chosen art'.[13] The legacy of the first hundred years of compound would create an institution which would prepare mechanics for eligibility for Franklin Fund loans offered from the compounding 1891–1991 portion of the fund.

It is highly significant that the Board of Managers would seek out an application that would address the need of young Boston citizens to achieve an education enabling them to become skilled workers. By attempting to overcome the problem of vanishing apprenticeship opportunities, the board contritely sought to rejuvenate the virtually moribund artificers loan fund. The Franklin Trade School was viewed as a way to finally honour Franklin's intent to empower a class of workers who would then serve others as enlightened citizens of Boston.

In late 1894 and early 1895, the Board of Managers advertised for bids on land that would be suitable for the construction of the Franklin Trade School. To that end on 29 June 1895 the board considered the responses and voted to purchase five acres of land referred to as the Parker Hill estate owned by H. J. Jaquith. While the Board of Managers were resolved on the use of Franklin's centennial bequest, the city Treasurer, Alfred Turner, believed that the people of Boston, as beneficiaries of the bequest, had ultimate discretion over the use of the city's portion and, after receiving the transfer of money from the Franklin Fund, refused to respond to any subsequent direction from the board of managers. The city Treasurer challenged the right of the managers to direct the City's application of the City's centennial share to purchase the Parker Hill estate and refused to cooperate.

In 1896 the Aldermen with Mayor Josiah Quincy and the three ministers filed a petition before the Probate Court of Suffolk County to be recognized as the trustees forcing Treasurer Turner to act upon their decisions. At the same time 'The Citizens' Association' asked the Probate Court to declare that there had been 'a failure of the Managers and Trustees' and that the three ministers of the oldest churches be reinstated along with four other individuals appointed through the wisdom of the court. The Attorney General of the Commonwealth filed a similar petition.

The Registry of Probate in March 1897, responding to the two petitions, appointed four individuals (Henry L. Higginson, Francis Welch, Abraham Shuman and Charles T. Gallagher) together with the three ministers of the oldest Episcopal, Congregational and Presbyterian churches, to serve as trustees with 'right of possession and control of funds'.[14] 'The court assumed that the managers were trustees and that when the town became a city there became a vacancy in trusteeship'.[15]

The new Board of Managers invoked their status as trustees of the Franklin Fund, granted by the Probate Court in 1897, and once again laid claim to the contested city share. After failing again to persuade Treasurer Turner, the board of managers sued Turner and the city for custody of the funds as the legitimate trustees.[16]

As a result of Higginson's (et al.) lawsuit against Turner, the Supreme Judicial Court of Massachusetts, in August, 1898, overturned the Probate Court's 1887 appointment of the individual managers as trustees, and restored the trusteeship to the City Alderman as well as granting 'possession and control of the fund' to the city of Boston as successor to the town of Boston.[17] While the bulk of the judgement simply voided the elevation of Higginson and other manager/trustees, the court offered an additional interpretive comment as follows:

> In the present case, the duties of the managers, though in some respects like those usually exercised by trustees, are not such as imply technical trusteeship. These duties bear some relation to those of visitors of a charity. The managers were probably intended to assist rather than supplant the inhabitants of the town in the administration of the fund. It is not necessary at this time to define the extent and limits of their authority.[18]

The new Board of Managers, under the leadership of Chairman William H. Lott, decided to reopen discussion on the proposal to build a trade school with Franklin's centennial bequest. The reconsideration process allowed popular alternatives to the trade school a chance to gain recognition and support.

One of the possible applications of the centennial distribution mentioned specifically by Franklin was public baths. The problem of urban sanitation and public health was still an issue one hundred years later in urban Boston. Mayor Josiah Quincy took the cue from Franklin's codicil and, in 1898, promoted the idea of using the Franklin Fund bequest for the construction of public baths instead of the trade school. Quincy's campaign for baths, which led to the construction of the elaborate Dover Street bath in Boston's South End opened in October, 1898, was premised on the connection between moral and spiritual well-being and physical cleanliness. Quincy's eloquent comments in March,

1897 on the subject are resonant with the resolves of Franklin's Junta of mid-eighteenth-century Philadelphia:

> The duty of a city is to promote the civilization, in the fullest sense of the word, of all its citizens. No true civilization can exist without the provision of some reasonable opportunities for exercising the physical and mental faculties, of experiencing something of the variety and of the healthful pleasures of life, or feeling at least the degree of self-respect which personal cleanliness brings with it. The people of a city constitute a community, in all which that significant term implies; their interests are inextricably bound together, and everything which promotes the well-being of a large part of the population benefits all.[19]

Mayor Quincy, and important political ally of reformer President Grover Cleveland and a former assistant US Secretary of State, forged an unlikely political partnership with the Irish political bosses to manage the City of Boston while advancing a tall agenda of municipal reforms. Literally and figuratively Quincy's ideas about the use of the Franklin Legacy for pubic baths squared with Franklin's intent. Quincy specifically disapproved of using the funds for the creation of a trades school which he felt 'might be possibly be of great special benefit to a very small fraction of the people, but it certainly would embody no such general utility to all as Franklin contemplated'.[20]

Powerful Mayor Quincy and Boston's labour unions who anticipated lucrative construction contracts to build the bath house were behind Treasurer Turner's artful obstruction of the Aldermen's plans for the centennial Franklin legacy.[21] Quincy opposed the plan to establish a trade school on the basis of its variance with Franklin's 'exact intentions'[22] but others were concerned about the burden placed on future taxpayers to pay the continuing costs of operation of the school. Ultimately, the political contest over what was to be done with the Franklin legacy and who was entitled to decide its fate would be resolved in the courts.

In the wake of the vote of 1893 to spend the centennial portion of the Franklin Fund on the establishment of a trade school, the Board Managers, in 1894, visited several trade and technical schools throughout the Northeast. They found distinctions in the types of institutions that taught vocational skills and abilities. Due to delays associated with the obstinate City Treasurer, the opposition of Mayor Quincy, and the final decision of the Supreme Judicial Court settling the authority issue in favour of the sitting Board of Alderman, a public hearing was called for 14 November 1898 and continued 25 November 1898 to record arguments for and against rescission of the 1893 vote to create a trade school. While the focus of the testimony was on the advisability of creating a trade school, witnesses were often favouring one of two alternative uses: the creation of public baths or the creation of an institute similar to the Cooper Institute in New York. Behind these partisan views loomed a growing tension between the Old Yankee interest shared with manufacturers and employers as well as gentlemen philanthropists (who favoured the trade school) and the Young Mechanic interests reflecting the viewpoint of the ethnic journeymen and labourers (who favoured either a self-improvement institute or public baths). Some of the testimony over the application of the Franklin Fund directly addressed the conflict in highly charged economic and social class terms. A collateral debate centred on the best way to educate workers in an increasingly industrialized economy and labour market.

At the time of the hearing, the Manual Training School phenomenon was well established in Boston. Becoming increasingly popular in the 1870s and 80s the Manual Training schools nationwide offered parallel curricula in 'intellectual and manual' subjects. Students pursued, over a three year course of full-time study, five simultaneous tracks: (1) mathematics, (2) science and applied mathematics, (3) language and literature, (4) Penmanship and drawing and (5) tool instruction.[23] The students learned broadly avoiding a 'narrow' education for a specific trade. Manual Training Schools also introduced pedagogical innovations by the use of the workshop method of teaching and learning. Boston's School Superintendent Seaver explained:

> Manual training is essential to the right and full development of the human mind, and therefore no less beneficial to those who are not going to become artisans than to those who are. The workshop method of instruction is of great value, for it brings the learner face to face with the facts of nature; his mind increases in knowledge by direct personal experience with forms of matter, and manifestations of force. No mere words intervene. The manual exercises of the shop train mental power, rather than load memory; they fill the mind with the solid merchandise of knowledge, and not with empty packing cases.[24]

The introduction of manual training into the public school curriculum did not, however, deal effectively with the problem of the atrophy of the apprenticeship system. Charles H. Morse, in his testimony at the November, 1898 hearing, distinguished trade schools from the manual training school, while admonishing trade unions for their opposition to the proposed Franklin Trade School:

> The trade school is intended for an entirely different purpose [than the manual training schools]. It takes the boy whose parents cannot possibly afford to send him to a high school and fits him for life ... There is at every manual training school almost daily application by parents to have pupils admitted for the purpose of becoming trained in mechanical work only ... In view of the fact that the manual training school cannon teach a trade, and in view of the fact that the apprenticeship system ... has gone to pieces ... [,] the only solution ... is ... establishment of schools which will make good mechanics.[25]

Characteristic of the rhetoric of labour during those halcyon days of the Knights of Labor, the tradesmen who testified against the Franklin Trade School in

November, 1898, objected to its narrow and applied curricular focus. George E. McNeill, representing the Central Labor Union, while declaring that 'Your trades school is simply reactionary process, an attempt to get back to the good old times of master and servant'.[26] advocated the use of the funds for an institute similar to the Cooper Institute in New York City. McNeill explains:

> I say we want an institute that shall include the trade school ... We want the education of the old barn chamber, the education of the old country home, where a boy is taught to nail on shingles or paint a house or lay a drain pipe or cultivate the farm, or do anything that is necessary. That is what the manual training school does. The manual training school, if it can have its full course through the high school, turns a boy out adapted to what comes next.[27]

McNeill sought a place where mechanics could come to learn citizenship, a place with public lectures, gymnasia, library, baths and a forum for exchange. Certainly McNeill invoked the spirit of Franklin when he ruminated: 'You may fill the streets of Boston with men who know how to handle the hammer or the saw or the plumbers' tools, or anything else, and you haven't raised the level of citizenship'. McNeill and several other witnesses before the Board of Managers 'want blacksmiths who are capable of being Congressmen ...'[28] McNeill echoed Franklin's conviction that skilled and industrious artificers, when presented with opportunity, substantially contributed to cities and made exceptionally benevolent and capable citizens and leaders. McNeill might have quoted Franklin with 'A rising tide floats all boats'.

Several speakers at the Board of Managers hearing in November of 1898 spoke in favour of sustaining the 1893 decision because they viewed the Franklin Trade School as a solution to the problem of under-qualified labourers entering the trades. William E. Wall, Secretary of the Master Painters and Decorators of the State of Massachusetts, claimed that as many as 50 per cent of the journeymen in his painting trade were incompetent due to lack of training.[29] Fred. J. Kneeland, President of the International Brotherhood of Painters and Decorators, refuted the claim by challenging the definition of competence. Kneeland argued that the 'master builders' and the 'professional philanthropists', those responsible for proposing the Franklin Trades School and several attending the hearing, knew little of the journeymen's business and defined competence according to the pace rather than the quality of performance. Not surprisingly, Kneeland touted an alternative application: 'I contend that public baths and a public forum are what we want, and that is what Ben Franklin wanted. If he had wanted something else he would have so stated'.[30]

John F. O'Sullivan, President of the Central Labor Union, pulled off the gloves and flatly declared that trade schools could not teach trades and inferred that their graduates had been taught to distrust trade unions. On-the-job training, or experience, was the only way to accomplish the education of fresh recruits to any trade.[31] O'Sullivan's testimony addressed the size of the work force and the larger problem of the unemployed and the underemployed. O'Sullivan, the last speaker of the evening of 14 November, concluded with the following impassioned plea:

> It can never be charged that the trades union is opposed to advancing intellectually, morally, and materially the wage workers interests. We stand here, not opposed to that, but opposed to creating an organized army of men who would come in and take our places. They say: 'What are we going to do with our boys?' My God! the proposition is: 'What are you going to do with their fathers?' What are we going to do with the boys! I appreciate that the problem of taking care of the child is a serious problem, but it is not to be considered with that of the man who starts out in the morning, walks over to Boston, goes down to the 'Globe' bulletin boards, where the paper is posted out on the outside, who is too poor to buy a paper, but who goes and scans that list, looking for the 'want ads.' to see where he can go for employment. With him the proposition is not what are you going to do with the boy, but the proposition is: 'What am I going to do with my family?'[32]

The hearing recorded an appendix listing forty-four witnesses in favour of and one witness opposed to rescinding the vote of 1893, the vote establishing the Franklin Trade School. On 15 December 1898 the managers voted to rescind the 1893 and 1895 decisions to establish the Franklin Trades School and purchase the Parker Hill Estate.[33]

Responding to the widespread interest in the creation of an institute patterned after new York City's Cooper Union (referred to as Cooper Institute in the City of Boston and Franklin Fund records), a five person committee of the Managers proposed on 1 August 1899 to 'lay out one-half of said Fund in the erection of a building on Washington street, in Boston, fitted with public conveniences, a library, reading-rooms, public hall, lecture rooms, ward-room, etc. and the other half in erecting a bath-house and gymnasium'.[34] The Cooper Union, created in 1859 through a substantial endowment given by industrialist -turned- philanthropist Peter Cooper, provided free instruction at night to working artisans seeking greater skill or knowledge of new technology. The record of the Franklin Fund is silent as to why the 1899 committee report was accepted but no action was taken. Another five person committee discarded the bath-house and gymnasium aspects of the earlier proposal and added shops and laboratories for 'theoretical and practical instruction in the applied arts and sciences'.[35] It was not until 17 April 1902 that the Board of Managers set forth the educational mission of the Franklin Institute as follows:

> 1. The general education of adults by classes and lectures in history, political and social science.

> 2. Theoretical and practical instruction in such applied arts and science and kindred subjects as shall be deemed by such managers best calculated to stimulate and broaden the intelligence, cultivate the taste, enhance the skill and increase the efficiency of the people of Boston and vicinity, giving special regard to artisans.[36]

With this iteration of a more expansive educational mission, the Franklin Institute's curricular parameters were gaining (what would become) final definition. The Board of Managers followed up its decisions with a public hearing on 13 May 1902 considering nine various lot locations for the new building. On 17 April 1902 they determined to 'lay out a portion of said fund for the erection of a building for the promotion of education ...'[37] By deciding to 'lay out' the Franklin Fund money, they thought their action could compel the City Treasurer to spend the funds as directed by the newly constituted, and court sanctioned, Board of Managers. It was not to be.

In 1903 Mayor Patrick A. Collins brought suit against the alderman acting as the board of managers of the Franklin Fund. The plaintiff was successful in challenging the legitimacy of the aldermen as the natural successors to the selectmen. After seventy-nine years (out of eighty-one years since 1822 and the incorporation of the City of Boston) of de facto authority, the Supreme Judicial Court, in 1904, voided all of the Aldermen's board membership leaving the Mayor and the three designated ministers. The court also affirmed the status of the Franklin Fund as a public charity of the City of Boston. This judgement effectively relegated the city's interests to that of beneficiary at the centennial and bicentennial of the trust pursuant to Franklin's testamentary construction. After stripping the aldermen from the management, the court recalled the Franklin's language in the following judgement:

> In regard to the administration of the charity the testator said in the codicil, 'It is presumed that there will always be in Boston virtuous and benevolent Citizens willing to bestow a part of their time in doing good to the rising Generation by Superintending and managing this Institution gratis', etc. We are of the opinion that managers should be appointed by the court from this class of citizens, chosen by reason of their qualifications, intellectual and moral, for this important service. We deem it proper that the mayor ex officio should be a member of the board, and that the whole number of lay members to act with the clerical members should be the same as the number of selectmen at the time of Dr. Franklin's death.[38]

To that end the Supreme Judicial Court appointed eight leading private citizens to fill the seats vacated by the Board of Selectmen in 1822, who with the Mayor and the three ministers would serve as the managers of the Franklin Funds (centennial and bicentennial portions). This governance structure endures to the present.

Of the eight appointees, two prominent lawyers (William Endicott and Richard Olney) had served in President Grover Cleveland's administration as Secretary of War and Secretary of State, respectively. Frank K. Foster and Charles T. Gallagher were distinguished professional men and state level politicians. Nathan Matthews had served as Mayor of Boston for four terms and was considered an expert on municipal governmental affairs. Henry P. Bowditch, Dean of the Harvard Medical School and Henry S. Pritchett, President of the Massachusetts Institute of Technology, represented the intellectual elite. Boston banker and industrialist James J. Storrow completed the Franklin Fund Board of Managers selected by Judge C. J. Knowlton of the Massachusetts Supreme Judicial Court. Despite this battery of political power brokers, the Managers of the Franklin Fund still had to negotiate several more twists and turns in the road on the way to spending the centennial legacy.

Although the ruling strengthened the independent and private nature of the Franklin Fund as a charitable trust, one other part of the judgement muddied the waters again insofar as the proper course for the expenditure of the centennial share that city Treasurer Turner still held hostage. In the favour of the managers, the court decreed that when Franklin used the term 'outlay' he meant the funds should be expended on public works projects and that the managers were empowered to develop a plan, establish the project and expend the money. In the city's favour, the court agreed with the plaintiffs that public works projects that created an ongoing 'burden of maintenance' compelling the commitment of public funds could be appropriately vetoed by city opposition. The City of Boston could, of course, voluntarily cooperate with the managers in support of the project within the scope of their public authority. However, the court ruled that the city could not be compelled to cooperate and the city showed every determination to block the trade school project. It took a confluence of the mightiest powers, political, economic and philanthropic, to finally achieve Franklin's centennial expectation. Enter Patrick A. Collins, Henry S. Pritchett, Andrew Carnegie and James J. Storrow.

Patrick A. Collins, the Mayor and the man responsible for the removal of the aldermen, grew up in Chelsea, Massachusetts, was educated in the public schools and apprenticed as an upholsterer. He rose through the artisan ranks, studied law and was graduated from the Harvard Law School in 1871. The finest example of Massachusetts Democratic Party leaders, Collins had the respect of the corporate community, the basis of his practice with Partner Judge John W. Corcoran, as well as the rather more boisterous Boston Irish politicos.[39] Collins, who could clearly identify with Franklin's platform promoting frugality and industry, was credited as having politically established the Franklin Fund as a proper, private charitable trust with capable trustees, able to withstand a second hundred years of challenges and trials.[40]

As President of Massachusetts Institute of Technology, Henry S. Pritchett was one of the citizens tapped in 1904 to serve on the court reconstituted board of the Franklin Fund. Pritchett's education and his university teaching appointments had been in the fields of astronomy and mathematics. President McKinley appointed him superintendent of the US Coast and Geodetic Survey. The ubiquitous Dr Pritchett, after serving ten years as President of MIT, became the first President of the Carnegie Foundation for the Advancement of Teaching. It was Pritchett, while visiting Andrew Carnegie in Scotland in 1904, who secured Carnegie's interest in the Franklin Trades School. While Pritchett served as Chairman of the board of managers, he negotiated an equal matching gift from Andrew Carnegie to the Fund's centenary distribution to the city of Boston. The Franklin Fund amount, which by 1904 had grown to $408,000, was available for erecting a building.[41] Carnegie's money was designated as an endowment for the ongoing support of the school and the maintenance of the building, which removed the objection that city officials had originally raised in 1895. Carnegie, made as his one condition to the gift, that the city of Boston acquire the site. The State Legislature of Massachusetts authorized a $100,000 bond issue under Statue 1905, Chapter 448 on behalf of the city of Boston in order to purchase a site for the new trades school, thus fulfilling Mr Carnegie's condition. It is highly significant that the enlightened and willing-to-be-helpful Patrick A. Collins was mayor of Boston when the deal was struck.[42]

Carnegie's interests in the education of tradesmen had concentrated on the Mechanics' and Tradesmen's School and the Cooper Union for the Advancement of Science and Art (also referred to as the Cooper Institute). As Trustee and Benefactor of both New York City institutions, Carnegie had an informed vision of the educational mission, the physical plant, the type of equipment appropriate for Boston's new Franklin Union (as it came to be called).[43] Carnegie's language in a letter to Dr Pritchett in 1904 summons up the philosophy and ethic of Benjamin Franklin:

> I think it is from the class who not only spend laborious days, but who also spend laborious nights fitting themselves to hard work, that the most valuable citizens are to come. We are here helping only those who show an intense desire, and strong determination, to help themselves, -- the only class worth helping, the only class that is possible to help to any great extent.[44]

Carnegie, whose first job was 'dipping bobbins into an oil bath and firing the factory boiler',[45] in a textile mill in Pittsburgh, worked his way up, according to the promise of America, amassing in the process one of the greatest of American industrial fortunes. Like Franklin, his early wealth came from the business of communication. As Franklin in his time utilized his printing business, the position of Deputy Postmaster and his incredible management skill, to profit from communications, Carnegie realized the reliance of business upon telegraphy, worked his way up through the Pittsburgh Telegraphy Company and utilized his extraordinary management ability to create a sound information network and financial base from which to build his corporate empire.[46] It is not surprising when Dr Pritchett told him of the Franklin Fund dilemma, Carnegie's immediate response was: 'I'll match Ben Franklin'.[47]

Carnegie's sway with Mayor Collins was also critical to making a deal. When the city balked at providing any support of the Franklin Union, Carnegie finessed the city with his offer of matching funds to be used to offset annual expenses. The fractious nature of private and public Boston at the time required someone of the international stature and economic power of Andrew Carnegie to successfully prod the city into partnership.

The Supreme Judicial Court by its 1904 decree also designated James J. Storrow as member of the board of managers. Elected as the board's secretary, Storrow was well known for his involvement with Boston charities. It was Storrow's election as President of the Boston Public School Committee that gave him the platform to implement much needed educational reforms. He expanded the services of the neighbourhood public schools, especially to adult learners as Evening Centres.[48] Storrow's fortune was built upon his high risk investment in 1910 in a struggling company that made automobiles. For five critical years, Storrow also chaired the finance committee of the fragile company, securing $24 million in loans on the strength of his character. At the end of the five years the General Motors Company was earning at the rate of $25 million annually.[49]

Like Franklin, Storrow believed in social clubs for self-improvement and civic concern. He founded the nondenominational City Club in order to promote consensus building at a time when Boston politics was especially factious, ethnically divisive and religion conscious.[50] Storrow not only increased the prestige of the Franklin Fund board of managers and served as secretary for many years, he also made a generous contribution to the endowment.[51]Collins, Storrow and Pritchett in the early years of the new Franklin Fund (1904–6) also successfully mollified the contending interests regarding the establishment of a trade/technical school. Franklin Fund chairman of the board and Boston Mayor Patrick Collins appointed James Storrow, Henry Pritchett and Frank Foster (a former Boston mayor) to serve as a committee to conduct more hearings on potential applications of the centennial Franklin Fund.[52] Held on 16 December 1904 the hearing that evening welcomed many of the same people who testified at a 1898 hearing with the old Board of Managers. Mrs E. A. Gleason, President of the Suffolk County Women's Temperance Union, advanced a large social reform agenda which 'recommended that the fund be used for furnishing (1) more playgrounds for children, (2) social centres, where the young men and women might spend their evenings and receive instruction and (3) health institutes, for the instruction of young boys and girls in reference to matters of health and the care of their bodies'.[53] Mr James A. Watson sought Franklin Fund money for 'the establishment of a tuberculosis hospital'.[54]

While the enthusiasm of the employers for applied education in specific trades (printing, plumbing, painting, etc.) clashed with the official representatives of the Central Labor Union and the Building Trades Council (now an affiliate of the American Federation of Labor), the reconstituted Board of Managers' conception of the Franklin Union had sufficiently broadened to subscribe many of its former detractors. The distinction was made between a 'trade school' teaching specific skills and an institution that would promote the general education (especially in English, applied science and mathematics), refinement and capability of Boston's working class. Like the earlier round of hearings, the Cooper Union in New York City gained nearly unanimous support as the institutional model for the Franklin Union. Also referred to as attractive models were the Polytechnic School of London and the Battersea Polytechnic School.[55]

The outcome of the 1904 testimony and deliberation was to fashion the Franklin Union as close as possible in purpose, structure, budget, facilities, and curriculum after Cooper Union, pleasing Andrew Carnegie as well as the acrimonious labour interest of Boston.[56] In the interest of establishing sufficient endowment to assist the new Union, an ad-hoc committee of Richard Olney and Nathan Matthews asked the advice of the Boston City Corporation Counsel Thomas Babson as to the propriety of using the Franklin Fund (Second Part) for income to the new institution. Taking on a protector's role (new for the city), Counsellor Babson advised that the managers of the Franklin Fund could not use any part of the (Second Part) income for operation of the Franklin Union and that it should accumulate as Franklin had directed until 1991.[57] The main purpose for the communication with Mr Babson was to ask if all of the Franklin Fund (First Part) had to be spent on the building or some amount of principal could be reserved to offset expenses of the union. The issue was the interpretation of Franklin's phrase 'lay out'. Babson reasoned that the phrase could mean:

> 'to plan for' or 'to arrange', as in the expression 'to lay out a park or garden'. If the Court should adopt this construction, which is probable, the Managers, if any considerable amount of money was left after the public work was built, might 'lay it out' or arrange for its expenditure by making a fund of it to be held by the city for the support of the institution.[58]

The Board of Managers, with the support of the Supreme Judicial Court, the Massachusetts General Assembly and in partnership with the Boston City Council, selected and acquired a site, recruited a Director and constructed a carefully designed facility at Appleton and Berkeley Streets which opened for students in 1908. The curriculum served those 'who desire to learn the underlying, fundamental principles of their trades or crafts so as to understand better the work which they are carrying out'.[59] With this avowed purpose the voice of Enlightenment philosopher, Benjamin Franklin, calling for 'useful' citizens in his codicil was echoed nearly 120 years after his death.

Also in 1908, and as a result of a petition from the managers, the legislature passed Chapter 569 of the Acts of the Massachusetts Legislature of 1908. This law established the Franklin Foundation as a new charitable corporation with a board identical to the Franklin Fund appointed by the Supreme Judicial Court in 1904 whose purpose was to operate the Franklin Union as a department of city government on behalf of the city. The Franklin Foundation completely controlled the management of the Franklin Fund (Second Part), as differentiated from the centennial gift, until its dissolution in 1991 while subject to the judgement and control of trusts by the Supreme Judicial Court. The City of Boston held title to all land, equipment and money that was part of the original Franklin Fund / Carnegie gift / state / city deal. The title to surplus funds from operations or other endowments was fully vested in the private, charitable corporation - the Franklin Foundation.

The powerful and benevolent Bostonians recruited by the Supreme Judicial Court who seized the reins of control of Benjamin Franklin's legacy in the early twentieth century were the type of citizens that Franklin had counted on to understand his priorities and help fulfil his vision for the future of the trust fund. With his designation of the municipal government as trustee, Franklin counted on a quality of stewardship that would rise above narrow self-interest and manage his trust fund in enlightened public interest. While the second half of the Franklin Trust life in Boston would be guided by an independent private charitable corporation at arm's length from the City of Boston, Franklin's wishes for the application of the trust fund were generally respected and protected.

Although in the codicil Franklin exhorted future managers to overcome 'unforeseen Difficulties' and stay the course, Franklin was aware of the frailty of American political system. From the admonishments in the codicil, it clearly occurred to Franklin that later generations might fail to see anything of value in his 200 year scheme beyond capturing the centennial and bicentennial booty.[60] Franklin, however, had confidence that Americans would develop a system of government with capacity for its own recovery, renewal, reform and growth. In a letter to General George Washington in 1780 he described the promise of America:

> I must soon quit the Scene, but you may live to see our Country flourish, as it will amazingly and rapidly after the War is over. Like a Field of young Indian Corn, which long Fair weather and Sunshine had enfeebled and discolour'd, and which in that weak State, by a Thunder Gust of violent Wind, Hail and Rain seem'd to be threatend with absolute Destruction; yet the Storm being once past, it recovers fresh Verdure,

> shoots up with double Vigour, and delights the Eye not of its Owner only, but of every observing Traveller.[61]

Having weathered several storms, albeit 'enfeebled and discolour'd', the Franklin Fund of Boston survived its first hundred years in order to grow for one hundred more.

Philadelphia

As the centennial bequest of 1891 was being anticipated, the size of the Franklin Fund of Philadelphia, $94,400, fell far short of Franklin's projection of £100,000 ($446,000). Based on the compounding action alone, embarrassing comparisons were made between Philadelphia's inept management and Boston's fiduciary success. Notwithstanding its under-achievement, the Franklin Fund was to be divided on a ratio of one hundred to 131 per Franklin's instructions with the larger portion of the accumulated principal to be distributed to the city of Philadelphia for public improvements. By 8 September 1890, the Board of Directors of City Trusts on behalf of the City of Philadelphia dutifully divided the Franklin Fund (the worth $100,000) into two parts, the first part totalling $76,000 for immediate outlay and the second part totalling $24,000 to be held in principal compounded by the earned interest until the bicentennial distribution in 1991. In the 21st Annual Report of the Board of Directors of City Trusts in 1890, just prior to the formal division the Fund was invested as follows: [62]

Municipal, state and federal bonds	$55,500
Other bonds and Mortgages	$30,450
Cash	$3,604
Balance of bonds, for loans	$330

The predominant investment in other bonds and mortgages continued in the Franklin Fund (Part II) after the funds were split in 1908 with no loans to married artificers among the investments.

Regrettably and predictably, the history of the centennial gift to the City of Philadelphia began with an inglorious legal battle. In 1890 Elizabeth Duane Gillespie, appointed by the Register of Wills of the City of Philadelphia as administrator of the Franklin Estate on 27 October, petitioned the Orphans' Court on behalf of the descendents of Franklin's primary heirs, Richard and Sarah Bache.[63]

The Orphans' Court, dating from William Penn's Proprietorship of Pennsylvania, expanded its function along with the provincial laws treating land as an asset suitable for payment of debts.[64] From 1791 until 1874 the business of the Orphans' Court was conducted by the Courts of Common Pleas. In 1832 laws were passed that empowered the Orphans' Court to facilitate 'the management of estates ... [and] to audit the accounts of executors, administrators and testamentary trustees ...' and Constitutional Convention of 1873 established an Orphans' Court in Philadelphia. In 1878 Judge Clement Penrose was elected and, then, re-elected in 1888, 1898 and 1908. Given his long and distinguished career as Judge of Orphans' Court, Penrose dominates the decisions affecting the Franklin Fund. His contemporaries summarized Penrose's omnipresence in the following conclusion to a eulogy:

> Indeed, it is not going too far to assert that the present laws affecting decedents' estates are and will remain a monument to the analytical faculties, legal acumen and secure logic of Judge Penrose.[65]

It was this judge who would be called to examine Benjamin Franklin's intent and sit in judgement of the City of Philadelphia and its management of the Franklin legacy at its centennial.

Elizabeth Duane Gillespie's status as a Franklin heir apparently qualified her for appointment as administrator of the Franklin Estate by the Register of Wills. Gillespie, wife of E. D. Gillespie, earned distinction as matron of the Christian Street Hospital tending to injured and ill veterans of the Civil War and as chairman of the Philadelphia committee to assist widows and mothers of Civil War casualties. Gillespie's duties as the post-office department chief of the Great Central Sanity Fair of 1864, prepared her for an expansive role as President of the Women's Centennial Executive Committee of the Centennial Exposition of 1876. Gillespie, coordinating a vast network of activist women in Philadelphia and throughout the US, organized the political lobby that convinced the Centennial Board of Finance of the US Congress that there existed strong local support as well as broad-based national interest in the Centennial Exhibition. Her effort helped secure a critically needed Congressional appropriation and made the exhibition, particularly the international aspect and the women's exhibition, possible. The explanation of why this powerful, effective and civic minded Philadelphian assumed the role in 1890 as administrator advancing the private individual interests of her fellow Franklin heirs in opposition to the public's interest is not evident in the record.[66]

Albert D. Bache, Franklin's great-great grandson, also filed an identical petition. The central purpose of the petitions was to void the original bequest to the city of Philadelphia (and the Town of Boston) and to ask the Orphans' Court to redistribute the estate.[67] The petitions also argued that the Court should award the residual estate, held by the city as the Franklin Fund, to the lineal descendents of Richard and Sarah Bache. Beyond the legal jurisdictional questions, there were three principal points set forth in the paper book of the petitioners dated March 1891.

Firstly, the Franklin Trust was subject to the law against perpetuities because the gift was not properly vested in the city. This contention was based on the remoteness of Franklin's gift for municipal public improvements (one hundred years and 200 years). The petition claimed that Franklin intentionally postponed the vesting.

Secondly, the Petitioners claimed that 'loans to married artificers', the ostensible application of the trust for the first one hundred years, did not constitute a charitable purpose. While conceding that Franklin's intent in the loan programme may have been benevolent, Gillespie and Bache contended that the Franklin Fund operated similar to a loan office of a bank or thrift institution with its principle function to enlarge the trust.[68] Contending that Franklin's sole purpose was to accumulate capital to a precise amount, the 'dereliction and negligence of the trustees'[69] had defeated this purpose.

Thirdly, the Statue of Limitation did not prevent the heirs from seeking recovery because the trust was a 'cestui que trust' (beneficiary trust) held by the trustees (the city officials). In other words, fulfilling the obligations of trustee, which the city had performed for better and for worse since 1790, did not automatically predict that the city would be beneficiary. The petition argued that since no distribution of the funds had been made, no precedent had been established as to beneficiary. Despite the passage of time the 'position of the parties has not undergone any material change ...'[70] therefore, the court, if it voided the initial testamentary act, could redistribute the estate.

The Orphans' Court found that while Franklin did not conform to the language of the law against perpetuities he did specify a one hundred year term similar to the 'life in being plus 21 years' prescription of the law. While holding that the law against perpetuities did not apply to charitable accumulations, and even discounting the charitable purpose of the loan programme, the centennial gift to the city constituted a substantial compliance with the law. Judge Clement Biddle Penrose was persuaded by the argument of the petitioners about the loans to married artisans. He states in his judicial opinion in 1893: 'It is argued ... with much force, that a scheme for increasing the size of the gift by making loans of small amount to poor men, from whom security was exacted for payment with interest, was not made a charity, taking effect at a time beyond the period allowed by the rules against perpetuities is void ...'[71] The judge went on to say that the city represented the trustee and beneficiary and the gift was vested immediately upon receipt of the original bequest in 1790. Having settled the vesting issue, 'all questions with regard to perpetuities and illegal accumulations disappear ...'[72] Moreover, Penrose determined that 'It is an established rule that if a testator leaves a legacy, absolutely as regards his estate, but restricts the mode of the legatee's enjoyment of it to certain objects for the benefit of the legatee, upon failure of such objects the absolute gift prevails'.[73]

Judge Penrose referred to the City of Philadelphia as a 'purchaser for value' not just a legatee. While he raised doubt about the technical ability of the municipal corporation to administer such a testamentary trust, he acknowledged the long stewardship of the city in the management of the Franklin Fund and considered the terms of the bequest as a contractual obligation to be honoured by the city as well as the descendents of Franklin.[74] On 21 March 1891, Judge Penrose of the Orphans' Court dismissed Gillespie's and Bache's petitions.[75]

Gillespie and Bache filed a combined appeal before the Supreme Court of the Commonwealth of Pennsylvania. While the attorneys representing the appellants made substantially the same case as before the Orphans' Court, the City mustered more argument refuting the contentions of the petitioners. They cited twelve relevant cases to establish the charitable nature of Franklin's loan programme for young married artificers. Despite extensive research and testimony, the Supreme Court ruled against Gillespie and Bache on two strict legal grounds: (1) the municipal corporation (City of Philadelphia) had no legal ability (i.e. a power expressly granted to it) to stand as a cestui que (beneficiary) trustee for a purely private trust benefiting the residual heirs of Benjamin Franklin's estate and (2) given the impossibility of this public-on-behalf-of-private trusteeship, the Orphans' Court is denied jurisdiction and can not compel the city to report to the Franklin's heirs. While this decision fundamentally supported the city's side, it did not resolve several of the more contentious aspects of Gillespie and Bache's challenge.

In a later judgement rendered by Judge J. Arnold of the Philadelphia County Court, issues regarding the nature of Franklin's charitable purpose were resolved forthrightly and finally as follows:

> The rule in Pennsylvania is that when a trust for charitable uses is created, every means to uphold it will be adopted; and every attack upon it, unless grounded upon the strongest reasons, shall fail.
>
> The essential part of the definition of a charity is that the persons who are to receive it must be indefinite and uncertain; in other words, they must be a class; for if a gift be made to individuals by name or description, so that they may be selected and set apart, although they are a class, the gift is not a charity.
>
> The gift of Benjamin Franklin by will to the City of Philadelphia to afford loans of £60 sterling at interest, to young married artificers, who have served an apprenticeship, to aid them in setting themselves up in business, is a charity.
>
> A gift of part of the accumulations of the trusts to the City of Philadelphia for public works at the end of the first hundred years is also a charity.
>
> The gift of the entire fund and its accumulations at the end of two hundred years to be divided between the inhabitants of the City of Philadelphia and the government of Pennsylvania, is also a charity.

> The fact that a charity is a perpetuity, is no objection to it; and a charity may be created either in perpetuity or for a term of years.[76]

For the first time the courts had found merit and charitable purpose in the loan fund aspect of Franklin's directives in the 1789 codicil.

During the litigation, the Board of Directors of City Trusts explored possible uses for the centennial gift to the city. Interest in erecting a public bath on the south side of Cherry Street and west of Ninth Street was pursued through discussion with the Commissioner of City Property. The Board of Directors entertained, although declined, an application of Franklin's bequest to expand the facility of the Girl's Normal School. It was not until 1895 that the Board emerged from the cloud of centennial-inspired litigation and began in earnest the process of spending the Franklin Fund legacy. In this year the Franklin Institute, the Pennsylvania Museum and School of Industrial Art, and the University of Pennsylvania applied for Franklin Funds.[77]

In March, 1895, the Board decided to expend the principal from the trust on the construction of a new museum building to replace Memorial Hall in Fairmont Park, a structure left over from Philadelphia's 1876 Centennial exposition. The Pennsylvania Museum and School of Industrial Art, the forerunner of the Philadelphia Museum of Art, had started with a collection focused mainly on industrial art supplemented by paintings donated by the Wiltach and Bloomfield Moore families. Of note was the early involvement with the museum of Elizabeth Duane Gillespie as Chairman of the Associate Committee of Women of the Trustees.[78] The Board of Directors of City Trusts saw the contribution to the museum as an opportunity to honour Franklin as well as support a public improvement according to Franklin's wishes.[79] The gift required matching money sufficient to construct a suitable building.[80]

Franklin had recommended in the 1789 codicil that the City use the funds for two purposes: (1) to pipe water from Wissahickon Creek to serve as a potable source for the municipal consumption and (2) to render the Schuylkill navigable. By the 1890s a growth of metropolitan Philadelphia had already extended deep into the watershed of Wissahickon Creek contaminating its waters and the cost of easing transportation on the Schuylkill was estimated far in excess of the resources of the Franklin legacy. Released from Franklin's specific recommendations, other public improvements could be designated.

The Board of Directors of City Trusts recorded its action in the Annual Report of 1895 as follows:

> The question of the expenditure of that portion of the BENJAMIN FRANKLIN FUND available since the expiration of the first one hundred years named in the will, has been finally settled by the acceptance, by the Commissioners of Fairmont Park, of the amount, $84,285.02, to be expended in the erection of an Art Gallery

> located in the Park, that portion of the building so paid for to have the name of BENJAMIN FRANKLIN connected with it in such a manner as to serve to perpetuate his memory.[81]

Due to the death of some of the museum's chief proponents and lack of council action, the prospect of expansion of museum space in Fairmont Part gradually lost favour and the project stalled for ten years. (The impressive Philadelphia Museum of Art's Greek Revival edifice perched on the high banks along the Schuylkill River and at the terminus of the Benjamin Franklin Parkway was finally built in 1928.)

During the period of limbo, the Master Builders Mechanical Trade School of Philadelphia approached the Board for building maintenance support and Swarthmore College requested funds to teach printing. The Board of City Trusts did not renege on its commitment, continuing to invest the city's centennial portion and compounding its value. In 1905 the Board gave its first warning of waning faith:

> The question of the Art Gallery is again receiving public attention, but if early action looking towards its erection is not soon had by authorities, it may become proper to reconsider the previous resolution of the Board, and to transfer this Fund to some other of the purposes named in Franklin's will.
>
> A Disposition of this kind would be very appropriate in connection with the celebration of the bi-centennial of Franklin's birth.[82]

While the Board had been kept abreast of the Commissioners of Fairmont Park's earnest efforts to secure funding from the City Councils, litigation had interrupted the progress of the museum project. By May of 1906, fifteen years beyond the 1891 date for distribution, Franklin's first gift to the City of Philadelphia had grown to $120,789.83. A special sub-committee was appointed to reconsider the application of the centennial bequest.[83]

On 4 May 1906 the Franklin Institute of Philadelphia, after consultation with James J. Storrow in Boston, made a proposal to the Board of Directors of City Trusts to re-designate the centennial expenditure to help build a new facility for the Franklin Institute. While noting the lack of the due diligence of the Fairmont Park art gallery initiative, the Franklin Institute promised to erect its new building in less than three years. The institute, in reaction to the centennial decisions affecting the Boston Franklin Fund, emphasized the desirability of supporting young artisans and offered scholarships to city residents as an added commemoration of Franklin. The proposal also pointed out the significance of its research library which was 'exclusively scientific and technical and consists of over 107,000 titles ...' The Institute listed fields of interest 'including electricity, chemistry, photography, mining, metallurgy, mechanics and engineering'. Its approximate 600 student annual enrolment studied in courses covering subject matter including 'Mechanical, architectural and free hand drawing, machine design and naval architecture'. The Trustees of the Franklin Institute also cited the work of the Committee on Sciences and Arts which had been voluntarily selecting winners for the John Scott Legacy metals on behalf of the Board of Directors of City Trusts.[84]

Squarely in the tradition of Franklin's Philadelphia Junto founded by a group of young men to provide mutual assistance and promote education, the Franklin Institute, established in 1824, provided the mechanics of Philadelphia a technical reference library, specialized instruction and a context for support and recognition of mechanical inventors and scientific innovators. Echoing Franklin's personal scientific discoveries and interests, the Franklin Institute had earned a significant reputation for its support of inquire into the nature and use of electricity culminating in the international Electrical Exhibition of 1884. Various medals (Cresson, Boyden, Longstreth, Potts and the highest award, the Franklin Medal) were awarded to outstanding scientists in recognition of their great achievement beginning as early as 1848. By the turn of the century, the Franklin Institute had established itself as a preeminent scientific publisher (*The Journal of The Franklin Institute*), society, school and museum. Prior to 1907 and the consummation of the deal with the Board of Directors of City Trusts, the Franklin Institute had received no public support from the City of Philadelphia.[85]

The Board of Directors of City Trusts, wishing to avoid supporting long postponed projects like the art museum for Fairmount Park, awarded the centennial Franklin Fund gift to the Franklin Institute. The Institute conveyed two properties at 16th and Arch Streets to be parlayed along with additional city land into a large and attractively located plot for the new building. The deal was contingent on the ability of the Institute to contribute (presumably from private donations) funds of an additional $175,000 or more. In exchange city residents would be given low cost or free lectures and offered scholarships to Institute classes. According to the agreement the Board of Directors of City Trusts would retain title to the site on behalf of the City of Philadelphia. The public contribution was mentioned in documents of exchange as a precondition to a prospective subscription of Andrew Carnegie to the building fund in Philadelphia along similar lines to his role in Boston.[86]

Despite its efforts to 'lay out' the centennial distribution within a short time frame, the Board of City Trusts served as custodian of the funds for many years as the Franklin Institute raised the balance of funds needed. Fundraising delays and shifts in site prevented the building known as the Franklin Institute including that portion designated as the Benjamin Franklin National Memorial on the Franklin Parkway from opening until 1934. By then a broad public subscription raised over $5 million in eleven days dwarfing the amount contributed by the Board of Directors of City Trusts Franklin Fund. Ironically, former United

States Senator George Wharton Pepper, who had served as counsel to the Franklin heirs in challenging the Board of Directors of City Trusts and the Franklin Fund in the 1890s, served as chairman of the Franklin Institute's highly successful building fund.[87]

A section of the Franklin Institute's 1934 building was designated the Benjamin Franklin National Memorial by an Act of Congress in 1973, becoming the only national memorial to a Founding Father outside Washington, D. C. Housed inside the eastern wing, the 'heroic statue' of Benjamin Franklin created by sculptor James Earle Fraser emphasizes the significance of Franklin as a Founding Father.

The 1824 founding of the Franklin Institute of Philadelphia as predicated on the notion that progress depends upon the successful dissemination of information about mechanical and technological advances. While the opportunities for other institutionalized forms of education greatly proliferated since its founding, the mission of the Franklin Institute, as it transformed into a major American museum, continued to be primarily the communication of significant scientific and technological achievements of the past and the present.

Franklin had suggested in the codicil that 'useful' improvements for both residents as well as visitors such as 'Fortifications, Bridges, Aqueducts, Public Buildings, Baths, Pavements or whatever may make living in the Town more convenient ...' be considered.[88] Franklin believed that 'convenient', i.e. successful, living in congested cities would depend on the adequacy of the transportation, housing and service delivery systems developed to support rapid population growth and physical expansion. John C. Calhoun's 1816 Bonus Bill and Henry Clay's 1824 General Survey Act advanced Franklin's localized and urban oriented notion to a rationalized national conception of vast 'internal improvements' such as roads and canals. The nineteenth century witnessed extraordinary advances in infrastructure often the result of private and public co-investment and American ingenuity. Technological invention (new building materials, industrial equipment, new sources of energy) and foresighted and innovative design ideas (urban planning, transportation systems, and scientific agriculture, for example) were always central to America's ability to accommodate its exponential population increases.[89]

The Franklin Institute served as a centre of information and switchboard of communication about science and technology. The Board of Directors of City Trusts had the insight to select the Franklin Institute as the recipient of the centennial share of the Franklin Fund, responding to the letter as well as the spirit of Franklin, the man. The portion of the building that houses the grand statue of Franklin designated by Congress as the National Benjamin Franklin Memorial is a physical manifestation of Franklin's importance to the nation and the power of Franklin's vision of an industrious and technologically superior America.

The beneficiary of progressive reform movements in Boston and Philadelphia, of greater protection from the judicial system of Massachusetts and Pennsylvania and of alerted public vigilance, the Franklin Funds gained integrity from the process of expending the compounded centennial portion of Franklin's bequest. Not only did Franklin's intent attract serious consideration and attention by the administration of the Franklin Funds for the second hundred years was brought under control and gained finer focus. Changes in management, henceforth, received the benefit of judicial review in both cities with formal judgements authorizing *cy pres* modifications.[90] As a result of the debate in both cities over the application of the centennial portion, Franklin's resolve to assist aspiring and industrious individuals gained status as a central and vital part of the testamentary trust agreement. The loan fund for the second hundred years was acknowledged by the courts as a legitimate charitable purpose, not secondary to the compounding aspect of the trust. While Franklin's interest in helping to establish small, independent business was all but abandoned by the time of the centennial, the Franklin Funds were generally rededicated to assistance of upwardly mobile individual citizens through support of occupational education (Franklin Institutes of Boston and Philadelphia) and urban residential settlement (home mortgages in Philadelphia). The managers of the Franklin Funds in both cities would, at least, struggle throughout the second hundred years to find the method by which Franklin's scheme could be found practicable, sometimes coming closer to Franklin's intent and sometimes drifting away again.

6 BOSTON: THE SECOND CENTURY

As the final judgement on decades of belligerence and contested authority and as an inaugural act for the second centenary of the Franklin Fund, in 1908, the Massachusetts Supreme Judicial Court made the board of managers of the Franklin Fund 'a body corporate under the name The Franklin Foundation'.[1] The decree built on the 1904 Supreme Judicial Court's construction of the board of managers, declaring the right of the court to appoint successors to the eight lay members and remove any of the eight managers for 'cause'. The three ministers would qualify as members as long as they held their appointments as the clergy of the three churches specified in the codicil. The court decreed that the board be 'deemed a board or department of the city of Boston and on behalf of the city should have custody, management and control of the Franklin Union and of part of the fund accumulating for the second hundred years'. The city retained title to the Franklin Union, the land it sat on, and any of the funds given to the city of Boston for the establishment of the trades school. The title to the second century fund was also recognized as vested in the city.[2] The Franklin Foundation was entitled to hold title to any funds donated to the Franklin Union after 1908.[3]

While the incorporation of the Franklin Foundation and the founding of the Franklin Union settled the issue of authority over the centennial gift from Franklin, the language establishing the foundation and the union lacked clarity and precision. While the school was a 'department of city government' and the Mayor of the City continued to sit on the Board of the Foundation, the issue of control, particularly over the Franklin Fund (sometimes referred to as the Second Part of the Accumulating Fund in the foundations accounting records), remained a matter of contention. Conflict between city officials and managers of the trust had first broken open in the 1890s over the application of the Franklin Fund First Part.

At that time, well educated, social and economic elites represented by the Board of Alderman and the gentlemen reformers interested in trade school education clashed with pragmatic City Hall politicians who sought funds for debt retirement (the Franklin Park initiative) or popular public improvements (the public baths project). Boston divided into at least two parts along class lines that formed during the days of the Early Republic, and became more pronounced as Boston industrialized throughout the nineteenth century. By the 1891 centennial of Franklin's gift, the stratification was fundamental to understanding Massachusetts and Boston politics. While Irish politicians beginning with Patrick Maguire were elected on the strength of ethnic solidarity, Mayor Patrick Collins was the last Irish Mayor to effectively blend urban new stock interests with entrenched Yankee/Mugwump interests in managing a progressive coalition. Collins, instrumental in finding a solution to the Franklin Centennial gift morass, echoed Franklin's sensibilities in his consensus building rhetoric:

> I love the land of my birth but in American politics I know neither race, nor color, nor creed. Let me say that there are no Irish voters among us. There are Irish-born citizens ... but the moment the seal of the court was impressed on our papers we ceased to be foreigners and became Americans.[4]

By the founding of the Franklin Union, rough and tumble ward healing characterized Boston politics. The Franklin Fund, through the act of the court and the appointment of esteemed citizens in a corporate body, was insulated from maladministration, political assault and chicanery – or so it seemed.

The Franklin Union admitted its first students in 1908 and in the next year offered six, two-year course options (Machine Construction, Industrial Electricity, Steam Engines and Boilers, Structures, Architectural Working Drawing and Industrial Chemistry) and six, one-year course options (Sheet Metal Drafting, Mechanical Drawing, Estimating for Architects and Builders, Heating and Ventilating, Gas and Gasoline Engines, and Practical Science).[5] A one-year introductory programme for under-prepared students who sought to enrol in the Lowell Institute School for Industrial Foremen was also created, representing the initial conviction of the school to provide the widest possible access to all people of Boston who sought vocational training. Having been created by Franklin's gift, the school was quite self-conscious, throughout the twentieth century, about its role in creating equal opportunity to education leading to gainful employment.

The vigilance about open access to Union programmes compensated for the inactivity of the loan programme in the investments of the Second Part of the Franklin Fund by the Franklin Foundation Board. The first time the minutes reflect a reconsideration of the enormous investment in the Massachusetts Hospital Life Insurance company came in 1917 not in the interest of adapting the moribund loan programme but to pursue greater yielding securities.[6] In this year the Franklin Fund was wholly invested in insurance policies representing a value of $256,892.

The Franklin Union, technically a public institution with no public funding, depended on student tuition and endowment income to meet all operating expenditures. By 1914, the school, with a facility constructed for 1,700 students, had enrolled 1,900, causing crowding and requiring more endowment revenue. Walter B. Russell, the Franklin Union's Director, stated the case as follows:

> Franklin Union illustrates the all too common condition of an institution with a magnificent plant, an unprecedented and increasing opportunity for usefulness, and, a meagre and almost negligible income from endowment. The Franklin Fund (first portion) was available only for the building and equipment. The Carnegie donation provides less than twenty-two thousand six hundred dollars ($22,600.) per year for maintenance. Except for Mr. Carnegie's gift, not one cent has ever been given for maintenance, and yet there is probably no public charity in or around Boston which brings greater return to the community for each dollar invested. The registration fees charged for instruction are designedly merely nominal and do not begin to pay the cost of the training offered.[7]

Russell, serving as Director from 1908 until 1937, continued to point out the inadequacy of the school's financial structure and plead for more endowment. He recognized the irony of a Boston institution, indeed a department of city government, supported exclusively by gifts from two private citizens: Franklin a Philadelphian, and Carnegie, a New Yorker. The Union did benefit from a 1926 bequest of $100,000 from James J. Storrow, the original secretary and member of the Franklin Foundation. However, the financial stress on the school was relieved by the contribution of the US government which contracted for training during and after World War I.[8]

The Franklin Union, utilizing its otherwise idle facility during daytime hours, became the headquarters for Franklin Union National Army Training Detachment for the US Army and its eight week educational and physical training programme. Navy aviation mechanics learned about gasoline engines in the classrooms of the Union. Boston female students were recruited to Boston School of Occupational Therapy, a course approved by the Surgeon General of the United States, in 1918 for training as military hospital rehabilitation assistants. For five years after the war, the Veterans Bureau used the Franklin Union as a training centre. With the wartime and post-war precedent set for active daytime enrolment, the Franklin Union established two-year programmes in Industrial Chemistry, Industrial Electricity and Pharmacy, and one year courses in Automobile Repair and Electrical Wiring Maintenance. All of this activity produced significant revenue and forestalled the financial crisis until the years following World War II.[9]

Probably as a result of Storrow's bequest in 1926, the twelve members of the Franklin Foundation Corporation sought the establishment of its powers to receive and totally control funds that were donated without requiring action of the city. The General Court of the Commonwealth of Massachusetts enacted in 1927 a law that broadened the powers of the Franklin Foundation, a corporation created and constituted by legislative act in 1908. Whether Storrow's donation and the subsequent expansion of Foundation power precipitated a reaction in City Hall or the offer of US Steel in 1929 to redeem $408,000 of its bonds at especially favourable rates, Mayor James Michael Curley and City Treasurer Edmund L. Dolan decided to challenge the right of the Franklin Foundation to direct the investments of both the Franklin Fund (Part Two) as well as the Carnegie Donation.[10]

During these decades of development, the Franklin Fund (Part Two) had been invested in certificates of deposit of Massachusetts Hospital Life Insurance Company valued as of 31 January 1930 at $476,348.99.[11] Dating from Franklin Fund Treasurer William Minot's investment in the insurance company in 1826, the substantial resources of the compounding fund were not invested in loans to married artificers. Beginning with the 1893 Pennsylvania court's decision in *Benjamin Franklin's Administratrix* v. *The City of Philadelphia* (also called *The Apprentices' Fund Case*), case law in both Pennsylvania and Massachusetts had tacitly accepted the contention that the dissolution of the apprenticeship system, among other factors, rendered Franklin's loan fund scheme impractical. From the words of Boston Franklin Fund historians William Minot and Samuel McCleary, Franklin's compounding scheme was the primary focus of the 200 year trust and the loan fund was considered only instrumental and clearly secondary. Given the masking of Franklin's intent to a savings account contrivance, it is no wonder that the City would look for ways to capture the substantial holdings of the Franklin Foundation.

When the Foundation, in 1930, directed Treasurer Dolan to cash in all of the certificates of deposits in the Massachusetts Hospital Life Insurance Company and repurchase $100,000 of the certificates of deposit as well as redeem the US Steel Company bonds, the City balked and filed suit against the members of the Franklin Foundation Corporation. (Ironically, Mayor Curley was a member of the corporation and thus a defendant in a suit brought by his political lieutenant, Treasurer Dolan.) The Finance Committee of the Foundation had recommended the sale action, based on advice from corporation counsel, Frank Deland, of the City Law Department, after reviewing the deposit agreement with Massachusetts Hospital Life Insurance Company dating from 1893. The Finance Committee was advised that the deposits with Massachusetts Hospital Life Insurance Company did not constitute a debt bearing a fixed rate of interest. The deposits were treated like insurance company capital and earned a return based on the performance of the company as a whole. Counsel advised that the investment strategy 'represented an improper delegation of the responsibility, power and discretion of the trustees'.[12]

Counsel also stated that the Franklin Foundation members would be ill advised to invest the entire Franklin Fund (Second Part) corpus in a single company. Multiple investing would spread risk and limit unexpected and/or catastrophic losses to the fund.[13] While Bentley Warren argued on behalf of the Massachusetts Hospital Life that the insurance company had a diversified investment portfolio, Everett Morss, Franklin Foundation President, agreed with legal counsel Deland.[14]

The city claimed before the court that incorporation of the Franklin Foundation was illegal and acted as a breach of the contract established between Franklin's executors and the town of Boston when the testamentary trust was first created. The city also argued that the selection of members by the court violated a 1909 statute that empowered the Mayor of Boston to appoint all department heads and municipal board members as well as the US Constitution separating the judicial branch from the executive and legislative branches.[15] The Supreme Judicial Court defended its earlier actions and explained:

> The departure from the precise plan of management outlined by the testator was required by the incorporation of the town of Boston as a city ... The corporation is simply a means to enable the trustees to execute the trust with less difficulty. The control of the funds has been always and still continues to be with designated individuals in their private capacities clothed with a corporate being. The title to the funds is continued in the city of Boston by explicit words. The beneficiaries and ultimate disposition of the fund are undisturbed. No change is attempted in the title, the management, or uses of the trust.[16]

The court among other judgements declared that 'members of the Franklin Foundation owe their selection to the will of the donor and the decrees of the court and not to any action on the part of the mayor of Boston'.[17] It also decreed that the city treasurer is 'bound to comply with all proper directions of the Franklin Foundation as to its management'.[18] The court determined that the Carnegie Endowment was intended to support the school and its management should 'follow the same course as that of the Franklin Fund'.[19] With this decision the 1930s city raid on the Franklin Fund (Second Part) led by Treasurer Dolan representing the Curley administration was over and the Foundation proceeded to diversify its court protected investment portfolio.

The Franklin Union offered courses with 'distinctly technological and industrial' content. The centrally located site was selected, according to the school's publication, expressly to serve the residents of lodging houses in South Boston 'who would otherwise spend their evenings at cheap playhouses and other places of amusement'.[20] The school's enrolment grew, especially as it addressed the need for trained electronic, electrical and mechanical technicians to support the armed services during World War II. In 1941 the Franklin Union changed its name to the Franklin Technical Institute 'clearly identifying it to the public as an alternative to vocational or collegiate education'.[21] Also at this time the Franklin

Technical Institute offered its first courses in photography, a curricular area that attracted students in large numbers for the next forty-five years.

In 1942 the Franklin Foundation purchased its first war bonds to support the war effort. By 1945, the Foundation held $133,200 worth of Series G, US War Savings Bonds as part of the Franklin Fund Second Part. The institute also served the nation as an important training facility for soldiers and sailors during World War II. Special programmes for the Army, Navy and Coast Guard in electronics, specialized engineering and telephone technology were created. The institute developed courses to assist Boston civilians in their preparation for civil defence.[22] Beyond serving a patriot cause, the Franklin Technical Institute sustained itself with government contracts (lasting through the Korean War) that produced a $500,000 surplus.[23]

Beginning in the mid-1950s peacetime contractions in enrolment and inadequate response of Director Brackett K. Thorogood (who had joined the faculty in 1908, served as Director from 1937, and who was in failing health), the institute encountered substantial annual deficits as follows: [24]

1954	$183,000
1955	$174,000
1956	$190,000
1957	$125,000 (estimated at 16 May 1957)

With this discouraging realization that the school could not support itself on tuition revenue, an ominous entry was placed in the minutes: 'If, as Mr. Thorogood believes, overall tuition charges cannon be raised appreciably, it seems obvious that the School must look elsewhere for funds to meet recurring deficits'.[25] The Board of Managers retired Director Thorogood and replaced him with faculty member, Louis Dunham who was able to balance the 1957–8 budget. Under Dunham's leadership the search for underwriting support had begun in earnest.

The first foray was directed at the Carnegie Donation endowment. At a meeting of the Franklin Foundation on 19 June 1956, the members directed the collector-treasurer of the City of Boston to use available cash from the Carnegie donation to pay 'requisitions of this corporation for payroll or other expenses of the Franklin Technical Institute'. Upon the refusal of the collector treasurer to honour this instruction, the Foundation borrowed money to make payroll and filed suit against the city. The Carnegie Donation had been used heretofore exclusively for the cost of maintaining and operating the Institute's physical plant per the agreement with Andrew Carnegie in 1905. In 1957, the Supreme Judicial Court agreed with the City of Boston and blocked the Foundation's efforts to use the Carnegie Donation to cover payroll and other non-facility related costs of operation.[26] This decision was still warm when the Foundation staged a raid on the Franklin Fund (Second Part) in June and July of 1957.

Ostensibly to 'expand our available supply of skilled technicians in the current race between Soviet Russia and our own nation in the important field of scientific competition', and, at the request of the Franklin Technical Institute, the Senate of the Commonwealth of Massachusetts considered Senate Bill 180 which responded to the Franklin Foundation's request for termination of the Franklin Fund (Second Part) and provide for the fund's immediate distribution for use by the financially strapped institute.[27]

Resolves, 1957, Chapter 111 called for the appointment a special commission in 1958 to make 'an investigation and study relative to the needs and problems of The Franklin Foundation and the Franklin Technical Institute generally, the possibility and feasibility of obtaining further aid from the Franklin Fund, the said city, the commonwealth or other sources, ... providing for the payment to the Franklin Foundation for the benefit of the Franklin Technical Institute of the trust fund bequeathed by Benjamin Franklin to the Inhabitants of the Town of Boston'.[28] The Foundation on behalf of the Institute sought an abrogation of Franklin's codicil plan for dissolution of the Franklin Trust after the second period of one hundred years. Franklin had specified:

> At the end of this second Term, if no unfortunate accident had prevented the operation the Sum will be Four Millions and Sixty on Thousand Pounds Sterling; of which I leave one Million sixty one Thousand Pounds to the Disposition of the Inhabitants of the Town of Boston and Three Millions to the Disposition of the Government of the State, not presuming to carry my Views farther.[29]

Differing from the centennial distribution formula, Franklin mentioned the 'inhabitants of Boston' as well as the government of Massachusetts as beneficiaries, crossing state and municipal legal jurisdictions. Fortunately, this instruction complicated the political process and maximized the chance for judicial intervention and ethical restraint.

Notwithstanding the built-in political impediments, the twelve member special commission, composed of two state senators, three state representatives, four citizens appointed by the Governor, two citizens appointed by the Mayor of Boston and a Secretary, made an affirmative recommendation to the Senate and House of Representatives providing for the payment of the entire Franklin Trust Fund - Second Part to the Franklin Foundation for the immediate benefit of the Franklin Technical Institute.[30]

The legislature officially approved the commission's proposal and passed an act on 30 September 1958, listed under Acts 1958 – Chapter 596, giving the state and the city portions of the bicentenary proceeds to the Franklin Foundation for operational support of the Franklin Technical Institute, contingent on acceptance by the city council of the city of Boston.[31] Of great significance the legislative act included a condition requiring the subsequent review and approval of the Supreme Judicial Court. Following the passage of the legislation, the Franklin Foundation brought suit against the Attorney General of the Commonwealth in the Supreme Judicial Court in order to receive the court's review and approval for the implementation of Statute 1958, Chapter 596.[32]

The bill in equity was filed on 19 March 1959. The principal argument of the board of managers was that the trust had failed, due to the inability of the trust fund to loan money to married artificers who had completed their apprenticeship and could produce two sureties as the testator had directed. The court was asked, presumably invoking its authority under the *cy pres* doctrine, to terminate the trust and decree the dissolution plan adopted by the Legislature.[33]

The Foundation claimed that the failure of the artificer loan programme was 'brought about by difficulty in finding sureties, changes in economic conditions, and decline in the number of articled apprentices'.[34] No evidence or detailed explanation of this contention was offered. Although the court accepted this thesis, the other purpose of the trust, i.e. to accumulate for centennial and bicentennial distributions to the beneficiaries identified in the codicil, was still viable. The judgement reads:

> ... we see an equally dominating intent to accumulate for the gifts of principal in one hundred and two hundred years. We also agree that Franklin did intend that the accumulations should be achieved by the device of making loans to young artificers. But we have been shown nothing to justify the suggestion that he would wish all accumulation to cease if not capable of accomplishment in that way. That the trust will not attain by the date set for termination the principal amount estimated by the testator is unimportant. We observe in the codicil an intent to provide substantial gifts to future generations in the two cities. We shall not defeat that intent by destroying the trust now as to the Commonwealth and the city of Boston.
>
> No useful purpose would be served by analysis of the cases cited by the plaintiff. Franklin's codicil is unique.[35]

The court determined that the trust was not terminated under St. 1958, c.596. Only the court can terminate trusts, it decreed, and the court was '... not convinced that his charitable objectives have ceased to be in accord with the public interest ...' and left Franklin's trust intact.[36]

While the court accepted the Franklin Foundation's contention that the loan programme as Franklin had prescribed was impracticable, it included the following resonant statement: 'although no present occasion has been shown for termination, there need be no sterile accumulation. Notwithstanding the plaintiff's contrary opinion alleged in the bill, some charitable outlet, even with the plaintiff, probably could be found for use of the income until 1991'.[37] Although the precise meaning of this comment is somewhat unclear, the court meant to challenge the Foundation to re-examine the feasibility of a revised loan programme. Unsure of the court's meaning and pestered by a request from a Boston attorney for loans to give two Wentworth Institute students, John Lunn, Foundation President and Noel Morss, Legal Counsel, co-authored a report considering the Foundation's policy regarding the Franklin Fund (Part Two). In this report, for the first time since the 1790s there was a thoughtful recapitulation of Franklin's instruction regarding the artificer's loan fund. An itemized list of ten qualifications (artificer, married, under twenty-five, apprenticed, two sureties, 5 per cent interest, ten year repayment, not to exceed £60, repayable in gold, for business) was tested for their validity in 1960 terms. While the apprenticeship requirement could not be accomplished 'literally', the gold repayment, Lunn and Morss concluded, was the only qualification that 'may be safely disregarded as invalidated by paramount federal law'.[38]

Lunn and Morss advised that the costs of managing a loan fund would also have to be authorized under a *cy pres* adjustment in light of Franklin's prohibition of taxing the trust for administrative costs. They further concluded that using the funds as scholarship for technical school or undergraduate students would not be honouring Franklin's interest in helping young men after they had completed their training (apprenticeship in Franklin's day) to establish a small business. While they remained open to providing loans to graduate school students, Lunn and Morss proposed the creation of a loan fund that might assist interns and residents at Boston hospitals, explaining that 'Such borrowers are responsible and are possibly more nearly analogous to persons who have "served their apprenticeship" and need assistance in "setting up their business"'.[39] A physician in Franklin's day would not have been considered a Leather-Apronman or fit the definition of artificer or artisan. The document authored by Lunn and Morss gives no further insight into their judgement that medicine as a service profession and a medical practice as a business should be considered 'more nearly analogous' than other conventional blue-collar vocational careers. However, the Lunn and Morss report prompted the creation of a Special Committee of the Foundation which reported on 1 May 1962 in favour of establishing a loan fund for medical students and hospital interns and residents. Perhaps the affluence of practising physicians after completing residency increased their attraction as prospects for loans.

The Institute returned, in 1962, to the Supreme Judicial Court and received approval of a *cy pres* modification to the loan programme that allowed the Foundation to make a new type of loan to third and fourth year medical students enrolled in Boston University, Tufts University and Harvard University as well as house officers (interns and residents) at Boston hospitals. In order to provide proper security for the loans a Medical Student and Resident Assistance Foundation acting as a guaranty fund was established with a gift from Louis E. Wolfson of $100,000 to be held by the Foundation. (After encountering an especially high amount of loan defaults in 1974 which reduced the Wolfson Guaranty Fund to $63,000, the Foundation obtained agreement from the three universities that they would additionally guarantee the loans.)[40]

The loan fund did a land office business from the start. Students borrowed at the rate of 2 per cent per annum while still enrolled in medical school or while interns/residents and 5 per cent or 6 per cent per annum upon completion. In a Report of the Loan Committee in 1976 a summary of activity for the fourteen year period beginning in 1962 claimed that $3,476,000 had been loaned to 1,749 different individuals. These borrowers had to be living at 'bare subsistence level' in order to qualify for the loans (fixed at $7,000 maximum gross income in 1962 and indexed upwards periodically). The only detailed profiled information recorded in the records is for the year 1979 for Tufts University when forty of the graduating class of 161 had received Franklin loans. Of the forty, 42 per cent were women and 30 per cent were married.

Also in 1979 the last major investment in Massachusetts Hospital Life Insurance Company was cashed in order to have enough funds to meet individual borrower's needs. In making this decision the Loan Committee stated: 'Indeed, since it was an important feature of the testator's that his bequest be invested in loans to young citizens, it is arguable that no part should be withheld from the Loan Program'.[41] This recognition had been a long time coming.

With a new director in Louis Dunham and careful financial management and slow and deliberate expansion, the Franklin Institute of Boston (a third name change granted by the legislature in 1958 along with degree granting authority) enlarged its educational mission beyond industrial technologies to include a wide array of engineering courses.[42] Two year curricula in chemical, civil, computer, electrical and mechanical engineering technology were developed with a long list of one-year course options ranging from automotive service and management to architectural and structural drafting.[43] Dunham who served as Director until 1975, and Michael C. Mazzola, Director until 1990, ingeniously developed programmes to meet students changing needs and kept the school financially stable. Functioning with insufficient endowment and with little resources for physical expansion, the Institute was necessarily quick on its feet. In the mid-1970s, the versatile Franklin Institute of Boston attracted the attention and affection of an equally entrepreneurial educational neighbour, Boston University (BU).

While students at BU Medical School had been benefiting from the Franklin Fund since 1962, in April of 1974, J. P. Kendall, in his capacity as Chairman of the Franklin Foundation Development Committee, introduced the subject of affiliation leading to merger with Boston University proposed by the University. Vaguely referred to as the prospective 'Franklin School' of Boston

University, R. I. Rossbacher, on the planning staff at BU, drafted a proposal entitled 'Potential Franklin Model' in early 1974. According to Director Mazzola, affiliation arrangements included 'admissions and recruitment of students with the assistance of Boston University's admissions staff, including the availability of University housing, etc'. The affiliation agreement became official on 2 June 1974 when the Vice Chairman of Boston University's Board of Trustees, Dr Gerhard D. Bleicken, formally announced the plan.[44]

The timing of the affiliation corresponded exactly to the creation of the 'Program in Artisanry' at Boston University, a freestanding academic programme offering course work in ceramics, metalsmithing, textile design, wood and furniture making with special emphasis on helping students learn to establish craft businesses upon graduation. The designation of a professional certificate and Master of Fine Arts degree-granting programme with an artisanry emphasis made it unique in the nation, signalling a return to early American craft traditions or, at least, a revival of an antiquated term. The Program in Artisanry (PIA) received an initial start-up grant from the Henry P. Kendall Foundation. The new 'Franklin School' was intended to eventually subsume the Franklin Institute and the Program in Artisanry as well as joint initiatives with BU's School of Engineering. Dr John Silber, BU President, toured the Institute's facility on 4 November 1974. In that same year, Franklin Foundation President and Development Committee Chairman J. P. Kendall and Vice President and Loan Committee Chairman C. W. Anderson joined the Boston University Board of Trustees.[45]

During the 1974–5 academic year Franklin students used BU dormitories, health services, physical education facilities, the library and the student union. The Franklin Institute changed its academic calendar to correspond with the University's calendar. Program in Artisanry students used photography labs and drafting rooms at the institute. Even the 1975–6 Franklin Institute and Boston University catalogues described the affiliation. The Institute's Director expressed his enthusiasm for the new University relations by stating 'that we stand at the threshold of a great new era in the history of Franklin Institute of Boston'.[46]

The University's involvement with the institute was also simultaneous with the effort to obtain a $250,000 mortgage on the building at 439–41 Tremont Street in order to solve an urgent and serious Institute cash flow problem. The Treasurer reported that 'a group of savings banks and individual insurance companies had declined to participate' but 'he felt that the Trustees of Boston University would be receptive'.[47] At the meeting on 4 June 1975 Treasurer Paul Hellmuth 'noted that the Director urged this action as soon as possible, preferably before 30 June 1975'. The action was recommended and Treasurer Hellmuth was instructed 'to contact Dr. John R. Silber, President of Boston University'.[48] The mortgage was structured with a five year term at an annual interest rate of 10 per cent paid quarterly and secured by a mortgage on 439–41 Tremont Street It was later extended for three more years at 12 per cent interest.[49]

Boston University's attention was contemporaneous with the institute's negotiation with the Boston Redevelopment Authority about an Institute Master Plan calling for expansion on a triangular piece of land adjacent to the institute building to be used for student housing. The Boston University planning staff were inserted in the negotiation and contributed to a revised facilities development plan that would provide support for the 'Franklin School' of Boston University. On 8 October 1975, BU staff member, R. I. Rossbacher, presented a planning study and schematics to the Institute Board reorganizing the institute's facility according to merged university/institute functions and programmes.[50]

As a part of the expanding influence of Boston University, the Loan Committee by June of 1975 discussed the need to truncate medical student loans to ensure funds from the Franklin Fund (Second Part) loan programme for students enrolled in Boston University's Program in Artisanry. Loans to medical students seemed less of an appropriate application given the language of Franklin's intent in the codicil and the foundation of PIA. Given the revival of the term 'artisan' and the PIA's avowed purpose to develop a graduate capable of establishing a craft business, PIA students seemed tailor-made for the loan programme. In 1976, Rossbacher proposed that PIA students would have to provide guarantors for their loans, use consultants to advise them on business start-up, display a notice of their status as Franklin Fund Borrowers, and submit to annual inspection.[51]

Ironically, it was not until 1977 that qualifying students of the Franklin Institute were allowed to borrow $2,000 at 6 per cent interest disbursed over fourteen quarters starting the year after they graduate. In addition to the two required guarantors, all loans were secured by the Franklin Institute as well. The great demand for the Franklin Fund loans beginning in 1962 coming from medical school students, artisanry students and technical institute students raises doubts about the claims of due diligence by the board of managers over the previous 150 years to loan money to young citizens who were 'most likely to make Good Citizens'. It seems odd that the choice in 1962 was medical education rather than a host of alternative fields some closer to Franklin's artificer.[52] The creation of Boston University's Program in Artisanry in 1975 demonstrated how close Franklin's design could come to meeting pressing needs nearly two centuries later.

Given the momentum built-up behind the merger plans, the Franklin Institute agreed to transfer a $200,000 gift from the Charles Hayden Foundation earmarked for the construction of Institute housing to Boston University to pay for the renovations of a University owned facility to house the Program in Artisanry. This former parking garage at 606 Commonwealth Avenue needed extensive improvements in order to become ceramics, metal, textile design and wood/furniture studios. There was apparently some confusion over whether the Hayden Foundation understood that Boston University, not the Franklin Institute, operated PIA. Eventually, the Hayden Foundation agreed to amend the purpose and re-designate the recipient of the grant. The money was given by the Franklin Institute in January 1975 to the university and the Commonwealth Ave. building was transformed into an excellent studio facility.[53]

By 1977 Dr Silber and the University had made it clear that the merger of the Franklin Institute and Boston University was predicated on the willingness of the Massachusetts General Assembly, the Boston City Council and the Supreme Judicial Court to allow a re-designation of title and beneficiary of Franklin's trust. BU Vice President for Alumni, Government and Community Relations Daniel Finn (BU Trustee from 1959–71 and 1983–94) explained that the $3.5 million Franklin Fund was 'necessary if Boston University was to carry out its own obligations since the University would be expending considerable funds to implement the merger'.[54] The Franklin Foundation in combination with Boston University proposed the adoption of a Legislative act (House Bill 5503) that would have accomplished the merger of the Franklin Institute of Boston with Boston University. The ostensible purpose of the merger was to maintain the 'viability' of the Franklin Institute.[55] The Bill 5503 also provided: 'That in order to promote the forgoing transfer, it is appropriate and advisable to authorize the present exercise of Boston and the Commonwealth of the powers given them by Franklin's *Will* to dispose of the portion of the Franklin Fund accumulating for a second hundred years, to designate that the Franklin Fund be distributed in 1991 to Boston University'.[56]

On 14 March after public hearing on Bill 5503 the Joint Education Committee acted favourably. On 28 March 1977 the Bill 5503 was presented in a third reading and met opposition from City Corporation Counsel, Gleason who 'contended that the Bill was home rule legislation and, therefore, should originate in the City Council'. If presented with this proposed act in City Council, Gleason doubted that a decision of a 1977 City Council could legally pre-empt a 1991 City Council prerogative. Gleason's reservations were shared by the Judiciary Committee which reported unfavourably on the bill. The Ways and Means Committee, chaired by the Institute's representative Barney Frank, held the bill pending a review by the Supreme Judicial Court.[57]

Of interest, Noel Morss, the Franklin Institute's legal counsel, advised the Franklin Foundation Board of Managers assembled with Boston University representatives that he believed that the transfer of the Franklin Funds (Part Two) was unconstitutional under the anti-aid amendment unless they were paid for at fair-market value.[58] The anti-aid amendment, Article XLVI of the Amendments to the Constitution of the Commonwealth of Massachusetts, prevented the transfer of public assets to private institutions and individuals without a fair market value exchange. Needless to say, the Boston University representatives took the lead in commissioning the legal preparation for the appeal to the Supreme Judicial Court.[59]

In January of 1978, the Supreme Judicial Court, in response to questions asked by the Legislature before formal action on the Bill, found that their proposed action would violate the Home rule Amendment which allows local communities, in this case the City of Boston, to control local governmental matters. The court also ruled that the intended plan constituted a legislative application of *cy pres* doctrine and the court concluded that 'the Legislature is not authorized to make these alterations'.[60] Given the change of title, use and management as well as beneficiaries implicit in the BU/FI merger and the corresponding effect on the Franklin Fund (Second Part), the changes were exclusively the court's to make. The court also ruled that the Legislature could not determine the future uses of the proceeds from the bicentennial dissolution in 1991 without violating the terms of the trust. The court reasoned that the 1978 designation of Boston University as the recipient of the 1991 distribution would pre-empt the decisions of the beneficiaries at the time of the dissolution of the trust (i.e., the citizens of Boston and the Commonwealth of Massachusetts in residence in 1991).[61] The concern expressed by Attorney Morss about the unconstitutionality of the act based on the anti-aid amendment was dismissed because the court regarded Franklin's trust as private money until the trust was ultimately dissolved and the bicentennial gifts were accepted by the state and city.

The proposed merger between Boston University and the Franklin Institute was dropped. The affiliation between the two institutions continued in modest ways until 1984. In that year the Franklin Institute as an economy move sought to use outside contractors for maintenance and custodial services. The Service Employees International Union, Local 254, thinking that the Institute was controlled by Boston University, enlisted the administration of Boston University to coerce the institute into dropping the plans. Boston University acting under pressure from Local 254, according to the Director's Report at the Annual Meeting on 23 February 1984 had:

> a) Informed the President of Franklin Institute of Boston that the affiliation agreement might have to be canceled.
>
> b) Withdrawn the bus service for Franklin students who are [*sic*] in residence at Boston University thereby requiring the Institute to provide transportation at a cost of $700 per month.
>
> c) Terminated all Franklin students who were employed in the Boston University cafeteria in part-time jobs.

> d) Suggested that our continued good relations with Boston University were in some ways related to the reversal of prior decisions and the signing of an agreement with local 254 for custodial/maintenance workers.[62]

Although the affiliation continued in 1985, the relationship was strained and thin.

In 1985, Dr John Silber announced that the Program in Artisanry would be eliminated and the Commonwealth Avenue building would be used to house scientific laboratories. The PIA faculty sought a merger with the Swain School of Design in New Bedford and Boston University helped finance the move of the studio equipment to new facilities at the Swain School. The Program in Artisanry and the Swain School of Design merged with Southeastern Massachusetts University in 1986–7, now the University of Massachusetts, Dartmouth.

As if to emphasize the lesson learned by the experience with Boston University, the Franklin Foundation Legal Counsel recorded in the minutes the following comment in June, 1978:

> Of lasting interest is the fact that the Court interprets Franklin's will as requiring the disposition of the Franklin Fund in 1991 to be made by the Legislature and City Government as then constituted and not before.[63]

The 1977 effort to prematurely terminate the trust represented the last of the raids on the Boston Franklin Fund. The fund continued to be loaned out to medical students and Franklin Institute students and had reached the compounded value of $4,500,000 by 1991.

7 PHILADELPHIA: THE SECOND CENTURY

Much earlier than Boston, Philadelphia recognized that in order to properly administer testamentary donated to the municipality, and independent group of distinguished individuals acting in a corporate body must be created. In 1869, with the creation of the Board of Directors of City Trusts, Philadelphia found a way to steadfastly and honourably administer the Franklin Fund, free of political interference. While the management of the Girard Estate and the administration of the Girard College dominated its time and attention, the Board adopted a committee system which accounted for the minor trusts including the Franklin Fund, the John Scott Loan Fund and the Wills Hospital Trust. In 1913, as a result of the Lybrand Report, the Board of Directors established three major administrative posts to better distribute leadership: the General Manager, the President of Girard College and the Executive of Wills Hospital. The minor trusts were under the purview of the General Manager and the Committee for Minor Trusts.

Accepting all of Franklin's restrictions as stated in the 1789 codicil, the Board of Directors of City Trusts was only able to make ten loans totalling $2,514 before it sought, in 1874, the first of several *cy pres* adjustments from the Court of Common Pleas in Philadelphia.[1] With the age limit extended to thirty-five year old artificers, the Board was optimistic about marketing the Franklin Loans.[2]

While seventy-eight borrowers came forward from 1875 until 1879, the numbers dwindled again with only thirteen loans from 1880 to 1885. The last five years before the one hundred year anniversary of Franklin's gift in 1790 yielded no loan applications. In 1895, the Board redoubled its efforts to popularize the loans by placing newspaper advertisements and circulation placards 'in as many shops and establishments as could be reached'.[3] The Board even placed a permanent brass plaque on the column outside their 12th Street offices announcing 'Loans to Artificers'. Despite this effort, the eligibility constraints discouraged prospective borrowers and no loans were made from 1885 until 1917.[4] The Board invested the Franklin Funds in public bonds.

In 1917, a typical year of the first several decades of the second hundred years, the Benjamin Franklin Fund had invested capital in the following:[5]

Philadelphia City	4 per cent loan	$9,400
Philadelphia City	3 ½ per cent loan	$10,100
Philadelphia City	3 per cent loan	$19,700
Pittsburgh School	4 ¼ per cent bond	$1,000
Allegheny County	4 per cent loan	$9,000
Beaver County	4 per cent loan	$1,000
Bonds and Mortgages on real estate		$3,600
Total		$53,800

Given the drop in prevailing interest rate for public bonds and loans, this contrary investment strategy did not even deliver the 5 per cent that Franklin had specified in the 1789 codicil. Perhaps the reduced interest rate gained by bond investment forced the reconsideration of whether the loan programme to individuals could or should be reinvigorated.

The Board of Directors of City Trusts worked to understand the reasons for the dissolution of interest of young Philadelphia artisans. They pointed out that indentures of apprenticeship, along with apprenticeship, in general, had lost favour and, while individuals who had served apprenticeships might still be located (graduates of Girard College, for example), the length and employment arrangements varied from the precise language of the codicil calling for apprentices who had 'faithfully fulfilled the Duties required in their Indentures'. The 5 per cent interest rate established by Franklin, that represented a discount in 1790, was no longer competitive with prevailing lending rates. The Board concluded that the interest rate for Franklin Fund loans had to be lowered in order to attract a new market of individual borrowers. While the Board's claims about changes wrought by the industrial revolution on urban Philadelphia may have been overstated or based on limited vision about the nature of capital and labour, their explanation for the obsolescence of the Franklin loan scheme, drafted as part of 1917 *cy pres* request to the Court of Common Pleas, is rich in connotative meaning:

> Industrial competition had undergone a radical change. In the eighteenth century, men worked at all trades individually. The development of machinery, the enormous multiplication of the productive power by its use, aided by steam and electricity, the concomitant growth of great plants and enormous aggregations of capital, have greatly reduced the possibility of individually competition in industrial work. In the same period both money and credit have enormously expanded. Enterprises are now undertaken involving money outlays, which in the testator's time, would have been impossible. As a consequence, ordinary workingmen not only enjoy certain advantages which would in the old times have been considered luxuries, buy by the rise of savings banks and building associations, they are able to begin the accumulation of property from surplus earnings and are also able to make loans on term more agree-

> able to them than those offered by this Fund ...The rise of great plants has specially tended to attract men of more than average ability giving them the opportunity of experimenting on a large scale in the effort to reduce the cost of production. This has become a function so well paid as to practically withdraw many ingenious men from individual competition.[6]

The elite world view conveyed by the Directors in this excerpt deserves careful examination.

The first assumption implicit in the BODCT narrative is that Franklin's eighteenth-century artificers translated into early twentieth-century industrial factory workers. This translation was unnecessarily delimiting. While shoe and textile manufacturing in Philadelphia, for example, were totally transformed by the advent of new machinery, specialization of labour, harnessed steam and electricity, aggregated capital and the factory work place, such trades as house carpentry, brick laying and baking functioned similarly to crafts in Franklin's day. These latter trades, among many other examples, saw equipment innovations, new technology, and changes in markets and products but sustained their small business, individual driven nature. Their needs for capital were still modest and they faced stiff competition from similar small scale operations. The Board's inculcation of large scale industrialization practically ignored the tradesmen who continued to operate in small, independent shops.

'Great plants', invoked the villain (or the hero depending on your perspective) of the industrial age, counterpoised to individual trade practice. While the perspective of capital seemed to lose touch with the motivations of the individual worker, other voices of the period expressed the needs and aspirations of the person in the factory or shop. The demand for continuing education in Philadelphia to keep apace of technological innovation in manufacturing processes and machinery found expression in the popularity of evening school. A 1914 Annual Report of the Pennsylvania Commissioner of Labor and Industry describes the industrial workers and their exemplary commitment to personal development and upward mobility as follows:

> The rapid changing industrial conditions are making a greater and greater demands upon the working man. [*sic*] Manufacturing processes are becoming more and more complex. The demand for skilled workmen is greater than ever before and increasing all the while. The job to to-day will require more extensive knowledge a year hence. Large numbers of men and women, at work in the industries with little or no opportunity for advancement unless they are trained, are now asking that they be given the opportunity to prepare themselves better for the fierce struggle of life. Thousands of boys and girls, who left school at an early age, are demanding a chance to secure the training needed to help advance in their vocations.[7]

The stultifying effect of industrialization upon the individual worker described by the Board of Directors of City Trusts narrative does not square with this persistent Franklinian notion of self-improvement and equal opportunity. The voice of these contemporary aspirants was, apparently, inaudible to the Board in 1917. Conceivably, those Philadelphians with need and qualification genuinely spoke a foreign language.

Artificers fitting the Franklin definition were particularly numerous in the ethnic neighbourhoods of Philadelphia in the first two decades of the twentieth century. During the period from 1901 to 1915, Philadelphia grew from 1,293,000 to 1,684,000 residents. For example, new immigrants from Italy joined settled residents of Italian descent in South Philadelphia filling the streets radiating from the intersection of Ninth and Christian Streets and supporting dozens of small shops, businesses and restaurants in 'little Italy'. While unskilled immigrants found wage work in housing and building construction, road building and cleaning, trash collection, etc., skilled workers served the city's needs for 'bakers, shoemakers, masons, plasterers, stone carvers, waiters, and garment workers'.[8] Most of these trades were organized as small, independent enterprises with less than a dozen employees, often member of the same family and similar in profile to Franklin's artificers. Recalling the repetition of borrowers with the same surnames as sureties in the early decades of the Franklin Fund loan programme (1791–1820), familial networks continued to be characteristic of small, localized business.

Likewise the Jewish immigrants from Russia, Poland and Eastern Europe, doubling their population from 1905 to 1918 from 100,000 to 200,000 residents, plied their trades in small, family owned and operated shops. Skilled artisans such as tailors, shoemakers, carpenters, butchers and coppersmiths served both the Jewish community as well as the whole of Philadelphia. The industrialization of Philadelphia did not dim the prospects of many artisans whose trades were not substantially transformed by advances in technology and who sought to sell their products and services to support the expanding population.[9]

The presumption of the narrative that 'ordinary workingmen' had surplus earnings and had ready access to conventional credit was not borne out by the reality of urban Philadelphia at the time. While the standard of living for most urban Americans increased during the period as measured by the amount of home owners and gross family income, these 'advantages' were frequently earned by multiple wage workers in the family. Physical and psychological health, education and religious practice were frequently sacrificed to the long hours of labour required of the upwardly mobile husband, wife and children. The reference in the narrative to 'luxuries' within the reach of the common workingman seems particularly gratuitous and patronizing given the modesty of the life style of Philadelphia labourers.

The BODCT's narrative of 1917 also described the co-optation of 'ingenious men' into the large management bureaucracies of an industrialized world.

The Board further asserted that 'men of more than average ability' or the 'good citizens' that Franklin sought to assist, would be drawn from the great corporations as part of management not from the rude ranks of labour. This expression tends to support to historian Robert Wiebe's theory that the leadership of Progressive reform in American cities sprang from an emergent, powerful and motivated middle class, made up of new professionals working within a scientifically and bureaucratically organized society. The Board of Directors of City Trusts believed, as Wiebe suggests, that the personalized, pre-industrialized world of the small town, small business, local politics and individual competition had been replaced by the impersonal, centralized, bureaucratic, industrial and urban world of big money, large corporations/trusts, factory production and boss politics. In the old order, American defined itself by 'Entrepreneurial genius, self interest, and habit'. In the new order, the society depended on formalized inter-relationships resembling 'well-oiled machinery' or a 'frictionless bureaucracy'.[10]

While the Board narrative tends to confirm Wiebe's theory, the Board's conclusions are gross and unrepresentative of the actual condition of a considerable labour force and range of small businesses thriving in Philadelphia in 1917. The Directors overlooked the differing values, perspectives and characteristics of their Philadelphia contemporaries which varied according to skill, occupation, income, ethnicity, race and religion. Given the Board's expectations and biases, it is predictable that the managers of the Franklin Fund would overlook suitable candidates for loans and attempt to modify the loan programme to ensure its success.

In 1917, the Court of Common Pleas agreed, under the *cy pres* doctrine, to increase the maximum amount of a loan from $300 to $500, lower the interest rate to 4 per cent and waive the requirement of indentured apprenticeship in the City of Philadelphia. The court sustained the Board's contention that attending a technical school in order to acquire skills of a trade was a modern equivalent to Franklin's requirement regarding apprenticeship. By alleviating the need for local apprenticeship the court also recognized the rapid growth of the greater metropolitan Philadelphia are and tacitly acknowledged the patterns of movement and relocation following education and employment opportunity. All three of these *cy pres* changes closely adhered to Franklin's intent as specified in the codicil.

By 1917, the City of Philadelphia had well established day time vocational education programmes that provided trade skills and general education for school-aged boys and girls. Of greater significance was the strong tradition of continuing education for artisans already employed who sought additional skill to qualify for promotion within the trade. William C. Ash, Superintendent of the Philadelphia Trade School testified in 1914 before the US Congressional Commission on Industrial Standards that while his school enrolled its capacity of 1,700 tradesmen and women in evening classes per session, he estimated the need to be as high as 15,000 prospective students. The Philadelphia Trade School functioned very similarly to the apprenticeship system as Superintendent Ash explained:

> In plumbing, our largest trade in the evening school, and the first class that graduated in 1909 – keep in mind that all of the young men who graduated were regularly employed during that time at the school at the trade during the day. Just as soon as they became of age and passed the State examination they were admitted as journeymen. Fifteen of those boys are master plumbers.[11]

The trade school structured its curriculum to provide a combination of general education and practical vocational skill to facilitate mastery and promotion to independent craftsman status. This was Franklin's expectation of indentured apprenticeship.

Removing the restriction regarding apprenticeship permitted a large group of young artisans trained through the vocational education system to apply for the Franklin Loans. While allowing this adjustment, the court indicated its conservative approach to *cy pres* modifications by additionally stating that: 'Preference shall be given to married artificers who have served an apprenticeship or received their training in Philadelphia'.[12]

Another major modification approved by the Court of Common Pleas in 1917 involved the security required for the loan. The 1917 petition had argued that two reputable citizens willing to act as sureties on a ten year bond could no longer be obtained and suggested that a 'well secured first or second mortgage on real estate within the City of Philadelphia' should be accepted as a suitable alternative. The court also sustained the petitioner with his request. This *cy pres* modification overcame the most frequently cited obstacle to attracting borrowers for Franklin Fund loans. As early as 1829, Philadelphia had accepted real estate in the City and Count of Philadelphia as collateral from the sureties in lieu of specie as required by Franklin in the codicil.[13] The 1917 court action allowed the borrower to offer real estate as collateral in lieu of sureties. The implication is that prospective borrowers owned real property, presumably residential, and could use it to leverage a business loan. While this was an inversion of the customary order of settling a freehold as in Franklin's day, the Board of Directors of City Trusts and the court believed that this liberalization would increase the pool of potential applicants.

The loans, spread over a ten year repayment period, were still to be used to establish the individual tradesman in an independent business. Despite the rhetoric to the contrary, the BODCT continued to help establish small artisanal shops in Philadelphia. In 1919, the Board established its own requirement, subsequent to the court liberalization, to accept only first mortgages on real property in Philadelphia in an effort to provide greater security to the fund.

Even with the 1917 *cy pres* adjustments the Board had to aggressively promote the availability of Franklin loans. It contacted the Council of Associated Building Trades of Philadelphia, American Federation of Labor, notifying the 50,000 workmen represented by these unions. It distributed literature at meeting rooms of several unions, including blank applications, attempting to recruit borrowers.[14] While the Franklin Loan Fund continued to grow as a result of investment in governmental bonds, the Board failed to attract people to its loan programme. In 1920, the exasperated Board of Directors of City Trusts sought the advice of the Board Solicitor in applying the income to Franklin's other instruction in the codicil: 'whatever may make living in the town more convenient'. (Franklin offered this suggestion regarding the use of the centennial gift of compounded principal available in 1890, but not as an alternative to the loans to married artisans during the second hundred years of the trust.) The Board thought that they might split the fund according to the proportions specified for the bicentennial and conclude their efforts.[15]

Counsel to the Board of Directors thwarted this effort to abrogate the trust by rendering an opinion that '... the Trustee has no right to use annual income ... for the purposes contemplated ... the effect of which is to spend it and not accumulate it ...' Further the Board Solicitor declared that the 200 year compounding scheme '... appears to have been the testator's main object, the lending of money from the fund ... in the meantime merely a means to an end'.[16] The conjecture that the compounding interest component of the codicil was Franklin's 'main object' went unchallenged.

The Board searched for innovative ways to offer the loans wholesale to an enabling institution. The Board encouraged the Pennsylvania Institution for the Instruction of the Blind to offer the loans to their graduates who were intent on establishing businesses. The institution was unable to arrange sufficient loan guarantees and was ultimately unsuccessful in deploying the Franklin Fund loan programme to the satisfaction of the BODCT.[17]

Certainly the marketability of the Franklin loan programme after 1929 was greatly affected by the nation's Great Depression in Philadelphia.[18] Given the failure of many small savings and loan associations, general contraction of credit and widespread unemployment in Philadelphia, it would seem that the generous terms of the Franklin loans would have attracted many more prospective borrowers. However, small business suffered from lack of demand just like large enterprises and the period witnessed many business failures. Even payment on 4 per cent loans with one tenth principal payment annually apparently presented insurmountable difficulty for the young entrepreneur during the Depression.[19] With well over $100,000 of Franklin Fund to loan (at a time when cash was hard to come by), the Board redoubled its effort through letter writing, aggressive advertising with circulars and posters and personal appearances at labour union halls and meetings. Notwithstanding the turbulent economic times, it is startling that the Board made no loans from 1917 until 1939.[20]

In 1939, the Board of Directors of City Trusts decided to petition the Court of Common Pleas for more modifications in the Franklin Loan Fund. The judges appointed a Master to 'take testimony and report' to them about the merits of the petition. The petition first requested that the loan limit be raised from $500 to $3,000. The Board had been offering loans for $1,000 by matching the Franklin maximum amount with an equivalent amount from the John Scott Loan Fund. The increase sought in the petition allowed the Board to offer loans totalling $6,000 under the new limit when matched with a Scott loan. Low-cost housing in this period ranged in price from $3,900 to $6,200, positioning the Franklin/Scott loan amount at an appropriate level.[21]

The petition also requested liberalization of the borrower's qualifications so that Philadelphia nativity was no longer required and the borrower could be a 'skilled, unskilled or clerical' worker, otherwise qualified. The waiver of Philadelphia nativity anticipated the large influx of workers associated with Philadelphia's booming war-time economy. Employment rebounded from the low Depression levels, particularly in metal, textile and construction industries, beginning in 1939, with 200 new businesses established in the city.[22] Historian Margaret Tinkham describes a dynamic Philadelphia:

> In November 1940 the [Chamber of Commerce's] Business Research Bureau could report that the production of durable goods was up 33 percent, that exports through Philadelphia's port were up 29 percent, car loadings up 20 percent, payrolls up 12 percent, and retail sales up 6 percent over those of 1939. About $1 Billion in defense contracts had been placed with Philadelphia firms.[23]

Without question Philadelphia underwent a radical economic recovery stimulating rapid expansion of business and employment opportunity in 1939–40. With this prosperity the pool of prospective Franklin Fund borrowers had to dramatically increase.

Yet the Master, appointed by the court in 1939, expressed scepticism about the prospects for the Franklin Loan Fund even with the adjustments, assigning it the role of 'secondary provisions' to Franklin's 'ultimate charitable intention'. The compounding of interest over 200 years was Franklin's principal objective according to the court appointed Master. He reported:

> The theory [*cy pres*] upon which is based the jurisdiction of the court to modify the terms of the loan scheme is that the scheme is modal merely – just an instrumentality for accumulating a larger fund for ultimate application to public charitable uses ... The Master ventures to suggest for future consideration the possibility that, for the sake of attaining the testator's primary purpose, it may at some time become neces-

> sary to substitute for the loan scheme a simple program of productive investment within the range of discretion permitted by law to trustees.[24]

Perhaps moved by the prospect of better economic times, the Board of Directors of City Trusts disagreed with the Master's conclusions and did not take advantage of the court sanctioned opportunity to abandon the loan programme. The Board continued to try to animate the loan programme. For their part, the court granted the modifications requested in 1939, including the allowance of female as well as male borrowers. Preference for married artificers who served apprenticeship or received training in Philadelphia remained a notation in the new language approved by court.[25]

Apparently not by design a major alteration in the use of the Franklin Fund was accomplished during this period. The practice of accepting real estate as collateral for business loans had led to a transmutation of purpose. The loan fund became a conventional home mortgage loan programme competing with savings and loans associations. While the Board still acknowledged that the avowed purpose of the Franklin Fund was to assist business development, the loans were approved for financing the purchase of residential real estate. Exactly how and why this conversion was accomplished is not recorded. It appears that it simply 'happened' over a period of years.

The early results of the 1939 *cy pres* adjustments, coupled with the new focus, showed progress with the approval of twelve loans for the period from 1940 to 1943. However, during the next five years, only $35,100, constituting fifteen loans to individuals for mortgages, were finalized. While the number of applications greatly increased, forty-eight of fifty applicants failed to meet the requirements in 1948. The record is silent as to why so many applicants were disqualified. The Republican city government including the Mayor and City Council, meanwhile, was under full-scale assault for widespread corruption associated with $40 million of unaccountable municipal expenditures. Even the president judge of the Court of Common Pleas, the erstwhile protector of the testamentary trusts, engaged in case tampering and collusion with the Philadelphia police as part of the larger scandal.[26] The Board of Directors of the City Trusts, while somewhat insulated from political machinations, did include the Mayor and the President of the City Council, as well as leading Republican business associates. Perhaps the malaise effecting the administration of the Franklin Fund was symptomatic of a general breakdown of government operations.

In 1949, the Board offered the explanation that few loans were demanded as a result of the suspension of home building during World War II causing a depression in the mortgage loan market. The BODCT alleged that the high cost of the housing constructed right after the war also discouraged young, married couples from buying their own home.[27] Once again the managers of the loan fund came up dry in their effort to loan Franklin's legacy. Strikingly, other contemporary sources refute the state of affairs as described by the Board.

While the house financing benefits of GI Bill might have created some competition in the market for Franklin loans, Philadelphia had a 'building boom' with unprecedented growth of smaller, affordable homes in the outlaying neighbourhoods of East Germantown, West Oak Lane and Northeast Philadelphia. As with many major cities the post-war period brought a wholesale demographic shift within Philadelphia's older neighbourhoods. Pre-World War II neighbourhoods identified with Italian and Jewish families attracted an immigration of African American residents.[28]

Philadelphia experienced 'white flight', the mass relocation of working class people of European descent from inner-city neighbourhoods, to fast growing middle-class suburbs of Philadelphia, particularly along corridors of mass transit (bus and street car lines). Redistributed Philadelphia, both in the inner-city with older multiple family dwellings and row houses, as well as the suburbs packed with new small single family homes, provided many people with the opportunity to purchase affordable urban housing.[29]

Record-breaking growth in housing was the order of the day in post-war Philadelphia. In order to keep pace with the high rates of employment and economic development, the companies doing business in the City of Philadelphia reported nearly $100 million of post war construction and upgrading.[30] Yet, the Board of Directors of City Trusts was unable to position the Franklin Loan programme to take advantage of this flood of urban development.

The concept of using the loans to establish independent business had been sacrificed in favour of the Franklin Fund as a first mortgage lender. In Philadelphia of Franklin's day, owning the tools of the trade earned the artisan rights to citizenship; hence, Franklin's emphasis on loans to help start up a business. Arguably, in Philadelphia in the late 1940s, owning your own home was a stakeholding equivalent for an upwardly mobile citizenry.[31] The vast post-war Philadelphia neighbourhoods populated by crowded row houses demonstrated the premium Philadelphians placed on living in a single family home, no matter how modest or compact.

To compete in the post-war housing finance market, the Board of Directors of City Trusts sought and received another modification from the Court of Common Pleas in 1949. With this alteration the Franklin Loans were offered for $6,000 (not counting the Scott Fund matching amount) at 4 per cent over fifteen years. The mortgage bond could not exceed 2/3 of the current appraised fair market value of the real estate. While the capital of the Franklin Fund in 1949 consisted of $204,559 available to loan and notwithstanding the court's granting of *cy pres* petition, only two loans were approved in 1949 and 1950. No loans were approved from 1951–4 despite an active marketing effort utilizing classified newspaper advertising in the *Philadelphia Evening Bulletin* and the *Philadelphia Inquirer*.[32]

Perhaps inspired by the dramatic municipal reforms of the new Democratic administration of Mayor Joseph S. Clark and city Council President James A. Finnegan operating under reforms associated with the new 1951 city charter, the Board of Directors of City Trusts, in 1952, undertook a fresh approach to invigorating the loans to young artisans for establishing businesses.[33] The BODCT solicited the assistance of the Metal Manufacturer's Association of Philadelphia to find young tradesmen that might need a loan to get started in their trade. The Association responded to the Board that $6,000 was insufficient capital for establishing a new small company in metal manufacturing. The senior tradesmen also explained that they did not encourage the formation of competitive companies and would prefer providing opportunity for young people within the brotherhood of existing companies. The self-serving opposition of unions to apprenticeship programmes and the concerted effort to limit the number of individuals admitted to their fellowship had plagued the managers of the Franklin Trusts in both Boston and Philadelphia from the mid-nineteenth century onward. The failure of organized labour to understand and identify with Benjamin Franklin's intent regarding young artisans and their growth into worthwhile citizens seriously undermined the ability of the trusts to compound human resources as Franklin had dreamed. Regrettably, labour, over and over again, resisted the extension of the franchise.

Undaunted, the Board contacted educators at the Philadelphia Board of Education to find out about the threshold costs for new businesses in other trades. They also studied the curricular offerings of the vocational programmes to discern what trades were open to young, newly skilled entrepreneurs. The Board of Education provided the Franklin Fund officials a list of vocations and the approximate cost of starting up in business as follows:[34]

Advertising	$1,400
Art Commercial	$1,500
Auto Body and Fender	$3,000
Cabinetmaking*	$9,000
Carpentry*	$2,000
Drapery*	$1,000
Dressmaking*	$1,000
Duplicate Service	$10,000
Electric Wiring and Appliance Repair	$3,000
Hair Dressing (Beauty Culture)*	$5,000
Interior Decorating*	$500
Job Printing*	$8,000
Millinery*	$300
Optical Mechanics	$10,000
Painting and Paperhanging*	$3,000
Photography	$5,000
Radio and Television	$7,000
Sheet Metal Repair	$5,000
Shoe Repair*	$6,000
Tailoring*	$700
Upholstery*	$1,000
Watch Repair*	$4,000
Welding (Gas and Electric)	$2,500

Of this list, thirteen trades (those marked with asterisks) were included in the list of occupations for those artisans who received loans in the late 1790s and early 1800s. Remarkably, this 1952 initiative with the public schools represented the first attempt to analyse the financial requirements of artisans as occupations had evolved over 162 years since Franklin's executors gave Philadelphia the original bequest.

Notwithstanding the erosion of the apprenticeship system in favour of systematic manual training, trade and technical education, and, notwithstanding the onset of the wide scale industrialization, there were still opportunities for enterprising and hardworking young people to establish independent small business. At least that is what the Board of Education in Philadelphia advised the Board of Directors of City Trusts in 1952. Considering the encouraging response of the school board, the abrupt conclusion printed in the records of the Board of Directors of City Trusts was unexpected: 'The possibility of making loans secured by bailment leases was investigated at length. The Board's Solicitor was of the opinion, however, that loans made on this basis by a trustee would not be favourably considered by the Court, and this thought was pursued no further'.[35]

Having come so close to recovering Franklin's intent, the Board of Directors of City Trusts demurred, apparently, believing that the risk to the interest compounding scheme would have jeopardized the 'primary purpose' of the trust. The failure to seek court opinion, at least, seems particularly odd given the several instances of successful petition to the Court of Common Pleas by the Board in 1874, 1917, 1939 and 1949. Unfortunately, the available records offer no further insight into the Board's decision. The Board of Directors of City Trusts also continued to serve as the administrator of the Stephen Girard Trust, the enormous $6 million bequest to the City in 1831 that was magnified exponentially due to the vast coal deposits discovered on Western Pennsylvania lad also bequeathed by Girard. Girard directed that his gift be left for the education of white male orphans resulting in the founding of Girard College. The Board of Directors of City Trusts acted as the Board of Trustees for the college, directing its development and controlling its huge endowment. Flush from the multi-million dollar sale of the Girardville Coal Mines, the Board of Directors of City Trusts, as a quasi-public institution just beyond the reach of the Mayor and the City Council, presided over a trust estimated to be worth $98,000,000 in 1965.[36] The Franklin Fund Loan Program and the John Scott Loan programmes were insignificant given the scale and status of the Girard Trust.

Given the tumultuous course of events from 1957 until 1968 affecting the Board of Directors of City Trusts, it is small wonder that the Franklin Fund received little quality attention. In 1954 the Supreme Court of the United States issued the *Brown* v. *the Board of Education* decision that outlawed racial segregation in the nation's public schools. While the Philadelphia public schools complied with the court ruling, the Board of Directors of City Trusts refused to integrate Girard College, citing the explicit testator's instructions to admit only white students. The directors argued that Girard's trust agreement from 1831 took precedence over the subsequent Fourteenth Amendment to the US Constitution and the *Brown* decision.[37]

Girard College became the object of protest for angry African American citizens of Philadelphia beginning in 1957 when a United States Supreme Court ruled that Girard College was sufficiently a 'public' educational institution to fall under the 1954 *Brown* decision and must not discriminate in admissions. Rather than integrate the school, the Court of Common Pleas, with the assent of the Board of Directors of City Trusts, and over the objection of two prominent reformers, Mayor Joseph Clark and city Council President James Finnegan, created a separate, private shadow Board of Trustees to govern the Girard College while it pursued its legal rights to exclude Black students through the Pennsylvania court system. For over ten years the BODCT and the Girard College were the object of public criticism and heated protest. Even the Rev. Martin Luther King became involved, encouraging non-violent confrontation. Finally, in 1968, the Supreme Court of Pennsylvania, having the jurisdiction over testamentary trusteeship in the Commonwealth of Pennsylvania, upheld the Supreme Court of the United States judgement that the *Brown* decision superseded the terms of Girard's will.[38]

The role of the Court of Common Pleas in protecting at great lengths the integrity of the Stephen Girard's intent placed it at odds with the opinions of the city government, rulings of the Supreme Court of Pennsylvania, and the Supreme Court of the United States. The extreme judicial conservatism of the Court of Common Pleas in interpretation of Girard's will and its unwillingness to grant a *cy pres* adjustment granting admission of non-white students to Girard College placed the Orphans' Court in the position of abetting illegal racial discrimination, and, thus obstructing justice. The Court of Common Pleas and the Board's intransigence on this issue seems inconsistent with their apparent liberalizations of Girard's intent when defining trusteeship and 'poor' children, arranging indentures, and permitting relatives to withdraw students.[39] The strict constructionist interpretation of college admissibility based on Stephen Girard's words by the Court of Common Pleas, along with the majority of the Board of Directors of City Trusts, also contrasts with the five separate *cy pres* adjustments (1917, 1939, 1949, 1963 and 1966) that varied from the expressed wishes of Benjamin Franklin's codicil. In the 1950s and 1960s, the Board of Directors were distracted by a landslide of litigation and political controversy, leaving the routine administration of the minor trusts, including the Franklin Fund, largely to staff. Perhaps this explains the contrasting styles of management.

In 1963, the Board sought and was granted another *cy pres* modification to the Franklin Trust increasing the maximum loan from $6,000 to $10,000 to be repaid over twenty years. In their petition the Board reported that only thirty-three loans had been made from 1949 until 1962. The increased amount available ($20,000 with the matching Scott fund loan) and, most especially, the very attractive interest rate of 5 per cent greatly increased the numbers of loans. The success suggested to the Board that the interest rate could be raised and remain competitive with building and loan associations and mortgage lending institutions and, in 1966, the Board petitioned the court for the sixth time to increase the maximum rate of interest to 6 per cent, while increasing the age limit to thirty-nine years. On 18 October 1966, the Court of Common Pleas approved an interest rate range of 5 per cent-5.5 per cent granted the age limit extension.[40] The higher yield on the Franklin bonds also helped the trust make up some lost ground in accumulation, compensating for the time when the funds lay dormant or under-invested.

In 1970, the Court and the Board agreed on *cy pres* modification on the rates that would prevent the constant re-petitioning activity. The court granted permission to index the interest rate to the maximum legal interest less ½ per cent. Recognizing that Franklin wished to offer a below market rate to encourage young borrowers, the action allowed the Franklin Fund Loan programme to always position itself as an attractive alternative. The court also allowed the mortgages to be for an amount up to 80 per cent of value and to be paid off in up to thirty years. This action completed the conventionalizing of the Franklin Loans, giving it normal mortgage loan characteristics and functionally abandoning the use of loans for establishing businesses.

By 1979, the prevailing mortgage interest rate stood at 11 per cent and the Franklin Fund loans were sought after. The Board returned to the Court of Common Pleas for the last time to increase the maximum loan to $20,000. The petition explained that the practice of doubling the loan amount available by using matching Scott Fund loans had fully invested the Scott Fund. In order to write mortgages of $20,000 the Franklin Fund would have to lend the whole amount. Given the rise in real estate prices the Board argued that the higher amount was nearly always justified based on 80 per cent value. The court agreed and granted the adjustment.

Kent Roberts, the Board of Directors of City Trusts administrator assigned to the Franklin Fund loan programme from 1950 until 1991, reported that the Board was willing to loan to borrowers who purchased homes in higher risk, older, inner city neighbourhoods. While they needed to be satisfied that the property was sufficient security for the amount of the first mortgage loan, they did not 'red line' areas of the city or block applicants based on preconceived notions of where the Board preferred its mortgaged property to be located. In Kent's words: 'we've always tried to use the Franklin money to make loans to needy people'.[41] The most effective, although circuitous, means of attracting applicants was by word of mouth. Roy Goodman, a librarian at the American

Philosophical Society, received a Franklin loan to purchase his home in a redevelopment area in the Northern Liberties neighbourhood. Goodman explained: 'I heard about [the Franklin Fund loans] through a custodian at the Society, who told me about an ad in the *Welcomat*'.[42]

While the precise demography of the bondholders in the last three decades of the Franklin Loan Fund's operation was determined to be confidential and not a public record, Roberts declared that the Board supported fair and open access to the loans without regard to race, sex, religion and ethnicity.[43] In 1989 the Board of Directors of City Trusts touted that the loan fund had supported 33,500 Philadelphia homeowners. Loans, averaging $12,900, carried a 9.5 per cent interest rate. Fund financial officer/accountant Michael Russo explained of the ninety-five mortgages outstanding in 1987: 'Most of our loans go to people living in working-class neighborhoods ... Firemen, policemen, nurses, not wealthy people'.[44]

Russo offered further insight into how the people who hear about the programme from 'word of mouth' are evaluated: 'To get one you must be 39 years old or younger, purchasing a house within the city limits. We use this rule of thumb: If single, you are not qualified if you make over $20,000 a year. If married, you are not qualified if you make over $35,000'.[45] The Board of City Trusts, depending on 'word of mouth' wrote only two mortgage loans in 1986.[46]

To its credit, the Board of Directors of City Trusts endeavoured to invest the Franklin Fund during the second hundred year period in loans to worthwhile individuals (some with business loans and most with home mortgage loans), encouraging young people to settle their families in Philadelphia and become solid citizens. While the BODCT found it necessary to repeatedly liberalize the requirements of the loan fund, drifting farther away from Franklin's young married artisans seeking to establish small businesses, and while it spent most of the century invested in municipal, state and federal bonds, the loan fund finally became a fully extended resource available to middle income workers in the city of Philadelphia. The BODCT, ultimately, understood the importance of helping to build a strong base of industrious citizens of Philadelphia and all of they *cy pres* modifications granted by the Court of Common Pleas at the behest of the Board were intended to serve that end.

However, the Directors of City Trusts also were limited by their biases and predilections in the administration of the Franklin Fund. Occasionally, the Board confessed through its own statements that it felt that the support of artisans was anachronistic and, thus, an inferior purpose of the trust. The steady compounding of the principal by prudent fiscal management responded to Franklin's ordinate purpose an fulfilled the Board's fiduciary responsibility. The Court of Common Pleas over the years sustained the Board's judgement in this matter. And yet, the Board acted over and over again to modify the loan programme, inspired by Franklin's hopeful notion that his fund could renew Philadelphia's ranks of enlightened citizens by supporting 'the rising Generation'. The 33,500 Philadelphia middle income citizens who purchased a home with the assistance of Franklin Fund mortgage in the last decades of the trust's life attest to the power of a compounding and revolving fund marshalled in support of a class of people, validating Benjamin Franklin's contention about the positive effect of extending credit to the industrious.

Unlike the Franklin Foundation in Boston, which sought to capture the Franklin Fund as a permanent endowment for the Franklin Institute, the Board of Directors of City Trusts had no such favoured application for the Philadelphia Franklin Fund upon its bicentennial dissolution. The only instruction that it sought from city officials in preparation for 1991 concerned the investment strategy. The BODCT sought to determine if mortgages should cease sufficiently in advance of the date providing an all-cash fund at the end of 200 years and facilitating the division between bicentennial beneficiaries: the Commonwealth of Pennsylvania and the City of Philadelphia. Declining to orchestrate the process of distribution, the Board of Directors of City Trusts left the city and state to their own devices and, as dutiful fiduciary, simply waited for instructions from the Court of Common Pleas. In Philadelphia, the stage was set for a last mad scramble for Franklin's bequest.

8 BICENTENNIAL: BOSTON AND PHILADELPHIA

The year 1990, 200 years after his death, was an auspicious year for Benjamin Franklin's sage admonitions to be remembered and his benevolent spirit to be rekindled. The coming of age of the Franklin Fund corresponded to an unprecedented and precipitous collapse of the economy of the Commonwealth of Massachusetts with a two-year budget deficit of nearly $1 Billion, a mass exodus of defence industry jobs, rising crime and highly partisan confrontational politics. Despite nearly two decades (1970–87) of relative prosperity with economic diversification, low unemployment and large investment in community development, the state and the City of Boston by the late 1980s was characterized by ethnic, racial and economic conflict and division. Certainly boasts about 'the Massachusetts Miracle', the condition of the state's economy, and commitment to equal opportunity were being reconsidered and redefined. Franklin, with the innovative codicil conceived a the dawn of a predominantly agrarian nation in the eighteenth century, figured out a way to boldly insert his views into public debated of a mature urban American on the brink of the twenty-first century. With the promise of a handsome reward, the citizens of Boston and Massachusetts had to listen one last time to the ruminations of the patriot statesman about virtue, citizenship and prosperity.

The value of the Franklin Fund in Boston from the end of Fiscal Year 1989 audited statements of the Franklin Foundation was $4,646,613.[1] Although far short of Franklin's forecast of £4,061,000 or $19,000,000, the city of Boston would receive 1061/4061 st of the value (or at least $1,214,001) and the Commonwealth of Massachusetts would receive 3000/4061 st of the value (or at least $3,432,613). But like the centennial benefit, the bicentennial gift came wrapped in litigation.

As early as 1981, the Franklin Foundation, acting as a neutral trustee of the Franklin Fund (Second Part), was forced to consider whether it should suspend making ten-year loans to medical students in order to have completely liquid investments in 1991 when the trust was terminated. Franklin did not instruct the managers of the trust to stop loaning the funds to married artificers in anticipation of the distribution at either the first or second century mark. The medical loan agreements called for full repayment by 'the seventh June 30 following June 30 of the year the borrower graduates'.[2] The Foundation petitioned the Supreme Judicial Court of Massachusetts for instruction. The Franklin Foundation recommended in the petition that the loan programme continue per Franklin's instructions and that the gift in 1991 represent some cash and mostly loans receivable. The Attorney General of the Commonwealth of Massachusetts filed answers to the petition indicating the state's agreement with the Franklin Foundation that the loan programme should not be terminated in order to provide all cash at the 1991 termination date. The City of Boston, however, disagreed and indicated that it wanted to be paid in cash in 1991, thereby, necessitating the termination of the loan programme in 1984. The court's decree followed the Foundation's recommendation and loans continued through 1991.

While the Franklin Foundation attempted to act as a neutral party, this action was the first of several that revealed a conflict of interest between the members of the foundation acting as managers of the Franklin Fund (Second Part) and, simultaneously, as the trustees (or governors) of the Franklin Institute. The special status of the Foundation as a state created corporate entity, distinct and removed from the direct authority of the state or city government allowed it to act, conceptually, as a neutral party.[3] However, the Foundation's additional governance role with the institute, especially given the institute's long-term interest in the Franklin Fund (Second Part) as endowment, prevented impartiality. Along with the medical students, since 1977, students of the Franklin Institute were eligible to borrow Franklin loan funds starting the year after they graduated. The Franklin Institute students benefited from the continued operation of the loan programme until the 1991 final dissolution of the trust. Regardless of the Foundation intent to act as a disinterested party in its petition to the court in 1981, its recommendation regarding the maintenance of the loan programme accepted by the court, was self-serving. Medical students at Tufts, Harvard and Boston Universities also benefited by having access to loans through 1991. Due to the merger of the Program in Artisanry with the Swain School of Design in New Bedford in 1985, students at Boston University, other than medical students, were never extended borrowing privileges.

While and item 'Boston University Relationship' continued in Director's Reports through 1987 and Daniel Finn, BU Vice President and longstanding BU Trustee, was elected as Vice President of the Foundation Board in 1987,the plans of Boston University to merge with the Franklin Institute, first developed in the 1975, were not reactivated. The Institute's long-range planning subcommittee, under Finn's chairmanship, proposed a plan to position the institute to independently attract the 1991 Franklin Fund disbursement as permanent endowment for the institute. To that end, the planning subcommittee, in 1988, drafted a legislative programme and initiated a campaign to enlist political support. A broad three-to-five year public relations programme, designed to raise the institute's visibility with the public, was also initiated with the commemoration of the 200th anniversary of Franklin's death in April of 1991 as a primary focus.[4] Foundation members Raymond L. Flynn, City of Boston Mayor, John E. Drew, Lawrence S. DiCara and John F. Smith served on this planning subcommittee.[5] The Foundation also retained lawyers to analyse the legal history of the Franklin Fund (First and Second Parts) and help target its legislative strategy to capture the entire 1991 distribution. Such were the Franklin Foundation's initial moves.

In preparation for the expenditure of the Commonwealth's portion of the bicentennial gift, Governor Michael Dukakis in Executive Order # 294 dated 31 December 1990 appointed a six (or up to eight) person advisory commission on the Benjamin Franklin Trust Fund, made of residents 'drawn from diverse racial, ethnic and socio-economic backgrounds'. The Commission members, serving as volunteers with two year terms, were charged with the following responsibilities:

> A. Investigate a range of potential uses in the Commonwealth for the Franklin Trust funds that would be in keeping with Benjamin Franklin's spirit and goals for the funds.
> B. Determine how best to spend and perpetuate the funds in ways keeping with Benjamin Franklin's spirit and goals for the funds.
> C. Inform itself of the plans of the City of Boston with respect to the portion of the funds Boston will receive, and the same with respect to the City of Philadelphia and the Commonwealth of Pennsylvania.
> D. The Advisory Commission shall present a report to the Governor on or before May 15, 1991 which will include the:
> a) results of its investigation and study, and
> b) recommendations to the Governor regarding the:
> 1) best use of the monies from Benjamin Franklin Trust Fund,
> 2) procedure for implementing its recommendations, and
> 3) proposed legislation which may be necessary.[6]

Governor Dukakis appointed Fredie Kay, Executive Director of the Office of Dispute Resolution for the Commonwealth, as Chairperson of the commission. In 1991, shortly after its creation, the commission was prorogued pending the outcome of litigation initiated by the Franklin Foundation. Denied the leadership which would have been provided through the instrumentality of the commission, various camps seeking to use Franklin's bequest began to form on their own.

The Mayor's Office and the Governor's Commission heard from Friends of the Museum of Printing who wanted the Franklin Fund to help establish a National Museum of Printing in Boston. The Town of Franklin in southeastern Massachusetts sought Franklin funds for several public improvement projects.

English interests attempting to save Margaret Stevenson's house on Craven Street (the house Franklin lived in while in London) from demolition requested help from the fund. Ideas for application of the funds, as might be expected, rapidly proliferated.

The new Mayor of Boston Thomas Flynn, despite his ex-officio membership in the Franklin Foundation, advocated the use of the Franklin bequest to underwrite the mayor's 'Safe Neighborhoods Plan' aimed at arresting the outbreaks of street violence and gang warfare. Other city officials expressed a desire to use Franklin Funds to establish a job-training programme for inner-city youth to be based in Roxbury, one of the most crime-ridden areas of the city.

While the state Commission began and, then, suspended the process of organized inquiry and the city publicly discussed alternatives, the Franklin Foundation, acting again as a 'neutral party', sought court advice on what precise date should be used for timing the termination of the trust. The Foundation recommended 30 June 1991. In this same civil action commenced on 20 June 1990, the Foundation, compromising its 'neutrality', asked certain questions of the Supreme Judicial Court, which assisted the Institute's effort to capture the Franklin Fund. In this litigation, the Foundation tried to maintain an independent posture, distinct from the voice of the institute. No matter how sincere the effort to maintain objectivity, the conflict of interest was unavoidable.

200 years after its creation, Benjamin Franklin provided for the simple dissolution of the testamentary trust spreading the benefit over the state government and the inhabitants of Boston to use as they wished. As a result of the court and legislative decisions of 1904–8, the break-up of the trust became a highly complex legal and political problem, a labyrinth of public and private interests in conflict. Careful attention should be given to the identifiers, especially Franklin Institute and Franklin Foundation.

The Franklin Institute, technically a department of the city of Boston, had never received any public appropriation, and was operated by the private, nonprofit corporation, Franklin Foundation, acting on behalf of the city of Boston. The Mayor and the city council of Boston presumed to act on behalf of the inhabitants of Boston as beneficiary, and direct the application of proceeds of dissolution, independent of any position taken by its agent, the Franklin Foundation. The Commonwealth of Massachusetts (with the executive branch and legislative branch differing on authority, approach and objective) acted as legislative enabler as well as direct beneficiary, also independent of the Franklin Foundation, a corporation of its making. The Supreme Judicial Court acted as adjudicator only until the trust terminated, and, thus, was concerned with the Franklin Foundation and its management of the Franklin Fund (Second Part) only until dissolution. The court was without opinion on how the proceeds of dissolution should be spent by the inhabitants of Boston and the state government. Before a rational and orderly process could be established for dissolution by the interested parties, the Franklin Foundation made a surprising legal move.

The Franklin Foundation, seeking a declaratory judgement, asked in 1990 that the court rule on the validity of the *1958* state statute (St. 1958, c. 596) and, subsequent, companion *1958* city council action that assigned the Franklin Fund (Second Part) to the Franklin Institute at the point of termination of the trust.[7] The Franklin Institute, acting independent of the Foundation, filed an answer to the 1990 request for declaratory judgement setting forth its point of view. The institute contended that legislation was passed in 1958, and while it failed to prompt the immediate termination of the trust, the law had never been repealed or modified since passage. The Institute sought to validate the 1958 legislation noting that the only reason the trust was not immediately terminated was the intervention of the 1960 Supreme Judicial Court's ruling in *Franklin Foundation* v. *Attorney General, supra*. Counsel for the city of Boston and Attorney General of the Commonwealth of Massachusetts countered in separate opinions that the 1958 statute had 'no applicability' in 1990 and the Franklin Funds should be distributed to the beneficiaries in 1991 as Franklin had instructed, with no strings attached.

The Institute's argument hinged on the notion that the court's premature termination of the trust (had the court agreed with the 1958 statute) was simply a 'procedural contingency', i.e., a technical requirement necessary to accomplish the intent of the act. The Institute offered its definition of 'procedural contingency' as 'a certain and predictable event which, when it actually happened, occurs, or has been performed, triggers off the legal effectiveness of the statute and transforms a dormant statute into and active statute'.[8] The 1990 court acknowledged that the 1958 statute had led to two diametrically opposed interpretation and, hence, decided to examine the 'intent' of the legislature at the time of passage in order to compensate for ambiguity in the law. The court examined the very subtle nuances of the legislative process in order to establish this intent.

The first draft of the legislation which appeared as 1957 Senate Doc. No. 180 with a preamble offered the first hint of legislative intent. The phrase '... public policy requires the termination of the trust, if lawfully terminable ...' made it clear that in this first Senate version termination was not provided for. The bill allowed that the fund would be retained by the Foundation for permanent benefit of the institute but not 'unless and until authorized by a decree of the supreme judicial court'.[9]

The special legislative commission studying the bill recommended a revision of the Senate version in its report published as Resolves 1957, c. 111. The commission altered the language of the preamble removing the question about the lawful ability to terminate the Fund and including new language that 'the public interest would be better served by presently applying the shares of the fund distributable to the city of Boston and to the commonwealth on the trust's termination to the advancement through technical education of such young men'.[10] The 1990 court emphasized the word 'presently' in this passage as a signal of intent. The legislation aimed to assist the financially precarious Franklin Institute as well as to 'expand our available supply of skilled technicians in the current race between Soviet Russia and our own nation ...'[11] The 1990 court noted the word 'current' used here and elsewhere in the report as defining the compelling need to act in 1958.

The special legislative commission in 1957 recommended that the legislature seek an advisory opinion from the supreme judicial court before advancing the bill rather than leave in 'the explicit statutory requirement of court authorization'. A contrary opinion about the desirability of this change was offered by Noel Morss, legal counsel to the Franklin Institute in 1957, who feared that a full legal argument would not be possible with the advisory approach. Atty. Morss explained that the bill was predicated upon the declaration that the trust had failed and the purpose of the testator was not served by continuing the trust, a judgement that only the court could make. He argued for the original language of the Senate version. The final 1958 statute included the proviso that distribution of the funds and termination depended on authorization decreed by the Supreme Judicial Court. The final statute dropped the preamble altogether that contained some of the language noted by the 1990 court as indications of the legislature's intent to act only with effect in 1958. The Franklin Institute argued in 1990 that the removal of the preamble was in indication that the act was not intended to be time certain, but rather indefinite, pending the termination of the trust. Left un-repealed, the force of the 1958 law should govern actions in 1991, argued the Franklin Institute.

In *Franklin Foundation* v. *Attorney General* (1993), the Supreme Judicial Court decreed that 'St. 1958, c. 596, expresses an intent to effect early termination, and that it cannot be reasonably interpreted to take effect now'. The court pointed out that had the statute been intended to bind the state thirty-three years after passage it would not have made provisions for termination, as the trust would have automatically terminated. References in the 1958 law referred to authorization from the court for termination, and action not required of a trust whose term had naturally expired according to the testator's instructions.[12] This decision left wide open the application of the funds to be distributed in 1991 to the city of Boston and Commonwealth of Massachusetts.

The Franklin Foundation member and Boston attorney, Larry DiCara, articulated the case for the institute in an interview with *The Boston Globe*. 'The money should stay with the institute. The likelihood of a kid out of the neighbourhoods getting a skill that will last him the rest of his life is probably greater at Franklin than anywhere else.'[13] The Franklin Institute's Associate Dean, Richard

D'Onofrio, later its President, declared his willingness to apply some of the Franklin Fund to a loan fund to help apprentices establish themselves in business.[14] D'Onofrio had a conviction that not only is such a use possible but, moreover, it is desirable. He expressed a faith in Franklin's vision missing for over 150 years of Franklin Fund management, seventy-two years of which were controlled by the Institute's trustees.

The Franklin Foundation dutifully maintained the trust beyond the 30 June 1991 termination date, pending the outcome of litigation. While daunted by the court's decision, the Franklin Institute launched a political campaign to capture the Franklin Fund through new legislative action. Through a supplemental appropriations bill, William Bulger, President of the Senate, championed, an 'outside section', # 127, that distributed the state's potion of the Franklin Fund ($3.2 million) to the Franklin Institute for its 'maintenance, extension and use'. There was no requirement to protect the principal or conditions of trust. The appropriation bill, after passing out of the legislative conference committee, passed on 4 January 1994 and Governor William Weld signed the bill making all of its provisions law. The city of Boston followed suit. After 200 years Franklin's estate had been settled and his legacy could perpetually support students seeking to improve themselves by acquiring technical educations.

Philadelphia

The year of dissolution of the Franklin Fund was equally calamitous in the city of brotherly love, Philadelphia. The city government teetered on the brink of bankruptcy while SEPTA (the metropolitan transit system) workers conducted a devastating strike that disrupted the city's basic operation. It was a propitious time to reconsider of Benjamin Franklin's beliefs that political and economic independence could be achieved through careful savings and that loss of freedom would result from uncontrolled debt. It was also an appropriate time for the city and state to reflect on what had been learned over 200 years when deploying the legacy funds. Seeing that its fiduciary responsibilities ended with the termination of the trust in 1990, the Board of Directors of City Trusts eagerly exempted itself from debate, leaving the gnashing to city and state officials and the public-at-large. The trust in Philadelphia, like Boston, had continued to make loans up to the termination date. The value of the total trust at the expiration in April of 1990 was approximately $2 million. Of this amount the city share represented 26.13 per cent (or $522,000) and the balance (73.87 per cent, or $1,478,000) went to the Commonwealth of Pennsylvania.[15] Despite the stature and magnitude of Franklin's bicentennial gift, there was very little consideration given by either state officials or city officials to the application of the funds until January 1990, less than three months before the Franklin Loan Fund trust expired.

The City Solicitor's Office had as early as March 1989 considered the process of dissolution offering the following opinion:

> These amounts are given without restriction ... Accordingly, the sum due to the City is for the City's unrestricted use. Pursuant to our Charter, the monies will go into the City Treasury general fund, and may be considered a revenue source to balance future appropriations. Thus the City would be free to spend its share of the trust funds for any valid municipal purpose, and the money would have to be spent pursuant to appropriations made by City Council.[16]

Deputy City Solicitor Eric H. Auerbach, having rendered this straightforward opinion, penned the following thoughtful footnote:

> Nevertheless, I believe it would be appropriate for the City to make special use of the funds in the spirit of Franklin's Will. As Franklin stated in his Will, '[i]t has been a opinion that he who receives an Estate from his Ancesters, is under some kind of obligation to transmit the same to their prosperity'. I note in the material you sent to me requests from the School District and from the Philadelphia Foundation for these funds, both of which requests seek to match the intent of Franklin's trust. Similarly, the City might approach the Commonwealth and seek a joint agreement to manage the total amount to be distributed from the trust.[17]

At least on the legal staff level, some informed judgement about the best application, beyond the minimum requirement, was being offered and considered.

Soon other oars were in the water. The Library Company of Philadelphia, founded by Franklin in 1731, under the leadership of Edwin Wolf, expressed an early interest in receiving Franklin Fund money to establish a scholarship for in-residence researchers to use the Library, a collection of more than 500,000 rare books, including many from Franklin's personal library. As early as 1987 Joel Bloom, President of the Franklin Institute, cited a need to reward distinguished leaders in the fields of diplomacy and communications with Franklin Fund money to complement other awards to scientists and business executive already granted by the Franklin Institute. However, the awkward idea, consisting of a medal and a cash prize paid out of Franklin bequest, got a cool reception from Whitfield Bell, eminent Franklin scholar, Director Emeritus of the American Philosophical Society and Editor Emeritus of the *Papers of Benjamin Franklin* who, remembering Franklin's wish to be 'useful', thought public education a more 'Franklinian' application.[18] Without publically soliciting proposals the city had been receiving suggestions such as a formal Franklin garden, a scholarship programme for students studying in vocational education programmes, city-wide free distribution of smoke alarms and a lecture series.

City of Philadelphia Mayor Wilson Goode's initial proposal for application of the Franklin bequest was met with public disapproval. In January 1990, Mayoral staff members Lana Felton-McGhee and Gerri Walker announced the City of Philadelphia's plans to use Franklin's bequest for promotion of tourism. Given the deficit facing the city budget, funds to support city-wide festivals had been cut back and Franklin's $500,000 gift would support the 'Freedom Festival' to be held on the Fourth of July weekend in 1990. To honour Benjamin Franklin, the festival organizers had planned to engage noted stage performer, *Ben* Vereen, and popular singer, Aretha *Franklin*, to provide entertainment. *The Philadelphia Inquirer* in breaking the news of the Mayor's plan on Page One quoted city official Felton-Ghee's additional commentary: 'It took us a long time to come up with those two names'.[19]

Lost in the press coverage was the intention of the city officials to support two other festivals with the Franklin money, the 'Festival of Firsts' held in June, 1990, which highlighted Philadelphia's unique contributions to history (first zoo, first library, etc.) and a programme called 'Music in Museums' where musicians would perform in various locations around independence Hall and along the Franklin Parkway. After all, the Mayor's staff reasoned, the various events were part of a summer long celebration of Benjamin Franklin. However, the cultural programming that might have been funded by the Franklin legacy, as deserving as it was, appeared to the public to be 'frivolous and shortsighted'.[20]

It did not take long for the public criticism to find expression. While some Philadelphians were simply incredulous, Edwin Wolf, Librarian Emeritus of the Library Company and a noted historian, spoke unequivocally: 'This is the old Roman bread and circuses. You have a circus to get people's mind off the awful state of the city administration. It is inexcusable'.[21] Considering the fact that the money had been saved over a 200 year period, demonstrating the virtue of frugality, Christopher van de Velde, President of the City Parks Association, reasoned that: 'Spending the money in one shot to blow out a candle doesn't do much for my soul at all'.[22] While Goode's staff garnered support from the Philadelphia Convention & Visitors Bureau, the public reception, fuelled by press coverage, a critical editorial and letters to the editor, was overwhelmingly negative.

They Mayor's proposal also received the criticism of the Museum Council of Philadelphia and Delaware Valley, an organization of approximately 400 museums directors and curators, who recommended the appointment of a panel that could advise the public about the best application of the Franklin bequest.[23] By 26 January 1990 Mayor Goode regrouped with the appointment of a seven member commission of Franklin scholars, historians and academics which received suggestions from the public from mid January until 15 March 1990.

The Mayor conveyed his expectations as follows: 'My hope is that you and the other scholars will be able to offer some insight as to how Dr. Franklin would have me dispose of the trust given the current problems of illiteracy, teenage pregnancy, homelessness, and high drop-out rates facing Philadelphia'.[24] With this instruction, Mayor Goode emphasized the value of applying the funds to education and social services for the disadvantaged citizens of Philadelphia, a significant departure from fireworks, festivals and concerts.

The Mayor's Advisory Committee, under the chairmanship of Whitfield J. Bell, adopted Franklin's guidelines for the centennial distribution as parameters for those who wished to submit proposals. Joining Dr Bell, the other members of the committee were Dr Richard Beeman, professor of American History University of Pennsylvania; A. Bruce Crawley, president, Crawley, Haskins & Rodgers Public Valley Grantmakers; Dr J. A. Leo Lemay, professor of English and noted Franklin scholar, University of Delaware; Dr Larry Tise, historian and executive director, Franklin National Memorial of the Franklin Institute; and Dr Michael Zuckerman, professor of History, University of Pennsylvania.[25] The Committee, in its call for suggestions, quoted Franklin's instructions for the centennial distribution and advised that the Franklin legacy should be expended for 'works which may be judged of the most general utility to the inhabitants ... or whatever may make living in the town more convenient to its people, and render it more agreeable to strangers ...'[26] The committee held five meetings and one public hearing, receiving 300 letters from '225 private citizens and charitable or community institutions and foundations'.[27]

Among the more novel proposals was that from the Fudan Museum Foundation which sought funds to construct a 'Goddess of Democracy' statue comparable to the one erected at Tianamen Square in the People's Republic of China during pro-democracy demonstrations of that year. An individual proposed using the funds to fill potholes in Philadelphia streets. A highly popular proposal advanced by the City Parks Association, supported by eighty-two correspondents, sought the funds to provide perpetual support of the public parks, especially the open spaces in the city. This proposal was grouped with several others, including a request from Edward H. Able of the American Museum Association for the restoration of Benjamin Franklin House in London, England, identified as large capital projects which were considered unfavourably by the Advisory Committee.[28]

Three significant organizations proposed to hold the Franklin Fund in trust and apply its income to human needs. The Office of the Superintendent of the School District of Philadelphia, Board of Education, sought to create a Common Trust Fund 'making possible the redemption of lives of a host of talented, civic minded students struggling against the indifference of poverty'. Superintendent Constance Clayton's cover letter cited the excellent record of the '... School District in managing of trust funds ...'[29] The proposal showed considerable knowledge about Franklin's original intent for the Franklin Fund and identified 'his abiding concern – the welfare of the needs'. In simple, yet powerful prose, the proposal contended (correctly) that Franklin 'envisioned citizens who were learned in hand, in mind, and in heart; economically self-sufficient and morally correct'. Given the exigency that 'survival comes before self-improvement', the School District proposed that a new Franklin Fund would provide special counselling, supervision, financial assistance for post-secondary education, starting a business or buying equipment.[30] A fascinating feature of the proposal was the expectation that students would be measured against Franklin's own list for self improvement. The School District attached Franklin's list of virtues which read: temperance, silence, order, resolution, frugality, industry, sincerity, justice, moderation, cleanliness, tranquillity and humility. Given that the long tradition of using Franklin's autobiography for teaching civics and morality has generally been lost, this was a surprising inclusion. While the Advisory Committee turned fore-square toward education, it did not recommend the School District as the recipient of the Franklin Fund.

The second proposal of significance came from the American Philosophical Society, an organization founded by Franklin, and also called for the fund to be held as a perpetual endowment. The income from investments would be used to loan inner-city secondary school graduates money to cover the costs of post-secondary education based on eligibility criteria including academic abilities and achievements and good citizenship. The loans would be forgiven if the students returned to Philadelphia and worked in public service careers. The Society also cited its experience in managing trust funds and grant making programmes. The records do not indicate why the committee declined to recommend this proposal.

The third of the three most substantial proposals won the support of the Advisory Committee. The Philadelphia Foundation submitted a proposal that included several attractive features, most notably a commitment to:

> – match the income from the Franklin Fund annually, thus doubling the latter's effect and usefulness;
>
> – administer the Franklin Fund for three years without charge, and to charge its standard rate of 6 per cent thereafter; and
>
> – announce the annual grants and awards 'at a special event that will insure high visibility'.[31]

The proposal sought to fund 'at least two programs in the fields of youth employment and/or community economic development' at the level of $30,000 annually. The Philadelphia Foundation's proposal included no more detailed information about what it meant by 'community economic development'.

At its earliest meeting the committee found consensus around certain hopes for the future of the Franklin Fund. The Fund should continue as an independent endowment, held in principal and invested from 'maximum income' which would be given away to 'encourage, recognize and reward *excellence in productive work* of any kind' with as much publicity as possible. Because of the small size of the fund, additional matching money from the private sector should give it a 'multiplier effect' and administrative fees should be avoided.[32] At this point in its deliberation the Committee had not identified education as a primary focus. The consensus that the Franklin Fund's work as an income producing trust reaching even beyond Franklin's extraordinary prescribed 200 year term was ironic given the periodic attempts to collapse the trust prematurely and expend the corpus before its scheduled dissolution. The lesson of frugality, of the productive capacity of savings had been taught, at least to the members of Mayor's Advisory Committee.

On the 17 April anniversary of Franklin's death, the Advisory Committee submitted its report. The report included an overview of the kinds of projects proposed:

> Some of the ideas presented to us would be difficult to implement (e.g., inculcating Franklinian virtues notably thrift); some fall within the legal responsibilities of the City or national government, which only they can carry out (e.g., increased police and fire protection, street repair, the reconstruction of Franklin's houses in Philadelphia and London); and others are far beyond the capacity of the Fund to achieve (e.g. care of the homeless).[33]

The committee, in discussion amongst its members and after review of proposals, determined that a consensus had formed around two significant principles. A majority of the submissions urged that the Franklin's legacy be used 'to promote education' and that the fund be maintained in some perpetual form, i.e., the 'principal be reinvested', the income only being spent annually'.[34] The committee recommended that the Franklin Funds be used to provide need-based financial assistance to currently enrolled students or recent graduates of Philadelphia high schools to help them pay for 'trade, craft, or applied science' education required for gainful employment. The Franklin Fund support might come in the form of 'grants for living expenses, guaranteed credit or loans, tools, or other necessary equipment'. Hoping to magnify the impact of the Franklin contribution, the Advisory Committee also recommended that students who receive matching grant support from their schools should be given first preference.[35] A second appropriate use would be the recognition (1) of individuals who have demonstrated excellence in the crafts or fields of applied science and (2) of educational institutions that have developed distinguished training programmes in the crafts or fields of applied science.[36]

Careful to conserve Franklin Fund resources, the Advisory Committee suggested that the city place the Franklin Fund with the Philadelphia Foundation, a charitable foundation serving the five counties of southeastern Pennsylvania designed to manage multiple trusts including trusts with narrowly focused purposes. The Philadelphia Foundation, governed by a racially and ethnically diverse, nine member Board of Managers, managed a large unrestricted endowment used to support worthy community wide projects as well as 130 individual trusts worth more than $61 million as of 1990. The Committee cited the Philadelphia Foundation's seventy years of successful management of individual trusts, the benefit of an in-place professional staff and a record of sound and resourceful investment.

The Advisory Committee submitted the report to Mayor Goode who thanked the Advisory Committee, accepted their report and forwarded their recommendations to the Court of Common Pleas, for final adjudication.

The Commonwealth of Pennsylvania proceeded more expeditiously in allocating its 73.87 per cent share. State Senator F. Joseph Loeper introduced a bill in 1989, passed by the Senate, which allocated all of the state portion to the Franklin Institute for the construction of the 'Futures Center', a $71.5 million addition which was under construction at the time. Loeper's bill stalled in the House of Representatives and State Representative Gordon J. Linton counter-proposed that the state's share be distributed to the twenty members of the Commonwealth Community Foundations throughout the Commonwealth. (The Philadelphia Foundation was a member of this consortium.) The alternative House bill proposed by Linton would have awarded from $40,000 to as much as $200,000 to the foundations to be held as endowments to be used for 'education, job training and economic development programs'.[37]

The compromise legislation referred to as Senate Bill 1135 and signed into law by Governor Robert P. Casey on 17 December 1990, designated the Franklin Institute of Philadelphia as the recipient of half of the state's portion, 'to support educational and training programs'.[38] The remaining amount was given to the Commonwealth Community Foundations to be distributed on a pro-rated basis to the Commonwealth's community foundations. Propagating Franklin's legacy, perpetual Franklin endowments were established in twenty towns and cities each with its own distinct civic purpose. The structure of community foundations implicitly encouraged gifts from other local sources to augment Franklin's legacy and were likely to continue to compound the resource. Remarkably, Franklin's bequest after 200 years continued to be useful in the way he intended. While the state law finally decided the question of where the money would go, the division and distribution of the proceeds required a final dissolution action by the Court of Common Pleas.[39]

In November, 1992, Judge Francis X. O'Brien of the Court of Common Pleas in Philadelphia appointed Gerard T. St John to act as Master to evaluate the city's petition based on the recommendations of the Mayor's Advisory Commission and advise the court on the division and distribution of the trust fund to both the city and the state. In particular St John was asked to review the

Fund Agreement with the Philadelphia Foundation to insure conformity with the testator's intent as expressed in Franklin's 1789 codicil.

The Fund Agreement, forwarded to the court by the Board of Directors of City Trusts on behalf of the Mayor, was predicated on the basis of the recommendations of the Mayor's Advisory Committee. The Fund Agreement purported to be a direct translation of the committee's report. However, St John, in his inquiry on behalf of Judge O'Brien, discovered significant changes in the Fund Agreement from the draft approved by the Advisory Committee that caused problems for the court. The Fund Agreement stated the purpose of the Benjamin Franklin Fund as follows:

> The purpose of the Fund is to provide funds for charitable and educational purposes ... for the benefit of the residents of the City ... including, but not limited to, the following:
>
> 1) to assist students and recent graduates of Philadelphia public high schools who need financial aid to obtain additional training in trades, crafts or applied science;
>
> 2) to make awards to schools or other organizations to provide education and training in such activities; and
>
> 3) to recognize individual excellence in such activities.[40]

St John felt that the insertion of the word 'public' as a qualifier to school students, a condition not found in the advisory committee's recommendation, exempted students and recent graduates of private schools, violating the testator's intent to benefit all of the inhabitants of Philadelphia. St John also felt that the change from recognition awards to exceptional schools, as the committee had proposed, to awards to provide education and training significantly redirected the trust's interest toward a bottomless pit of need, quite outside the testator's intent.

Section 5 of the Fund Agreement was flawed in one major respect with its provision that: 'in the event that it becomes unnecessary, undesirable, impractical or impossible to utilize the Fund for any or all of such purposes, the Foundation shall have the right to utilize the Benjamin Franklin Fund for such other charitable purposes as it deems appropriate in accordance with its governing instruments'.[41] St John recommended to Judge O'Brien that this language provided too much flexibility, allowing the Benjamin Franklin Fund to deviate from the testator's intent without court review and approval.

The court, on the advice of the Master's Report, decreed that access to financial assistance must be available to all Philadelphia high school students and recent graduates, and that the use of the funds must conform closely to Franklin's intent as stated in the codicil. The judge also required an accounting to the court every five years reconciling the progress of the Benjamin Franklin Fund with Franklin's intent. Copies of the accounting would also be shared with the Attorney General of the Commonwealth, the Board of Directors of City Trusts and with an advisory committee made up of representatives of institutions founded by Franklin including the American Philosophical Society, the Philadelphia Contributorship, the Library Company, the Pennsylvania Hospital and the University of Pennsylvania. The court also encouraged the Philadelphia Foundation to raise more money for the Benjamin Franklin Fund to compensate for its slow growth over the first 200 years.

The final financial accounting issued by the court on 15 January 1993 assigned 36.935 per cent of $2,256,952.05 (or $833,605.24) to the Franklin Institute of Philadelphia and a like amount to the Commonwealth of Community Foundations, according to the division of the Commonwealth of Pennsylvania's portion as specified in Senate Bill 1135. A sum of $589,741.57 (or 26.13 per cent), the city's portion, was distributed to the Philadelphia Foundation after the Fund Agreement was edited to conform with the decree of the Court of Common Pleas. Thus, began the third century of the Benjamin Franklin Fund in Philadelphia. Ironically, after two centuries of shallow understanding and very limited public involvement, the beneficiaries in Philadelphia and Pennsylvania sought applications for the bequest that (1) had relevance to Franklin's life and his message to posterity and (2) that converted his trusts into perpetual form continuing to contribute to the welfare of the people. Franklin's grand scheme, originating in the 1789 codicil, had successfully promoted the virtues of frugality and industry and proven not only 'practicable', as Franklin had anticipated, but instructive and estimable.

CONCLUSION: VIRTUES IN CONFLICT

Thirty-six years before the writing of his codicil, in a letter written in 1753 to 'a zealous Religionist' whom he had aided, Benjamin Franklin shared his views about eternal life after death. Franklin was piqued by sanctimonious expressions of faith intended to curry God's favour in lieu of conduct which demonstrated 'loving thy neighbour as thyself'. In this revealing correspondence Franklin established his reason for creating his testamentary trusts:

> As to the Kindness you mention, I wish it could have been of more Service to you. But if it had, the only Thanks I should desire is, that you would always be equally ready to serve any other Person that may need your Assistance, and so let Good Offices go round, for Mankind are all of a Family.
>
> For my own Part, when I am employed in serving others, I do not look upon myself as conferring Favours, but as paying Debts. In my Travels and since my Settlement I have received much Kindness from Men, to whom I shall never have any Opportunity of making the least direct Return. And numberless Mercies from God, who is infinitely above being benefited by our Services. These Kindness from Men I can therefore only return on their Fellow-Men; and I can only show my Gratitude for those Mercies from God, by a Readiness to help his other Children and my Brethren. For I do not think that Thanks, and Compliments, tho' repeated Weekly, can discharge our real Obligations to each other and much less those to our Creator.
>
> You will see in this my notion of Good Works, that I am far from expecting (as you suppose) that I shall merit Heaven by them. By Heaven we understand, a State of Happiness, infinite in Degree, and eternal in Duration: I can do nothing to deserve such a Reward ... For my own part, I have not the Vanity to think I deserve it, the Folly to expect it, nor the Ambition to desire it; but content myself in submitting to the Will and Disposal of that God who made me, who has hitherto preserv'd and bless'd me ...
>
> The Faith you mention has doubtless its use in the World; I do not desire to see it diminished, nor would I endeavor to lessen it in any Man. But I wish it were more productive of Good Works than I have generally seen it: I mean real good Works, Works of Kindness, Charity, Mercy, and Public Spirit ... The worship of God is a Duty, the hearing and reading of sermons may be useful; but if Men rest in Hearing and Praying, as too many do, it is as if a Tree should value itself on being water'd and putting forth Leaves, tho' it never produc'd any Fruit.[1]

As a final payment of debt to Mankind and as a tribute to God's beneficence, Franklin devised a gift to the people of Boston and Philadelphia that was meant to produce fruit. Hardly 'a vain Fancy', Franklin's intent was profoundly serious, morally earnest and religious in nature. Investment in his fellow man represented an ultimate affirmation of Franklin's beliefs, not just a testamentary contrivance.

Franklin worked under the assumption that a free society as a matter of public policy would promote the rise in the standard and quality of living for all of its citizens. American government, particularly on the local and state level, would have as its primary purpose, and consequently, the focus of all its activity, improvement in the health and welfare of the public. Enlightened leaders, elected to represent the people and regularly drawn from the ranks, would have the privilege of protecting the inalienable rights of citizens: life, liberty and the pursuit of happiness. Unfortunately, the two cities and states Franklin chose to honour with his bequest failed to be consistent champions of freedom and enfranchisement. No worse or better than other governments, Boston and Philadelphia, Massachusetts and Pennsylvania ploughed through decades of faction, indifference, misfeasance, corruption, reform, reorganization and renaissance struggling to meet the challenge and fulfil the promise of democracy.

Franklin offered the cities a formula for building a strong democracy based on individual empowerment, broad enfranchisement and collective responsibility. Political theorist Benjamin Barber's definition of strong democracy echoes Franklin's conception of the role of government in the following passage written in 1984:

> ... strong democracy in the participatory mode resolves conflict in the absence of an independent ground through a participatory process of ongoing, proximate self-legislation and the creation of a political community capable of transforming dependent private individuals into free citizens and partial and private interests into public goods.[2]

While Barber's emphasis on process is resonant with Franklin's political theory, the transformation from dependence to independence and from private to public exactly describes Franklin's intent in the 1789 codicil.

However, Boston and Philadelphia repeatedly chose to build the democracy on a rigid class system, characterized by conflict and dominated by the economic and social elite, that provided scant opportunity for shifts in power and upward mobility. The Franklin Funds serve as a window through which to view the evolution of the urban brand of American democracy.

After 200 years, the successes and failures of the two philanthropic trusts, established in Boston and Philadelphia according to Franklin's wishes, are as instructive as the lessons offered by Franklin in his oft-quoted autobiography, vast correspondence, *Poor Richard's Almanac* and in his many essays and tracts. Although the trusts did not generate the $36 million largess forecast by Franklin in the codicil, and although in both cities the trusts were taken under the wings of the courts for protection from neglect, diversion and abuse, the 1991 combined value of the two Franklin Trusts reached a substantial sum of $6.5 million.[3] Although a diminution of Franklin's projection, the original capital compounded by interest income accumulated into a large sum and the lesson of frugality was, to some degree, learned. While the final contests to capture the bicentennial windfall have only recently been decided, Franklin's scheme gained some modest recognition for the value of compounded savings to two cities and a new nation swamped in debt. However, the relevancy of Franklin's conception of political and economic freedom predicated on the virtue of the people (expressed by their industry and frugality) had been missed on many agents of modern systems of government. The persistence of massive public debt and the inability to retire the debt, or even retard its growth, thwarts the growth of the nation and limits the enfranchisement of all of its citizens. Franklin's larger point about accepting constraints on prosperity commensurate with available resources, and retiring debt responsibly, has often fallen on deaf ears throughout the 200 year life of Franklin's trust scheme.

Nevertheless, the 'sinking fund' idea, popular with Franklin, Richard Price and other of their contemporaries, persists in most American municipalities as a device to retire debts associated with major capital projects, like sewage treatment plants, street improvements, public buildings, etc. In some cases sinking funds are used to retire debt encumbered through years of excessive operation. Sinking funds still have some of the fundamental features that Franklin and Price recognized: the need to be treated inviolate and to have a designated source of revenue beyond interest earnings, and to be invested for maximum yield. Much has been written about the absurdity of sinking funds as contrivances that permit cities to live beyond their available resources, pushing sacrifice off to future generations in favour of profligacy of the present. Once the debt has been incurred for whatever noble or dishonourable purpose, the sinking fund is still considered a viable way to retire debt. Throughout the 200 years of the Franklin Trust's operations no manager, trustee, agent or judge ever made the connection between (1) the compounding charitable trust, designed to compound by capturing its own interest while amassing a credit and (2) the characteristic of a sinking fund, also designed to compound by capturing its own interest and intended to redeem debt. Unfortunately, Franklin made no direct reference to his fascination with sinking funds in the language of the codicil and the broader economic point never came to light.

As the Franklin Funds increased through compounding of principal, notwithstanding occasional attempts to raid the funds, the citizens of Boston and

Philadelphia benefited by distributed accumulations in the 1890s and 1990s. On this ostensible level of performance, the codicil met the first of its two objectives, to demonstrate the virtue of frugality.

A second major feature of the codicil, however, was a resounding failure. Franklin wanted the funds to be invested in the form of low interest loans to married artificers, who after completing their apprenticeship, sought to establish their own business, thus illustrating the virtue of industry. For Franklin, the value of work did not spring from an exaggerated affection for money and the power associated with prosperity and affluence, although he has been regarded as the first great apologist for capitalism. In fact, Franklin decried ambition, avarice and those who would seek 'profitable Preëminence, thro' all the Bustle of Cabal, the Heat of Contention, the infinite mutual Abuse of Parties, tearing to Pieces the best of Characters'.[4] Franklin assigned gainful employment an exalted status for an entirely different reason, a reason frequently obscured by the dense clouds of popular Franklin mythology.

Franklin saw industry, i.e. work, as the means to independence and as the guardian of liberty. As if he were providing additional instruction and inspiration to the leadership of Boston and Philadelphia beyond the terms of his codicil, Franklin wrote in *Poor Richard Improved, 1758* the following:

> But, ah think what you do when you run in Debt; You give to another Power over your Liberty ... Poverty often deprives a Man of all Spirit and Virtue: '*Tis hard for an empty Bag to stand upright*, as *Poor Richard* truly says ... Then since, he says, *The Borrower is a slave to the Lender, and the Debtor to the Creditor*, disdain the Chain, preserve your Freedom; and maintain your Independency: Be *industrious* and *free*; be *frugal* and *free*.[5]

In Franklin's terms the young urban artisan without access to financial capital would be an 'empty Bag' and nothing less than America's unprecedented aspiration to be politically and economically free hung in the balance. In its small way, the loans to artificers from a neutral source, i.e. the Franklin Trust, was intended to circumvent the economic tyranny of a creditor class over a debtor class.

The meaning and significance of this second purpose of the codicil was diminished and ignored by the board of managers of both cities throughout most of the 200 year history. While in both cities the loan funds were successfully loaned to artisans in the first few decades of operation, the managers of the Franklin Funds in the nineteenth century concluded that Franklin had defined the borrowers in overly narrow occupational and social terms and had hopelessly constrained the loan conditions. Therefore, Franklin's directions were found insufficient in the face of rapid industrialization and the changing nature of labour, capital and society in Boston and Philadelphia. The managers undervalued Franklin's proposition that each citizen, working for a higher standard of living and financial independence, when joined by other industrious individuals, would establish a strong moral and ethical community and a broad economic base capable of metabolizing change associated with urbanization and industrialization.

The disappearance of apprenticeship in many trades during the nineteenth century created a ruse used to arrest the artisan loan programme. It was a commonplace understanding that the system of indentured apprenticeship under a skilled master craftsman had been gradually and successfully replaced with a combination of general education in the public schools, technical education in manual training and trade schools as well as mechanics unions, and on-the-job training. By requiring the bondsmen to have completed their apprenticeships, Franklin simply wanted them to have the basic skills of trade as a prerequisite to a start in business. With a modicum of imagination and desire, the managers could have adjusted then loan requirements (with or without court sanction) and stayed well within the tolerances of fiduciary propriety. The recitation of a collapse of the apprenticeship system represented a thin excuse for abandoning the loan programme.

Philadelphia's protest about apprenticeship appeared most disingenuous (or, at least, unimaginative) given the responsibility the Board of Directors of City Trusts had for administering Girard College as well as the Franklin Legacy. Stephen Girard required as a condition of his huge bequest that created the college that Girard graduates be indentured as apprentices as a transition to gainful employment in a trade after completing their education. While the records of the college indicate that the placement of its graduates as apprentices became increasingly difficult as the nineteenth century wore on, the college managed to fulfil Girard's testamentary instructions. Surprisingly, the Board of Directors of City Trusts never saw the potential of using Franklin's loan programme to launch Girard College graduates in the trades, all qualifying as young artisans having completed apprenticeships.

While the problem of sureties represented a more genuine obstacle to the prospective Franklin Fund borrower, the Boston records failed to verify Treasurer Minot's report that sureties got routinely abused by the bondsmen in the early decades of the programme. A high proportion of the required payments were apparently made by the borrower himself according to Minot's own receipts journal. When sureties contributed to repayment there was no evidence of coercion or complaint. They may well have been enthusiastic in helping out a friend, neighbour or protégé. Frequently, the young man carried the same surname as at least one of the sureties indicating a likely prospect of kinship.

A solution to the problem of security for the Franklin loans in Philadelphia, while extending credit to individuals, permanently shifted the type of loan offered. By requiring real estate in Philadelphia as security for the loans, the Board of Directors of City Trusts, without court approval, circumvented the requirement of two sureties as specified by Franklin while converting the programme from business loans to mortgage loans. The Directors recognized that real estate equity as opposed to personal property provided more conventional and reliable security. The managers of the Franklin Fund in Boston failed to consider this alternative.

Very late in the history of the Boston trust the Franklin Foundation executives devised a strategy for providing a substitute to the sureties system as specified by Franklin. The construction of the Wolfson Guarantee Fund to make payments on defaulted loans extended to medical students at Boston University, Harvard University and Tufts University allowed the Franklin Funds to be loaned risk-free to individuals who completed their qualifying medical education and needed financial assistance while meeting residency requirements. Subsequently, the universities themselves enthusiastically agreed to serve as the guarantor when the Wolfson Fund proved insufficient. Finding institutional guarantors for Franklin loans allowed Boston to support individuals per Franklin's wishes without jeopardizing the sacrosanct compounding of interest with principal. For most of the Boston trust's history the inability of loan applicants to obtain two acceptable sureties was recited as an explanation for the moribund Franklin artisan loan fund.

The managers in Boston, while alleging that the Franklin loans were unmarketable, purposefully defeated the revolving loan function of the trust early in the nineteenth century in favour of consolidating the Franklin fund with other private resources on deposit with the Massachusetts Hospital Life Insurance Company serving the special interests of the Boston Associates. In Philadelphia, the managers allowed the fund to languish through mismanagement and disinterest, only later to be contrarily invested, through political subterfuge, in public utilities. In both cities the Franklin Fund provided little opportunity to individuals for upward mobility and economic sufficiency. Likewise, Boston's and Philadelphia's torches of political liberty, especially as they illuminated the citizenry of these cities, seemed to flicker and dim with each passing decade after the Declaration of Independence.

Only as a result of imbroglios over the use of the centenary gift did the conscience of the two cities reawaken enough to reconsider Franklin's original intent in serving the Middling Interest, specifically the mechanics of the cities. After thoughtful consideration and some public debate, both Boston and Philadelphia applied the centennial portion of the Franklin Funds to institutions that served the educational and vocational needs of skilled workers through the Franklin Institute of Boston and the Franklin Institute of Philadelphia. Even in 1991-3 the authorities, particularly, city, state and court officials, who directed the application of the bicentennial portion, while free to consider any legal use, felt compelled to weigh Franklin's interest in assistance to artisans as a significant criteria. The final distribution plans in both cities sought legitimacy by tracking much of Franklin's original language in the codicil. The Franklin Institute of Boston argued that the use of the funds as a permanent endowment would serve the very population Franklin sought to assist. The Court of Common Pleas (Philadelphia) through court appointed Master, Gerard T. St John carefully evaluated and pursued Franklin's expressed wishes in sanctioning the final disposition.

Insofar as the Cities of Boston and Philadelphia constitute separate legal jurisdictions, the legal history is not identical and the course of legislative acts and judicial decisions allows the trust management of each of the two cities to serve as a basis of comparison for the other. As a practical matter, the managers of both trusts denied judicial review of digressions from Franklin's explicit wishes until the latter half of the nineteenth century. In Boston, first contact with any legal authority came with the decree in 1887 from the Probate Court of the county of Suffolk that established the Alderman as the legitimate successors to the Town of Boston Selectmen. This declaratory judgement only confirmed an arrangement accomplished by presumption sixty-five years earlier. The earliest serious challenge to the City of Boston's fiduciary competence as manager or trustee resulted from an internecine battle over how to expend the centenary distribution, not from review of the chequered record of the Franklin Fund managers during the first hundred years. The sudden expansion of the Massachusetts courts protection of the Franklin Trust in the early twentieth century, ultimately leading to the establishment of a charitable corporation controlled by the court beyond the City of Boston's political reach in 1906, was a reaction to waves of controversy and rancour. Even the Supreme Judicial Court of Massachusetts had to be prodded by numerous law suits into the position of demanding the accountability and probity of the trust's management. Short of court vigilance the city of Boston managed the trust from 1791 until 1887 outside the purview of any authority higher than itself. The decision of the Managers to meet for nearly a half century without the three ministers specified in Franklin's codicil symbolized management's willingness to suspend the explicit terms of the testamentary trust when convenient. That same easy adaptability to changed circumstances outside of judicial review did not cross over to the administration of the artisan loan fund.

Prior to the creation of the Board of Directors of City Trusts in Philadelphia in 1869, the virtually autonomous public entity given the authority to manage the city's charitable trusts, decisions affecting the Franklin Legacy were accomplished by the simple action of the Select and Common Council committee. The Board through an act of the Pennsylvania legislature and with the blessing of the Supreme Court of Pennsylvania, the District Court and the Court of Common Pleas was assigned the role of management, leaving the City of Philadelphia with the trusteeship of the Franklin Fund. As managers, the Board established a tangible relationship of accountability with the Pennsylvania judicial system which presided over testamentary trusts at arm's length from the machinations of local government. Changes in the administration of the Franklin Fund, henceforth, required *cy pres* modification to the trust instrument.

Although the intent and instructions of Franklin's codicil were virtually identical, the respective histories of the trusts reveal some contrasting priorities and concerns. Boston's Franklin Foundation for most of its history prided itself on the success of its compounding, placing greatest emphasis on the virtue of saving. The managers of the fund determined that the careful stewardship of the investment capital constituted complete fulfilment of their fiduciary responsibility, neglecting to regard the full extent of the testator's instructions. It wasn't until the closing years of the life of the trust that assisting individuals gained status was a principal purpose by an averment of the Massachusetts Supreme Judicial Court leading to the advent of the medical student loan programme of the 1960s. Although the creation of a strong trade school, now institute, effectively addressed Franklin's interest in Boston's skilled workers, the use of the principal to support individuals who have completed their studies and seek a start in business was largely defeated by the investment decisions of the trustees.

While the trustees of the Franklin Trust in Philadelphia also directed investment away from loans to young married artisans, it did continue to obtain court approval for modifications in Franklin's conditions in order to animate the fund. When the Board of Directors of City Trusts converted the investments into a low maintenance fund for long-term, low interest, home mortgages, with competitive interest rates and terms, they found sufficient borrowers. While the endless arguments for not loaning the Franklin Funds to married artisans to establish small business are unconvincing, the Philadelphia Franklin Fund, to its credit, continued to make loans to upwardly mobile, low and moderate income residents of Philadelphia, a segment of the population congruent with Franklin's Leather Apronmen. In this regard, Philadelphia's performance as fiduciary of the Franklin Fund achieved a better balance of commitment to compounding the fund and loaning out the fund than Boston, notwithstanding the lower value of the Philadelphia trust at the one hundred and 200 year mark.

The litigation, particularly the language of the plaintiffs, defendants and the judgements, at the centenary and bicentenary of the trusts has yielded some insightful and some dubious interpretations of Franklin's intent. As history, the case law regarding the Franklin trusts was limited by the lack of initially correct information about artificers, apprenticeship, credit and employment. Due to faithful recitation of legal precedent, initial mistaken judgements were canonized, if not compounded, and only rarely revisited for judicial reconsideration.

Regrettably, no complete study of the efficacy of the loan programme in the earliest decades of the trusts was ever undertaken.

Fortunately, in both cities primary records of the early years of the Franklin Trusts exist. The financial record books, particularly the general ledger and some of the bond books, in Philadelphia were transferred to the American Philosophical Society by the City of Philadelphia for safe keeping. The remainder of Philadelphia records are maintained by the City Archives or by the Board of City Trusts. In Boston, the Massachusetts Historical Society has a large un-catalogued collection of the financial records of William Minot (1783–1873) who served as Treasurer and Manager of the Franklin Fund from 1811 to 1866. The City of Boston's burgeoning and undermanned archived located in its collection the general ledger and some minute books of the managers of the Franklin Fund from the earliest decades. The Franklin Institute of Boston and the Board of Directors of City Trusts in Philadelphia have maintained excellent and complete records (minutes, correspondence, legal brief and other documentation) since the founding of their agencies. These primary documents present a contrasting view of the early successes and difficulties of both trusts and augment the evidence in the official court records and formally commissioned early histories. From these records it could be determined that artisans did seek, borrow and repay the loans according to Franklin's plan. From 1790 until 1830 in Boston and Philadelphia Franklin's private capital became a publicly managed revolving fund which empowered young men. The records proved that these artisans earned their way to self sufficiency, establishing independent small businesses and becoming a fresh reservoir of useful citizens as Franklin intended.

Public and private charities have served as a principal conduit for the redistribution of power in cultures which allow capital accumulation by individuals and corporations (acting as individuals). Financial assistance provided to the accidentally poor (ignorant, ill, disabled and elderly) and compensated work for the unemployed have been the centrepieces of charity whether administered by the church or other instruments of public will. Franklin was foremost in insisting that charitable aid be of an empowering nature.

Fresh from close readings of Enlightenment ideologues, America's Founding Fathers were keenly aware of the theory of natural rights for all of humanity. The familiar distillation of these natural and inalienable rights as framed by Jefferson ... Life, Liberty and the Pursuit of Happiness ... was a convenient reinterpretation of the more common litany ... Life, Liberty and Property. With the issue of American chattel slavery confusing the concepts of universal individual liberty and the definition of private property, Jefferson adroitly avoided this irresolvable conflict. Benjamin Franklin not only forthrightly opposed the institution of slavery while advocating universal manhood suffrage but he also demonstrated, by personal example as well as articulated philosophy, how a new nation could accumulate and redistribute capital providing equal opportunity for the industrious and the able and an adequate living for all citizens. In his words ... 'A rising tide lifts all boats'.

Franklin advocated the application of surplus personal wealth toward good works, i.e. philanthropic projects that would make life more convenient and fulfilling for all. He also believed that prosperous citizens had a duty to serve in government, to nourish the 'rising Generation' and to assist the disfranchised and disadvantaged. This calling of stewardship persists in the last of the twentieth century, not so much from elective political office-holders but through the instrumentality of trusteeship of non-profit organizations, deliverers of human service called charity in Franklin's day. The hospitals, churches, social service agencies, schools, museums, fraternal organizations, etc. represent a modern embodiment of Franklin's notion of capital redistribution by personal financial contribution, careful management of government grants and private gifts, and social, economic and political influence trading. The vast non-profit sector in cities like Boston and Philadelphia, just outside the orb of local government, constitute the modern manifestation of Franklin's theory of mutual assistance first articulated in the 1727 organization of the Junta in Philadelphia and based on Franklin's readings of Cotton Mather's *Essays to Do Good* and Daniel Defoe's *Essay on Projects*. Franklin can justifiably be honoured as the Father of American voluntarism.

Virtually all of the applicants for Franklin's bequest, both the centennial and the bicentennial portions, were charities and non-profit organizations seeking the funds on behalf of sectors of the population that were in need. Even the Roxbury park proposal in Boston in 1890s and the Fairmont Park and City Parks initiatives in Philadelphia in the 1890s and in the 1990s, respectively, were the type of public improvement that were intended to uplift all of the citizens. At the heart of the charitable or public service cause, in 1700s and 1800s, or in modern times, is compassion, mutuality and the belief that the environment and the standard of living can be improved by hard work and proper marshalling of natural and human resources.

Beyond Franklin's contribution to the theoretical evolution of American citizenship and trusteeship, in 1789, Franklin devised his ingenious plan for the establishment of the two Franklin Funds. While the values of patience and steadfast frugality were being taught by the compounding of principal with interest, Franklin wanted the trust funds invested continually as a low interest revolving loan fund with conditions that attempted to underscore the value of family, education, industriousness, steadfastness and growth. The force of the Franklin Fund would have been exponentially magnified not only by the increasing amount of money available to loan but by the effect of the rising and expanding generation's contribution as a class of enlightened citizens. The Franklin Funds could have contributed greatly to the building of 'strong democracy'. While his wee-conceived plan was defeated in this regard, the legacy of care lives on in the proliferation of non-profit organizations and the expanding number of citizens that provide leadership and share their resources.

Despite the long history of the troubled Franklin Funds which speaks volumes about America since 1790, Benjamin Franklin, the philanthropist, deserves to be heard again:

> ... I have, perhaps, too much flattered myself with a vain Fancy, that these Dispositions, if carried into execution, will be continued without interruption and have the Effects proposed. I hope however that if the Inhabitants of the two Cities should not think fit to undertake the execution, they will at least accept the offer of these Donations as a Mark of my good Will, a token of my gratitude, and a Testimony of my earnest desire to be useful to them even after my departure. I wish indeed that they may both undertake to endeavor the Execution of the Project because I think that unforeseen Difficulties may arise, expedients will be found to remove them, and the Scheme to be found practicable.[6]

Even the eminent Dr Franklin did not envision the full scope of social, political and economic upheaval that resulted from industrialization. He could not know how labour would be reshaped by changes in production driven by a market economy. He seems to have been more prescient regarding the progress of state and local governments, the evolution of American politics and the gradual disestablishment of religion. While realistic about the discord of partisans and the difficulty of managing a republic, he believed that America would attract and nurture rational and enlightened leaders who would strive to improve life for all citizens. He also expected that the leaders of Boston and Philadelphia would always understand the critical relationship between the gainful employment of all citizens of the republic and the condition of liberty and independence.

The standards that he set during his lifetime and after death were too high for his successors. The placement of priority on accumulation and the virtue of frugality only amplified half of his message to posterity. The citizens of Boston, and to a lesser degree also Philadelphia, failed to understand the virtue of individual industry. But his overriding success at keeping America's eyes fixed on the future, as made manifest in the course of Franklin Funds over 200 years, is a remarkable achievement.

APPENDIX A: TRANSCRIPTION OF THE 1789 CODICIL

Benjamin Franklin, excerpted from 'My Last Will and Testament dated July 17, 1788 with a Codicil or Addition dated June 3, 1789', signed and witnessed in his own hand, p. 6 to the top half of p. 10:[1]

I, Benjamin Franklin, in the foregoing, or annexed last Will and Testament named, having further considered the same, do think proper to make and publish the following Codicil or Addition thereto.

It having long been a fixed political opinion of mine, that in a democratical State, there ought to be no Offices of Profit for the reasons I had given in an Article of my drawing in our Constitution, it was my intention when I accepted the Office of President, to devote the appointed Salary to some public Uses. Accordingly, I had already, before I made my Will in July last, given large Sums of it to Colleges, Schools, Building of Churches, &c. and in that Will I bequeathed Two thousand Pounds more to the State for the purpose of making the Schuylkill navigable. But understanding since, that such a Sum will do little toward accomplishing such a Work, and that the project is not likely to be undertaken for many Years to come; and having entertained another Idea, that I hope may be more extensively useful, I do hereby revoke and annul that Bequest, and direct that the Certificates I have for what remains due to me of that Salary be sold, towards raising the Sum of Two Thousand Pounds Sterling, to be disposed of as I am no about to order.

It has been an opinion that he who receives an Estate from his Ancestors, is under some kind of obligation to transmit the same to their Posterity: This obligation does not lie on me, who never inherited a Shilling from any Ancestor or Relation. I shall, however, if it is not diminished by some accident before my Death, leave a considerable Estate among my Decendants and Relations. The above observation is made merely as some apology to my family for making Bequests that do not appear to have any immediate relation to their advantage.

I was born in Boston, New England, and owe my first instructions in Literature to the free Grammar Schools established there. I have, therefore, already considered these Schools in my Will. But I am under obligations to the State of Massachusetts for having, unasked, appointed me formerly their Agent in England, with a handsome Salary, which continued some Years, and, altho I accidentally lost, in their service, by transmitting Governor Hutchinson's Letters, much more that the amount of what they gave me, I do not think that ought in the least to diminish my Gratitude.

I have considered that, among Artisans, good Apprentices are most likely to make good Citizens; and having myself been bred to the Manual Art, Printing, in my native Town, and afterwards assisted to set up my business in Philadelphia by kind Loan of Money from two Friends there, which was the foundation of my Fortune, and of all the utility in life that may be ascribed to me, I wish to be useful even after my Death, if possible, in forming and advancing other young men that may be serviceable to their Country in both those Towns. To this End, I devote Two Thousand Pounds Sterling, of which I give one thousand thereof to the Inhabitants of Boston, in Massachusetts, and the other thousand to the Inhabitants of Philadelphia, in Trust, to and for the Uses, Intents, and Purposes hereinafter mentioned and declared.

The said Sum of One thousand Pounds Sterling, if accepted by the Inhabitants of the Town of Boston, shall be managed under the direction of Select Men, united with the Ministers of the oldest episcopalian, Congregational, and Presbyterian Churches in that Town, who are to let out the same upon Interest at five per Cent per Annum to such young married Artificers, under the Age of twenty-five Years, as have served an Apprenticeship in the said Town; and faithfully fulfilled the Duties of their Indentures, so as to obtain a good moral Character from at least two respectable Citizens, who are willing to become their Sureties, in a Bond with the Applicants, for the Repayment of moneys so lent, with Interest, according to the Terms herein after prescribed; all which Bonds are to be taken for Spanish milled Dollars, or the value thereof in current Gold Coin; and the Managers shall keep a bound Book or Books wherein shall be entered the Names of those who shall apply for and receive the benefit of this Institution and of their sureties together with the Sums lent, the Dates, and other necessary and proper Records respecting the Business and Concerns of this Institution. And as these Loans are intended to assist young married Artificers in setting up their Business, they are to be proportioned by the discretion of the Managers, so as not to exceed Sixty Pounds Sterling to one Person, nor to be less than fifteen Pounds. And if the number of Appliers so entitled should be so large as that the Sum will not suffice to afford to each as much as might be otherwise not be improper, the proportion to each shall be diminished so as to afford every one some Assistance. These aids may, therefore, be small at first, but as the capital increases by the accumulated Interest, they will be more ample. And, in order to serve as many as possible in turn, as well as make the Repayment of the principal borrowed more easy, each Borrower shall be obligated to pay, with yearly Interest, one-tenth part of the principal, which Sums of Principal and Interest, so paid in, shall be again let out to fresh Borrowers. And as it is presumed that there will always be found in Boston virtuous and benevolent Citizens, willing to bestow a part of their Time in doing good to the rising Generation by Superintending and managing this Institution gratis, it is hoped that no part of the Money will at any time lie dead or be diverted to other purposes, but be continually augmenting by the Interest, in which case there may in time be more than the occasions in Boston shall require, and then some may be spared to the Neighboring or other Towns in the said State of Massachusetts, who may desire to have it; such Towns engaging to pay punctually the Interest and the Portions of the principal, annually, to the Inhabitants of the Town of Boston.

If this plan is executed, and succeeds as projected without interruption for one hundred years the Sum will then be one hundred and thirty-one thousand Pounds; of which I would have the Managers of the Donation to the Town of Boston, then lay out at their discretion one hundred thousand Pounds in Public Works which may be judged of most general utility to the Inhabitants, such as Fortifications, Bridges, Aqueducts, Public Buildings, Baths, Pavements or whatever may make living in the Town more convenient to its People and render it more agreeable to Strangers, resorting thither for Health or a temporary residence. The remaining thirty-one thousand Pounds, I would have continued to be let out on Interest in the manner above directed for another hundred Years, as I hope it will have been found that the Institution has had a good effect on the conduct of Youth, and been of Service to many worthy Characters and useful Citizens. At the end of this second Term, if no unfortunate accident has prevented the operation the Sum will be Four Millions and Sixty one Thousand Pounds Sterling; of which I leave one Million sixty one Thousand Pounds to the Disposition of the Inhabitants of the Town of Boston and Three Millions to the Disposition of the Government of the State, not presuming to carry my Views farther.

All the directions herein given respecting the Disposition and Management of the Donation to the Inhabitants of Boston, I would have observed respecting that to the Inhabitants of Philadelphia: only as Philadelphia is incorporated, I request the Corporation of that City to undertake the Management agreeable to the said Directors, and I do hereby vest them with full and ample Powers for the purpose. And, having considered that the covering its Ground Plot with Buildings and Pavements, which carry off most of the Rain and prevent soaking into the Earth and renewing and purifying the Springs, whence the Water of the Wells must gradually grow worse, and in time be unfit for use, as I find has happened in all old Cities, I recommend that at the end of the first hundred Years, of not done before, the Corporation of the City employ a part of the Hundred Thousand Pounds in bringing by Pipes the Water of Wissahickon Creek into the

Town, so as to supply the Inhabitants, which I apprehend may be done without great difficulty, the level of the Creek being much above that of the City, and may be made higher by a Dam. I also recommend making the Schuylkill compleatly navigable. At the end of the second Hundred Years, I would have the disposition of the Four and Sixty one thousand Pounds divided between the Inhabitants of the City of Philadelphia and the Government of Pennsylvania, in the same manner as herein directed to that of the Inhabitants of Boston and the Government of Massachusetts.

It is my desire that this Institution should take place and begin to operate within one year of my decease, for which purpose due notice should be publickly given previous to the expiration of that Year, that those for whose benefit this establishment is intended may make their respective applications; And I hereby direct my Executors, the survivors, or survivor of them, within six Months after my decease, to pay over the said Sum of Two thousand Pounds Sterling, to such Persons as shall be duly appointed by the Select Men of Boston, and the Corporation of Philadelphia, to receive and take charge of their respective Sums, of One Thousand Pounds each, for the Purposes aforesaid.

Considering the accidents to which all human Affairs and Projects are subject in such a length of Time, I have, perhaps, too much flattered myself with a vain Fancy, that these Dispositions, if carried into execution, will be continued without interruption and have the Effects proposed. I hope however that if the Inhabitants of the two Cities should not think fit to undertake the execution, they will at least accept the offer of these Donations, as a Mark of my good-Will, a token of my Gratitude,and a Testimony of my earnest desire to be useful to them even after my departure. I wish indeed that they both undertake to endeavour the Execution of the Project: because I think that tho' unforeseen Difficulties may arise, expedients will be found to remove them, and the Scheme be found practicable. If one of them accepts the Money with the Conditions, and the other refuses; my Will then is that both Sums be given to the Inhabitants of the City accepting the Whole, to be applied to the same purposes and under the same Regulations directed for the separate Parts; and, if both refuse, the Money of course, remains in the Mass of my Estate, and is to be disposed of therewith according to my Will made the seventeenth day of July, 1788.

APPENDIX B: BOSTON ARTISAN LIST

Adams, Abraham Jr	3 May 1799
Adams, Benj. F.	12 February 1806
Adams, Daniel	28 August 1806
Adams, John I.	12 September 1826
Adams, Samuel Jr	7 March 1816
Adams, Samuel	18 January 1810
Allen, Joseph	21 November 1799
Allen, Josiah Jr	10 May 1791
Bacon, Nathan	18 June 1798
Bacon, Robert	19 August 1802
Bacon, William	7 August 1807
Badger, Daniel	25 June 1799
Badger, Daniel	30 January 1812
Badger, James	16 April 1814
Badger, William	5 May 1791
Baker, William	10 March 1815
Baker, William	2 January 1824
Bangs, James C. R.	10 October 1815
Bangs, Thomas G.	25 June 1812
Barrington, Edward	18 March 1813
Barry, James	4 May 1791
Barry, Thomas	28 November 1808
Baxter, Rufus	1 January 1791
Bell, Samuel	10 February 1798
Bell, Samuel	24 March 1815
Bell, Shubael	5 May 1791
Bently, Wm	27 May 1798
Bird, James	13 February 1798
Bird, Michael	5 May 1791
Blake, James Jr	17 August 1795
Bound, Ephraim	1 June 1792
Bradford, Charles T.	29 July 1853
Bradford, Thomas	4 April 1838
Bradley, Nathaniel, Jr	17 August 1795
Brazer, William	30 December 1796
Breed, Aaron Jr	30 March 1812
Brewer, Natha.	5 June 1794
Brigham, Jabez	7 December 1804
Burbeck, Thomas	1 January 1823
Cade, Peter	19 August 1793
Campbell, Charles H.	1 August 1878
Carroll, Thomas	18 March 1851
Chase, Stephen	28 May 1833
Clark, James Jr.	4 March 1835
Clement, Charles	23 May 1792
Cobb, Cyrus W.	24 April 1850
Codman, Thomas	16 September 1828
Coolidge, Charles	14 July 1815
Copeland, John	19 March 1812
Copeland, Nathaniel	30 May 1791
Copeland, Robert M.	7 May 1825
Copeland, William H.	16 December 1820
Corbett, David	23 October 1795
Cox, Thomas	20 January 1815
Crain, George W. (Cr)	14 May 1828
Creech, Samuel W.	2 April 1836
Crocker, Robert	6 May 1791
Crooker, Abel	26 April 1802
Crosby, William	23 May 1792
Cummings, William	7 May 1795
Cunningham, William	22 November 1855
Cushing, Joel	6 August 1800
Cushing, John	2 July 1818
Cushing, Samuel N.	28 February 1798
Cushman, Elkanah	6 May 1791
Cutler, Daniel	26 November 1820
Cutler, Nathan	7 October 1801
Dana, John	26 February 1807
Darling, Samuel Jr	30 November 1839
Davis, Samuel	16 February 1815

Dean, Faxson	9 January 1814	Goff, Stephen	20 May 1793
Dean, Thomas	1 May 1803	Goss, Sylvester T.	20 October 1820
Derby, John	18 April 1805	Gould, Joseph	29 August 1849
Dickman, Joseph	2 June 1791	Gould, Thomas	4 December 1807
Divine, Michael	1 May 1850	Gustine, Joel	2 October 1801
Dodge, William S.	9 September 1858	Hale, John B.	8 August 1833
Doggett, Noah Jr	10 June 1793	Hall, Edward	19 November 1796
Dorr, Joseph	1 May 1803	Hall, Milton	18 April 1805
Dow, Simeon Jr	15 March 1825	Hall, Samuel	26 October 1809
Dow, William A.	24 April 1827	Hammond, Joseph L.	3 Sept 1825
Drayton, John	14 February 1804	Hansell, Robert	8 November 1816
Drummond, James F.	29 August 1849	Harlow, —	1 October 1801
Dwelle, Elisha	13 March 1822	Harlow, Asaph	6 January 1801
Dyer, Eben.	2 December 1823	Hartshorne, Caleb	1 October 1810
Dyer, George Henry	30 April 1877	Hartshorne, Joseph	4 August 1808
Dyers, James	25 November 1819	Hartshorne, Rolun	27 August 1805
Eaton, Benjamin	3 May 1799	Hatch, Joseph	27 February 1818
Eaton, Benjamin	8 September 1800	Hawkes, Joseph	15 May 1805
Eayres, Moses, Jr	17 August 1795	Hay, William	25 June 1799
Eayres, Thomas S.	18 May 1791	Hayden, Robert	16 February 1812
Edwards, George W.	3 February 1824	Hayward, John	1 January 1791
Elder, Robert A.	4 September 1876	Healy, William P.	17 August 1839
Elder, Samuel	15 July 1879	Heard, Robert	24 December 1808
Ellison, William	17 August 1795	Hearsey, Ebed	4 April 1811
Emmes, Nathaniel Jr	18 January 1811	Hearsey, Thomas	1 January 1791
Emmons, Joshua Jr	1 January 1821	Hearsey, William G.	5 January 1838
Emmons, William H.	24 June 1835	Hearsy, Naaman	10 June 1814
Etheridge, Samuel	16 May 1793	Hinds, Frederic	10 August 1859
Evans, William	27 April 1870	Holmes, Chester D.	3 January 1855
Faxson, Nath.	20 August 1814	Hoogs, William Jr	30 July 1796
Felt, David	2 January 1816	Horn, Joshua	21 November 1799
Feritter, James	5 November 1814	Horton, Jotham	29 July 1800
Fletcher, Walter E.	15 August 1878	Howe, John	27 January 1797
Fogg, Hiram J.	17 July 1848	Howe, Joseph	1 August 1795
Foster, Nathan	15 July 1796	Hower, Thompson K.	25 October 1833
Francis, John	23 August 1796	Hubbard, William H.	12 October 1843
Francis, Joseph	13 May 1793	Hudson, Hezekiah	22 May 1792
Francis, Thomas D.	15 May 1805	Hunt, Joseph R.	14 February 1804
Fraser, Edwin L.	10 July 1876	Hunter, John P.	16 March 1816
Freeman, Francis O.	18 February 1859	Hyde, Henry	2 May 1807
French, Abijah	5 May 1791	Jenkins, Joseph	11 February 1805
Gardner, Deren	18 May 1809	Jenks, John	5 May 1791
Gardner, Jeremiah	22 August 1795	Jenks, Samuel Jr	5 May 1791
Gardner, Obadiah	10 October 1807	Jewett, Edmund M.	7 August 1807
Gilkie, Robert J.	10 March 1874	Johnson, Nathaniel	6 July 1816
Gill, Perez	16 May 1801	Jones, Nathan W.	12 July 1824
Gleason, Herbert	1 January 1853	Kendall, Thomas	27 May 1794
Glynn, John	19 October 1815	Kendall, William	19 September 1806

Kimball, John Jr	16 December 1823
King, William	16 January 1809
Kinnaird, Michael	7 August 1807
Kuhn, George	29 April 1800
Kuhn, John	16 May 1793
Lecain, Francis	13 January 1807
Leeds, Charles	27 February 1806
Lewis, Asa	17 October 1806
Lewis, David	25 July 1791
Lewis, John	14 November 1794
Lincoln, Charles	7 September 1795
Lincoln, Heman	21 October 1803
Littlefield, George E.	23 February 1886
Locke, Herbert C.	30 April 1873
Loring, Isaac	3 May 1799
Loring, William	25 June 1799
Lovell, Christian	17 May 1800
Lovell, Samuel Jr	2 May 1807
Lovering, John	14 July 1791
Mair, Thomas	26 April 1822
Martin, James P.	1 January 1813
Mayo, Joseph	5 February 1819
Mead, Demase	21 February 1807
Mellus, Joseph	3 November 1807
Michell, Thomas	4 May 1811
Miller, John Jr.	3 May 1799
Miller, Robert	14 February 1804
Moores, John R.	18 April 1811
Motley, William M.	24 March 1815
Munroe, Charles A.	10 October 1838
Munroe, Isaac	1 March 1808
Nason, Levitt	4 September 1808
Newhall, Edward	1 May 1803
Nichols, Jerome.	3 February 1814
Nichols, John	1 November 1800
Nickoles, Eleazer	21 November 1799
Norcross, Joseph	24 January 1810
Norcross, Nehemiah J.	28 May 1791
Osborne, John	29 May 1818
Osgood, James	28 March 1811
Otis, Isaac	13 November 1818
Page, Benj. Jr	3 May 1799
Page, William Wingfie-	31 May 1791
Paget, Joseph F.	6 April 1870
Park, Francis E.	26 October 1859
Patten, Nathaniel	6 September 1796
Peake, John	1 May 1803
Pelham, Thomas	4 April 1809
Pepper, Solomon	20 February 1810
Perkins, Jabez	5 May 1802
Phipps, William K.	March 1815
Pierce, James	16 September 1813
Pierce, Samuel	24 May 1792
Pike, John K.	10 August 1832
Pike, Jonathan	24 August 1792
Pook, Charles L. Jr	1 July 1827
Potter, John	3 July 1809
Pratt, John Jr	4 March 1826
Pratt, John	1 October 1801
Prowse, Daniel	8 May 1823
Quimby, Ira B.	9 May 1855
Ray, Caleb	25 May 1792
Reed, George Jr	22 May 1818
Rider, Thomas	16 February 1798
Rockwood, Albert G.	5 July 1877
Ross, Joshua	1 October 1801
Roulestone, John	16 August 1791
Roulston, Michael	25 June 1799
Salisbury, William	20 October 1820
Sanger, Zed.h	16 June 1826
Sawin, Silas W.	22 May 1823
Scott, Isaac	1 January 1812
Seward, Benjamin	16 July 1792
Sholes, John Jr	11 July 1810
Shores, James	1 June 1791
Simons, Joseph N.	7 December 1808
Smallridge, Jeremiah	13 September 1809
Smith, Jacob	26 April 1809
Smith, John	9 June 1794
Smith, Robert	22 November 1803
Smith, Stephen	25 June 1799
Snow, Prince	7 September 1795
Spear, John	22 May 1800
Spear, Nathaniel	5 December 1810
Spear, William T.	5 June 1818
Speed, Robert	1 May 1817
Spence, John	18 October 1817
Stacey, M. Leland	6 July 1885
Stacey, Philemon	13 May 1819
Steven, John C.	11 March 1823
Stevens, George	11 October 1824
Stevens, Robert C.	26 December 1805
Stickney, John B.	7 December 1842
Stimpson, Charles Jr	8 June 1819
Stoddard, Samuel	29 March 1805
Stodder, Bartlet	10 July 1811

Stodder, Jonathan	4 May 1791	Vanneman, John	1 January 1813
Tate, William	1 January 1791	Vannemar, James	2 December 1823
Tead, Nathaniel	10 March 1826	Waterman, John	13 October 1804
Thayer, Zebath Jr	17 September 1818	Webber, John	25 April 1815
Thompson, William	14 February 1815	Wedger, John	7 February 1822
Thorp, Thomas	11 July 1810	Weld, Giles E.	18 May 1816
Tilden, Thomas	2 March 1798	Weld, James	28 March 1811
Tilton, William P.	26 March 1816	Welles, Henry P.	11 November 1820
Toney, Eben O.	1 January 1816	Wells, Charles A.	14 February 1808
Tower?, Elisha	4 June 1825	Whitcomb, Lot	9 September 1811
Trask, Edward	17 February 1812	Whiting, Kimbell	16 September 1809
Turner, Abel	13 December 1817	Whitney, Alfred	5 January 1838
Tuttle, Daniel	3 May 1791	Willis, H. P.	1 January 1820
Tuttle, Edward	28 December 1815	Winnek, John	31 May 1791
Vallett, Peter	29 April 1808		

APPENDIX C: PHILADELPHIA ARTISAN LIST

Abbott, Thomas B	1810
Adolph, George	1822
Albertson, Niscon	1812
Allen, Edward A	1835
Allen, Edward A.	1835
Altemus, Isaac	1812
Atkinson, Asher	1820
Bacon, Benjamin	1830
Baker, Jm. S	1828
Barker, Burton	1830
Barker, James P.	1832
Barras, John B	1822
Bartman, Jacob	1829
Bavis, Aaron	1814
Bearlit, Mathias	1791
Beck, Martin	1809
Belair, Lewis	1813
Bell, James	1834
Benninghove, Jacob	1791
Bennis, Henry	1821
Bevens, William	1811
Bickham, Joshua	1814
Bickham, Joshua	1814
Biedman, Samuel C.	1834
Birchall, Caleb H.	1798
Boddy, M.John	1814
Borton, Abraham	1809
Boyer, John	1817
Boyle, James	1822
Brooks, James	1802
Brown, Christian D	1836
Browne, Liberty	1800
Browne, William	1811
Buchanan, Alexander	1802
Buckhard, Samuel	1798
Burden, Henry R	1806
Burkhart, Adam	1817
Butler, Courtland	1842
Cain, Joseph	1815
Calvert, Thomas	1826
Davison, Arthur	1795
Deal, Christian	1811
Deal, Daniel Jr	1820
Death, John	1816
Dietz, William	1826
Divine, J. T.	1827
Donaldson, David	1831
Doogan, Thomas M.	1820
Douglass, William	1840
Drane, William	1835
Drysdale, William, Jr	1844
Dubosq, Francis P.	1833
Duffield, James	1803
Dye, William	1832
Emerick, Benjamin	1815
Emerick, Henry	1817
Emerick, William B.	1815
Emmerick, George	1791
Errickson, James S.	1841
Evans, John B.	1802
Evans, Peter H.	1817
Evans, Richard C.	1829
Fagundis, Peter	1791
Faures, Lawrence P.	1819

Feeney, Patrick	1806
Fenner, Thomas	1819
Fenner, William	1831
Finn, William P.	1835
Foering, Frederick	1800
Foote, Lewis H.	1812
Ford, Jacob H.	1793
Fox, Joseph	1800
Fox, Peter	1820
Franklin, Benjamin	1827
Fraser, John Jr	1813
Freytag, Philip Daniel	1805
Freytag, Philip Daniel	1805
Gardy, John C.	1829
Garner, Henry	1821
Garriques, William	1818
Kite, Isaac Jr	1814
Kneass, Christian	1811
Kreider, Henry	1816
Lair, Philip	1828
Lancaster, Richard	1816
Lazar, Jacob	1791
Lewis, David	1817
Linker, Henry	1817
Lowder, George	1832
Lower, George	1792
Maas, David J.	1807
Marley, Joseph D.	1819
Martin, Marmaduke	1813
Mathias, Joseph J.	1827
McCalla, John H.	1847
McCauley, John	1791
McGill, Stephen	1800
McGlathery, George	1801
McGrath, Thomas	1831
McKane, William	1816
McKeage, William	1814
McKenzie, Caleb	1804
McLaughlin, George	1824
McLaurin, George S.	1832
McMaken, Samuel	1819
Metcalf, William W.	1816
Miles, William H.	1836
Miller, George	1814
Miller, Henry	1802
Miller, Jacob	1808
Miller, Joseph A.	1832
Miller, Lewis T.	1829
Mitchell, Benjamin Jr	1805
Monroe, John	1826
Mooney, William	1831
Moore, Chas.	1801
Morris, John	1820
Morrison, Hugh	1791
Mosely, George H.	1823
Moser, George H.	1792
Shultz, John	1814
Shulze, William	1823
Shute, William	1819
Slahter, Jacob	1808
Smith, James B.	1834
Smith, John M.	1801
Smith, Joseph	1808
Smith, Ralph	1804
Smith, Ralph Jr	1808
Smith, Rowland T.	1819
Snider, John	1804
Snyder, Christian	1804
Souder, John	1791
South, William	1828
Stackhouse, Charles P.	1844
Stackhouse, Samuel	1813
Steel, Canby	1825
Stokes, William Jr	1841
Straley, Frederick	1825
Streeper, Leonard	1807
Street, Robert	1791
Strock, Joseph	1818
Sutton, Martin	1805
Syfrid, Jacob	1792
Tage, Benjamin Jr	1831
Tage, William	1826
Tatem, Samuel	1802
Tatem, Thomas J. ?	1832
Taylor, Isaac W.	1849
Taylor, Michael	1830
Taylor, Robert	1800
Taylor, Robert	1812
Test, John	1802
Thomas, David	1791
Thomas, Issachar E.	1833
Thomas, Jonathan	1810
Thomas, Lewis	1807
Tounsend, Henry H.	1792
Underwood, James	1827
Van dyke, John	1825

Campbell, James	1828
Cansler, William W.	1838
Cassaday, John	1825
Chamberlain, Lewis	1828
Chambers, Samuel	1803
Chance, Marinus	1817
Chancellor, William H.	1793
Charleton, Benjamin H	1794
Chattin, James N.	1815
Chattin, Josiah M	1829
Church, Isaac	1812
Clark, George D.	1818
Clark, Samuel	1800
Clawges, John, Jr	
Clogher, John H.	1793
Colladay, Theodore	1818
Colliday, Joseph L.	1810
Collins, Charles	1809
Conrow, William G	1828
Cook, George H.	1807
Cook, Samuel	1821
Coppuch, John	1812
Coppuck, George W.	1825
Corman, Adam Jr	1809
Costen, Ezekiel	1833
Cox, Aaron F	1831
Cox, George	1812
Cox, John	1815
Cox, John R.	1815
Cromwell, James S.	1825
Cromwell, John	1827
Cromwell, Oliver	1800
Cryder, Thomas C.	1825
Curry, James M.	1825
Curtis, John	1791
Daniel, James	1825
Daniels, Joseph	1827
Davis, Benjamin F.	1826
Davis, Evan	1810
Davis, Thomas	1791
Garrison, Henry H.	1796
Garwood, Joseph	1804
Gaw, Gilbert	1827
Gaw, Robert Jr	1825
Gillingham, Henry B.	1828
Grant, John	1791
Grieb, Henry	1835
Groves, Robert F.	1830
Hains, Adam	1791
Hains, Henry H.	1794
Halt-, Valentine Van	1801
Halzel, John G.	1793
Hamilton, George	1819
Hampton, John	1807
Harmer, Francis	1811
Harrison, Henry K.	1827
Hartley, Mark	1806
Hett, John H.	1800
Hook, William	1804
Hooton, Andrew	1809
Hopper, Levi Jr	1800
Horner, Fountain	1820
Hotz, Daniel	1802
House, William	1804
Howell, William	1841
Hufty, Joseph	1801
Hutchins, Thomas	1801
Hutchinson, Charles H.	1796
James, Israel E.	1815
Jenkins, George W.	1844
Jenkins, John	1811
Johnston, Andrew	1821
Jones, Daniel	1806
Jones, George	1809
Katz, John	1809
Kelley, David	1808
Kellum, Charles	1805
Kellum, James	1807
Kinley, Henry	1819
Kinsley, Samuel	1805
Murdock, Thomas	1811
Murfin, Jehu	1828
Mustin, Eli	1816
Myers, Warnett	1818
Myrick, Jacob H.	1792
Nushag, William	1803
Parent, Thomas	1805
Parent, Thomas	1806
Pearl, Abraham	1825
Pearson, David Jr	1824
Peck, Benjamin G.	1840
Perpignan, Stephen	1835
Philips, Thomas D.	1821
Phillips, John	1792
Pidgeon, Christopher	1792
Poineer, William H.	1845

Point, Charles Jr	1830
Porter, Samuel	1808
Poulson, John	1809
Prettyman, William K.	1835
Price, Joseph	1791
Probasco, Peter	1823
Ralston, Isaac	1800
Read, Benjamin Frankl	1846
Reap, Philip	1809
Reese, Samuel	1813
Regnault, James	1819
Richards, George	1827
Rink, John	1808
Robbins, Enoch	1820
Roberts, Thomas	1822
Rose, Benjamin	1807
Ruse, John	1810
Rutherford, Thomas M.	1829
Sailor, George M.	1836
Schell, Henry Jr	1823
Schooley, Joseph K.	1827
Schreimer, Charles W.	1811
Shaw, James M.	1810
Shugart, Simon J.	1821
Van Holt, Valentine	1801
Vanderslice, George Jr	1818
Vantine, Joseph	1816
Wallace, John	1804
Walton, Frances C. N.	1828
Ward, Isaac	1811
Warner, Philip	1825
Warner, William Jr	1800
Watson, John M.	1832
Weldon, James D.	1846
Welsh, William M.	1843
West, Job	1803
Weyant, Peter	1813
Whartenby, Thomas	1810
Wheeler, Henry	1812
Wiell, John	1818
Wien, John Jr	1808
Wile, John	1813
Wile, William	1815
Willits, William R.	1831
Wintzell, George	1833
Wisdom, Samuel M.	1822
Wood, George	1828
Work, Frazier	1817
Yeager, Michael	1801
Yerger, George	1806
Young, Isaac	1827
Young, Philip	1826
Young, William	1828

APPENDIX D: SUMMARY OF LITIGATION AND STATE LAWS

Litigation in Massachusetts Courts:

Henry L. Higginson v. *Alfred T. Turner*, 171 Mass. 586 (1898).
Daniel A. Madden v. *City of Boston*, 177 Mass. 350 (1901).
City of Boston v. *James H. Doyle & others*, 184 Mass. 373 (1903).
City of Boston & another v. *James M. Curley & others.*, 276 Mass. 549 (1931).
The Franklin Foundation v. *City of Boston & others*, 336 Mass. 39 (1957).
The Franklin Foundation v. *Attorney General & others*, 340 Mass. 197 (1960).
Franklin Foundation v. *McCormack*, Suffolk No. 6198, eq. (1962).
The Franklin Foundation v. *Collector-Treasurer of Boston & others.*, 344 Mass. 573 (1962).
Massachusetts Supreme Judicial Court, 374 Mass. 843 (1978).
The Franklin Foundation v. *Attorney General*, 416 Mass. 483 (1993).

Acts of the Massachusetts Legislature:

Chapter 569 and 276, Acts of the Massachusetts General Assembly of 1908.
Chapter 212, Acts of the Massachusetts General Assembly of 1941.
Chapter 596, Acts of the Massachusetts General Assembly of 1958
Report of the Special Commission Established to Investigate and Study Certain Matters Relating to the Franklin Technical Institute, Chapter 111, Resolve of The Commonwealth of Massachusetts, 1957.
House Bill No 5503 of Massachusetts General Assembly of 1977
'An Act to Authorize Transfer to Trustees of Boston University by the Franklin Foundation and the City of Boston of the ownership and control of Franklin Institute of Boston and exercise by the city of the city's power to dispose of its share of the accumulating bequest of Benjamin Franklin, and to exercise in favor of the Trustees of Boston University of the Commonwealth's power to dispose of its share of said bequest'.

Supplemental Appropriations Bill of Massachusetts General Assembly of 1994, 'outside section - #127'.

Litigation in Pennsylvania Courts:

Board of Directors of City Trusts Petition before the Court of Common Pleas, 7 November 1874.
Franklin's Administratrix, Elizabeth Duane Gillespie et al. v. *City of Philadelphia*, 214 PA CC 484, (1890).
Franklin's Administratrix v. *City of Philadelphia*, 9 Pa. Court of Common Pleas 484, (1891).
Franklin's Administratrix v. *City of Philadelphia*, 150 Pa. Supreme Court 437 (1892).
Franklin's Administratrix v. *City of Philadelphia*, 13 Pa. Court of Common Pleas 241 (1893).
Board of Directors of City Trusts Petition before the Court of Common Pleas, No. 685, decree dated 11 June 1917.
Board of Directors of City Trusts Petition before the Court of Common Pleas, decree dated 17 August 1939.
Board of Directors of City Trusts Petition before the Court of Common Pleas, decree dated 20 May 1949.
Board of Directors of City Trusts Petition before the Court of Common Pleas, decree dated 16 April 1963.
Board of Directors of City Trusts Petition before the Court of Common Pleas, decreed dated 18 October 1966.
Board of Directors of City Trusts Petition before the Court of Common Pleas, decree dated 17 December 1970.
Board of Directors of City Trusts Petition before the Court of Common Pleas, decree dated 3 April 1979.
Report of the Master, Court of Common Pleas, 24 December 1992.

APPENDIX E: CHRONOLOGY

1788 Benjamin Franklin drafts *Last Will and Testament*
1789 Franklin drafts codicil to the Will
1790 Franklin dies 17 April 1790
1811 William Minot appointed Treasurer of Franklin Fund-Boston (FF-B)
1813 Liberty Browne, Franklin Fund- Philadelphia (FF-P) borrower, elected Pres. of Select Council of Philadelphia
1822 Boston becomes City, Selectman replaced by Alderman
1827 First FF-B investment in Mass. Hospital Life Insurance Co.
1829 Real estate first required of sureties in FF-P
1829 John Scott Legacy established in Philadelphia
1831 FF-B loan recipient Chas. Wells, first elected mayor of Boston
1831 Stephen Girard dies, leaving $7 million to Philadelphia for Girard College
1834 Pennsylvania creates statewide system of public education
1837 Philadelphia Committee on Legacies and Trusts takes stock ofFF-P failure
1841 First investment in gas works stock in FF-P
1847 A Presbyterian church is established in Boston, minister joins Board of Managers
1854 Consolidation of Philadelphia city and county government
1855 Boston Bd of Alderman expand, nine to twelve members, increasing Bd. of Managers – FF-B
1861 End of applicants for loans in FF-P until 1874
1866 Minot Resigns as Treasurer FF-B
1869 Board of Directors of City Trusts Philadelphia created
1870 FF-P invested in municipal bonds at 6 per cent
1874 First *cy pres* adjustment granted to FF-P by Ct of Common Pleas-age to thirty-five years
1874/6 Eighteen loans in FF-P
1882 FF-B to use money to pay off Roxbury Park debt, renames Franklin Park

1882	Fifty-five loans outstanding in FF-P
1883/5	FF-P makes nine loans and two loans completely paid off
1885	Bullitt Bill- reorganization of Philadelphia city government
1885–1917	No applicants FF-P
1891/3	(Philadelphia & Boston) Gillespie/Bache litigation for Franklin Trusts
1892	Only $209 in loans outstand in FF-P
1893	Hearings on what to do with centenary division – FF-B
1893	Initial decision of FF-B to create a trade school
1894	Franklin Fund(Boston)= $329,300; Franklin Fund(Philadelphia) = $90,000
1894	Boston Aldermen tour six cities to observe trade schools
1894	Centenary division-Boston turned over to Treasurer Turner
1895	BODCT Philadelphia decides to spend centenary division on art museum
1896	Boston Probate Court commutes Mayor and Alderman as Trustees
1898	MA Sup. Jud. Ct reinstates twelve Aldermen, Mayor and three ministers as managers
1902	FF-B managers approve plan for technical school
1903/4	Boston Mayor Collins sues managers. Pritchett, et al. become new Managers
1904	Andrew Carnegie's gift to Boston to build Franklin Union
1906	BODCT Philadelphia decides to contribute to construction of Franklin Institute
1908	Franklin Foundation created by MA Sup. Jud. Ct. to manage Institute & FF-B(II)
1908	Franklin Union in Boston founded
1917	Army and Navy take over Franklin Union for military training
1917–1939	BODCT Philadelphia makes no loans from FF-P
1917	FF-P *cy pres*,- $300–500, 4 per cent drop apprentice, mortgage instead of sureties
1930	BODCT Philadelphia turns over custody account to Franklin Institute
1934	Franklin Institute is completed
1939	FF-P *cy pres*, $500–$3,000
1941	Franklin Union becomes Franklin Institute
1940s	BODCT Philadelphia fifteen loans from FF-P
1942	Army, Navy and Coast Guard run programs out of the Franklin Institute
1949	FF-P *cy-pres,* $3,000-$6,000, 4 per cent, fifteen years

1957	Girard College focus of desegregation protests
1958	Boston Commission Rept, Legislation for Franklin Institute to take endowment
1958	MA Supreme Judicial Court blocks premature dissolution of Franklin Fund
1960	Court allows Boston managers to use funds for loans to needy medical students
1962	FF-B sold Ma. General Hospital Life Insurance stock
1962	FF-P *cy pres*, $6,000-$10,000, 66 per cent of value of real estate
1966	FF-P *cy pres,* 5-6 per cent, age from thirty-five to thirty-nine
1970	FF-P *cy pres*, thirty years, up to 80 per cent, max. interest less ½ per cent or lower
1975/6	Boston plans to merge with Boston University Program in Artisanry
1977	BU attempt to merge with Franklin Institute and capture FF-B
1979	Boston sells last of Mass. Hospital Life Insurance Co. stock
1979	FF-P *cy pres*, from $10,000–$20,000
1987	33,500 Philadelphians have had home mortgages from FF-P
1990	Franklin Fund-Phila.=$2 million and Franklin Fund-Boston=$4.5 million
1990	Gov. Dukakis appoints Advisory Commis, re. '91 disposition -FF-B
1991	Phila. Mayor Goode's proposal to spend money on festival and concert
1991	Phila. Mayor Good appoints Advisory Commission
1992	Boston litigation, Franklin Fund vs. MA and City of Boston
1993	Ct. of Com. Pleas approves FF-P plan, Fran. Institute, Phil. Found. get Frank. Fund
1993	MA Supreme Judicial Court decree denying validity of 1958 law
1994	Senate Supplemental Appropriation Bill, FF-B to Frank. Institute Boston

APPENDIX F: FRANKLIN'S CALCULATION AND ACTUAL VALUE

Year	B. Franklin's Calculation in £'s	B. Franklin's Calculation in $'s	Actual value: Boston	Actual Value: Philadelphia
1791	£1,000	$4,444	$4,444	$4,444
1792	£1,050	$4,667	$4,544	
1793	£1,103	$4,900		
1794	£1,158	$5,145		
1795	£1,216	$5,402		
1796	£1,276	$5,672		
1797	£1,340	$5,956		
1798	£1,407	$6,254		
1799	£1,477	$6,566		
1800	£1,551	$6,895		
1801	£1,629	$7,240		
1802	£1,710	$7,602		
1803	£1,796	$7,982		
1804	£1,886	$8,381		
1805	£1,980	$8,800		
1806	£2,079	$9,240		
1807	£2,183	$9,702		
1808	£2,292	$10,187		
1809	£2,407	$10,696		
1810	£2,527	$11,231		
1811	£2,653	$11,792		
1812	£2,786	$12,382	$9,000	
1813	£2,925	$13,001		
1814	£3,072	$13,651		
1815	£3,225	$14,334		
1816	£3,386	$15,050		
1817	£3,556	$15,803		
1818	£3,733	$16,593		
1819	£3,920	$17,423		
1820	£4,116	$18,294	$11,251	
1821	£4,322	$19,209	$11,767	

Year	B. Franklin's Calculation in £'s	B. Franklin's Calculation in $'s	Actual value: Boston	Actual Value: Philadelphia
1822	£4,538	$20,169	$12,356	
1823	£4,765	$21,177		
1824	£5,003	$22,236	$13,222	$23,059
1825	£5,253	$23,348	$13,783	
1826	£5,516	$24,516	$14,452	
1827	£5,792	$25,741	$15,102	
1828	£6,081	$27,028	$15,782	
1829	£6,385	$28,380	$16,492	
1830	£6,705	$29,799	$17,234	
1831	£7,040	$31,289	$18,010	
1832	£7,392	$32,853		
1833	£7,762	$34,496		
1834	£8,150	$36,221	$19,667	
1835	£8,557	$38,032	$20,552	
1836	£8,985	$39,933	$21,477	
1837	£9,434	$41,930	$22,443	
1838	£9,906	$44,026	$23,453	$16,192
1839	£10,401	$46,228	$27,006	
1840	£10,921	$48,539	$28,442	
1841	£11,467	$50,966	$28,442	
1842	£12,041	$53,514	$29,788	
1843	£12,643	$56,190	$31,338	
1844	£13,275	$59,000	$33,058	
1845	£13,939	$61,950	$34,879	
1846	£14,636	$65,047	$36,730	
1847	£15,367	$68,300	$38,536	
1848	£16,136	$71,715	$40,465	
1849	£16,943	$75,300	$42,494	
1850	£17,790	$79,065	$44,530	
1851	£18,679	$83,019	$46,389	
1852	£19,613	$87,169	$48,788	
1853	£20,594	$91,528	$51,469	
1854	£21,623	$96,104	$54,281	
1855	£22,705	$100,910	$57,286	$20,600
1856	£23,840	$105,955	$60,364	
1857	£25,032	$111,253	$63,645	
1858	£26,283	$116,815	$67,115	
1859	£27,598	$122,656	$70,764	
1860	£28,978	$128,789	$74,616	
1861	£30,426	$135,228	$78,679	
1862	£31,948	$141,990	$82,932	
1863	£33,545	$149,089	$87,497	
1864	£35,222	$156,544	$91,823	
1865	£36,984	$164,371	$96,824	

Year	B. Franklin's Calculation in £'s	B. Franklin's Calculation in $'s	Actual value: Boston	Actual Value: Philadelphia
1866	£38,833	$172,590	$102,159	
1867	£40,774	$181,219	$110,167	
1868	£42,813	$190,280	$117,692	
1869	£44,954	$199,794	$125,366	
1870	£47,201	$209,784	$133,493	
1871	£49,561	$220,273	$142,069	$38,900
1872	£52,040	$231,286	$151,193	$40,018
1873	£54,641	$242,851	$160,911	$53,150
1874	£57,374	$254,993	$171,316	
1875	£60,242	$267,743	$182,279	$48,305
1876	£63,254	$281,130	$193,985	$51,880
1877	£66,417	$295,187	$206,501	$49,420
1878	£69,738	$309,946	$218,800	$55,400
1879	£73,225	$325,443	$229,726	$58,992
1880	£76,886	$341,715	$234,489	$68,169
1881	£80,730	$358,801	$249,095	$68,874
1882	£84,767	$376,741	$259,069	$67,712
1883	£89,005	$395,578	$269,431	$70,657
1884	£93,455	$415,357	$280,225	$69,481
1885	£98,128	$436,125	$291,439	$71,443
1886	£103,035	$457,931	$303,096	$75,768
1887	£108,186	$480,828		$81,802
1888	£113,596	$504,869		$80,638
1889	£119,276	$530,113		$88,998
1890	£125,239	$556,619		$94,821
1891	£131,501	$584,449		$89,884
Centenary	**£100,000**	**$446,145**	**$402,718**	**$94,400**

Division – Part II

Year	B. Franklin's Calculation in £'s	B. Franklin's Calculation in $'s	Actual value: Boston	Actual Value: Philadelphia
Initial Balance	**£ 31,000**	**$138,305**	**$124,843**	**$22,339**
1892	£32,550	$145,220		
1893	£34,178	$152,481		
1894	£35,886	$160,105		$24,000
1895	£37,681	$168,110	$102,245	
1896	£39,565	$176,516		
1897	£41,543	$185,342		
1898	£43,620	$194,609		
1899	£45,801	$204,339		
1900	£48,091	$214,556		
1901	£50,496	$225,284		$136,600
1902	£53,021	$236,548		
1903	£55,672	$248,376		
1904	£58,455	$260,794		
1905	£61,378	$273,834	$151,636	
1906	£64,447	$287,526		$159,000
1907	£67,669	$301,902	$163,971	
1908	£71,053	$316,997	$177,523	$40,481
1909	£74,605	$332,847		$41,254
1910	£78,335	$349,489	$185,065	
1911	£82,252	$366,964	$192,689	
1912	£86,365	$385,312	$200,629	
1913	£90,683	$404,578	$208,898	
1914	£95,217	$424,807	$217,511	
1915	£99,978	$446,047	$226,751	
1916	£104,977	$468,349	$236,260	
1917	£110,226	$491,767	$246,424	$58,453
1918	£115,737	$516,355	$256,892	
1919	£121,524	$542,173	$267,805	
1920	£127,600	$569,281	$279,851	
1921	£133,980	$597,746	$292,439	$80,403
1922	£140,679	$627,633	$306,329	
1923	£147,713	$659,014	$321,646	
1924	£155,099	$691,965	$337,728	
1925	£162,854	$726,563		
1926	£170,996	$762,892	$373,232	
1927	£179,546	$801,036		
1928	£188,524	$841,088	$411,488	
1929	£197,950	$883,142	$432,063	
1930	£207,847	$927,299	$453,666	
1931	£218,240	$973,664		

Year	B. Franklin's Calculation in £'s	B. Franklin's Calculation in $'s	Actual value: Boston	Actual Value: Philadelphia
1932	£229,152	$1,022,348	$498,976	
1933	£240,609	$1,073,465	$533,318	
1934	£252,640	$1,127,138	$559,731	
1935	£265,272	$1,183,495	$583,126	
1936	£278,535	$1,242,670	$598,799	
1937	£292,462	$1,304,803	$628,281	
1938	£307,085	$1,370,044	$649,060	
1939	£322,439	$1,438,546	$678,933	
1940	£338,561	$1,510,473	$703,291	$144,000
1941	£355,489	$1,585,997	$729,611	
1942	£373,264	$1,665,297	$760,272	
1943	£391,927	$1,748,561	$777,700	
1944	£411,523	$1,835,990	$799,922	
1945	£432,100	$1,927,789	$841,320	
1946	£453,705	$2,024,178	$866,222	
1947	£476,390	$2,125,387	$875,193	
1948	£500,209	$2,231,657	$935,034	
1949	£525,220	$2,343,240	$964,449	
1950	£551,481	$2,460,402	$1,027,036	$204,599
1951	£579,055	$2,583,422		
1952	£608,008	$2,712,593	$1,043,981	
1953	£638,408	$2,848,222	$1,077,185	
1954	£670,328	$2,990,634	$1,116,185	
1955	£703,845	$3,140,165	$1,174,317	
1956	£739,037	$3,297,173	$1,314,090	
1957	£775,989	$3,462,032	$1,391,445	
1958	£814,788	$3,635,134	$1,343,306	
1959	£855,528	$3,816,890	$1,403,252	
1960	£898,304	$4,007,735	$1,559,200	
1961	£943,219	$4,208,122	$1,468,236	
1962	£990,380	$4,418,528	$1,545,734	
1963	£1,039,899	$4,639,454	$1,617,889	$314,835
1964	£1,091,894	$4,871,427	$1,683,537	
1965	£1,146,489	$5,114,998	$1,763,511	
1966	£1,203,813	$5,370,748	$1,837,769	
1967	£1,264,004	$5,639,285	$1,997,823	
1968	£1,327,204	$5,921,250	$2,095,117	
1969	£1,393,564	$6,217,312	$2,210,222	
1970	£1,463,243	$6,528,178	$2,326,716	
1971	£1,536,405	$6,854,587	$2,307,964	
1972	£1,613,225	$7,197,316	$2,534,956	
1973	£1,693,886	$7,557,182	$2,695,122	
1974	£1,778,580	$7,935,041	$2,809,305	
1975	£1,867,509	$8,331,793	$2,688,986	

Year	B. Franklin's Calculation in £'s	B. Franklin's Calculation in $'s	Actual value: Boston	Actual Value: Philadelphia
1976	£1,960,885	$8,748,383	$2,825,473	
1977	£2,058,929	$9,185,802	$2,969,225	
1978	£2,161,876	$9,645,092	$3,055,724	
1979	£2,269,969	$10,127,347	$3,134,405	
1980	£2,383,468	$10,663,714	$3,274,283	
1981	£2,502,641	$11,165,400	$3,458,797	
1982	£2,627,773	$11,723,670	$3,578,069	
1983	£2,759,162	$12,309,853	$3,672,144	
1984	£2,897,120	$12,925,346	$3,812,183	
1985	£3,041,976	$13,571,613	$3,893,251	
1986	£3,194,075	$14,250,194	$3,974,688	
1987	£3,353,779	$14,962,703	$4,060,009	
1988	£3,521,468	$15,710,838	$4,190,720	
1989	£3,697,541	$16,496,380	$4,286,642	
1990	£3,882,418	$17,321,199	$4,400,159	
1991	**£4,076,539**	**$18,187,259**	**$4,500,000**	**$2,000,000**

Franklin's calculation, unaided by computer calculation, was £4,061,000.

NOTES

Introduction

1. R. Ketcham, *Presidents Above Parties: The First American Presidency, 1789–1829* (Chapel Hill, NC: The University of North Carolina Press, 1984), pp. 178–9.
2. The term 'artificers' described a type of occupational group and also referred to a middling class of citizens with social status inferior to the merchants, clergy and professionals but superior to the unskilled labourers, apprentices, slaves and servants. Skilled craftsmen, builders, small scale manufacturers and other producers were considered artificers. See C. S. Olton, *Artisans for Independence: Philadelphia Mechanics and the American Revolution* (Syracuse, NY: Syracuse University Press, 1975), ch. 1, and T. J. Schlereth, 'Artisans and Craftsmen: A Historical Perspective' in I. M. G. Quimby (ed.), *The Craftsman in Early America* (New York: W. W. Norton & Company, 1984), pp. 34–61.
3. B. Yenawine, 'Benjamin Franklin's Legacy of Virtue, The Franklin Trusts of Boston and Philadelphia', (PhD dissertation, Syracuse University, 1997).
4. Accion International was founded in 1961 to address poverty in Latin America, and is now one of the largest microcredit providers in that region. Opportunity International was formed in the early 1970s when both an Indonesian and a Latin American start-up microcredit programme were merged. Today, Opportunity International is serving borrowers in over thirty countries. Grameen was founded in 1976 by Muhammad Yunus in Bangladesh to address poverty and has a global presence and thought leadership position today. See P. Smith and E. Thurman, *A Billion Bootstraps* (New York: McGraw Hill, 2007), p. 179–80.
5. B. Armendariz and J. Morduch, *The Economics of Microfinance* (Cambridge, MA: MIT Press, 2007), Preface.
6. J. Ledgerwood, *Microfinance Handbook: An Institutional and Financial Perspective* (Washington, DC: The World Bank, 2001), p. 2.
7. Ledgerwood, *Microfinance Handbook*, p. 1.
8. P. Burgess, 'Is microfinance the answer to the missing middle?', *Microfinance Focus*, 2 January 2010, online posting (no pagination). Burgess explains, 'What is the missing middle? A small business can be started using the resources of family and friends. While big business can be expanded using all sorts of financing instruments ... stock, bonds, bank lines of credit, leasing, etc., a small business that want to expand to be a big business is faced with a terrible problem ... virtually no financial services that are serving this critical part of the economy. This missing middle problem is not new ... a commission in the United Kingdom in the 1930s, headed by Harold Macmillan, who later became

the Prime Minister, identified this problem and it became known as the Macmillan Gap. The problem has never been successfully addressed ... though there have been attempts. In the USA the Small Business Administration (SBA) is an initiative that has this as part of its mandate ... but has only had modest impact. The concern for the microfinance industry is that the perceived advantage of bigger loans to improve financial performance is a mirage. It needs to be recognized that loans to SMEs, while they are obviously bigger than typical microfinance loans, are also, less obviously, very different...'

9. The Nobel Committee commented, 'Lasting peace cannot be achieved unless large population groups find ways in which to break out of poverty. Microcredit is one such means, development from below also serves to advance democracy and human rights...' as noted in Smith and Thurman, *A Billion Bootstraps*, p. 180.
10. B. Franklin, *My Last Will and Testament dated July 17, 1788 with a Codicil or Addition dated June 3, 1789 (Original in collection of the American Philosophical Society)*, p. 7.
11. M. Yunus and K. Weber, *Creating a World Without Poverty* (New York: Public Affairs, 2007), pp. 68–70.
12. As Robinson describes in *The Microfinance Revolution*, the 1980s demonstrated that '... microfinance could provide large-scale outreach profitably,' and in the 1990s, '... microfinance began to develop as an industry.' M. Robinson, *The Microfinance Revolution* (Washington, DC; The World Bank, 2001), p. 54.
13. K. Epstein and G. Smith, 'Compartamos: From Nonprofit to Profit', *Business Week*, 13 December 2007.
14. K. Heim, 'Making a Profit while helping the Poor', *Seattle Times*, 29 April 2007.
15. Franklin's codicil outlined an itemized list of ten loan qualifications: artificer, married, under twenty-five, apprenticed, two sureties, 5 per cent interest, ten year repayment, not to exceed £60, repayable in gold, use for business.
16. Franklin, *1788 Will and 1789 Codicil*, pp. 7–8.
17. E. Rhyne, *Microfinance for Bankers and Investors* (New York: McGraw Hill, 2009), p.107.
18. Franklin, *1788 Will and 1789 Codicil*, pp. 7–8.
19. In the context of modern microfinance, 'group lending' refers to a self-selected group of individuals who apply for un-collateralized loans that are made to individuals in the group but where repayment is the responsibility of the entire group. Group lending is described in detail in Armendariz and Morduch, *The Economics of Microfinance*, pp. 85–93. For an example, see solidarity group lending to urban vendors by Accion International in Latin America referenced in Ledgerwood, *Microfinance Handbook*, p. 2.
20. Armendariz and Morduch, *The Economics of Microfinance*, p. 202.
21. Fonkoze has created a figurative ladder that consists of four steps that together constitute the core programmes through which clients work with staff and volunteers to pull themselves out of poverty and create a financially secure future for themselves and their families. Before entering into a Fonkoze loan programme, clients must complete the first step on the ladder, referred to as 'Chemen Lavi Miyò', or the Road to a Better Life. This programme reaches out to the poorest of the poor. It provides clients with training, one-on-one supervision and encouragement, confidence building and other services like health care and home repair. It protects clients as they move forward along a two-year road from abject misery to a point where clients have their own functioning microenterprise and are ready to enter a microfinance programme. http://fonkoze.org/aboutfonkoze/whoweare/howworks

22. M. Berger, L. Goldmark, T. M. Sanabria (eds), *An Inside View of Latin American Microfinance* (Washington, DC: Inter-American Development Bank, 2006), p.199.
23. In 2001, the Consultative Group to Assist the Poor (CGAP) published a study which defined mission drift as loss of focus on the poor and examined whether changes in the industry had left poor clients behind. See R. Christen, 'Commercialization and Mission Drift: The Transformation of Microfinance in Latin America', CGAP Occasional Paper Number 5 (2001), pp.13–17.
24. Each new Grameen member bank is required to learn and pledge to follow the Sixteen Decisions which outline principles of sustainability and social impact. Yunus and Weber, *Creating a World Without Poverty*, pp. 58–9.
25. Rhyne, *Microfinance for Bankers and Investors*, p. 162.
26. *Records*, Report from President John Lunn and Counsel Noel Morss, dated 5 October 1960, pp. 2380–1.
27. City of Boston, Committee of the Board of Mayor and Alderman appointed to examine the Accounts of the Treasurer of the Franklin Report dated 11 April 1853, identified as City Document #26, p. 6.

1 Franklin's Intent: the Autobiographical Origins of the Codicil

1. Franklin had drafted two former wills which were relatively short, undistinguished and straightforward, suited to the small size of his estate in 1750 and 1757. The two wills are reprinted in: B. Franklin, *The Papers of Benjamin Franklin*, ed. L. W. Labaree and W. J. Bell (New Haven, CT: Yale University Press, 1961–), vol. 3, pp. 480–2, and vol. 7, pp. 199–205. Reflecting his considerable estate of 1788, the third will was lengthy. It bequeathed generous portions of property and money to his daughter and her husband, Sarah and Richard Bache, his favorite grandsons, Will Temple Franklin, and Benjamin Franklin Bache and his sister, Jane Mecom. This will is notorious for Franklin's virtual disinheritance of his Loyalist son, William. The primary source for this note is Benjamin Franklin's 'My Last Will and Testament dated July 17, 1788 with a Codicil or Addition dated June 3, 1789' signed and witnessed in his own hand, pp. 6–10. The original will is held by the American Philosophical Society on behalf of the City of Philadelphia, Registry of Wills. A full transcript is included as Appendix A.
2. Franklin, *1788 Will and 1789 Codicil*, p. 9.
3. B. Franklin, *Benjamin Franklin's Memoirs: Parallel Text Edition*, ed. M. Farrand (Berkeley and Los Angeles, CA: University of California Press, 1949) p. 234.
4. R. Ketcham, *Presidents Above Parties*, pp. 178–9.
5. F. Butterfield, 'From Ben Franklin, a Gift that's worth Two Fights (Boston and Philadelphia become Beneficiaries of Benjamin Franklin's Will)', *New York Times*, 21 April 1990, p.1.
6. B. Franklin, 'Advice to a Young Tradesman, written by an Old One', Dated 21 July 1748, *The Papers*, vol. 3, pp. 306–8.
7. R. Ketcham, *Benjamin Franklin* (New York: Washington Square Press, 1966), ch. 4.
8. Franklin, 'Advice to a young Tradesman, written by an old One', p. 306.
9. Franklin, *Memoirs*, p. 38 and the 'Plan of Conduct', 1726 from *The Papers*, vol. 1, pp. 99–100.
10. Franklin, *Memoirs*, p. 172.

11. For example: Franklin, *Poor Richard's Almanack*, 'Hints for those that would be Rich', 1737, *The Papers*, vol. 2, p. 165, and *Poor Richard's Almanack Improved*, 'How to get RICHES', 1749, *The Papers*, vol. 3, p. 349.
12. B. Franklin, 'Rules Proper to be Observed in Trade', 15 November 1750, in *Benjamin Franklin: Writings*, ed. J. A. Leo Lemay (New York: The Library of America, 1987) , pp. 345–7.
13. Franklin, *1788 Will and 1789 Codicil*, p. 9. The features of the codicil are nearly identical as they relate to Boston and Massachusetts and Philadelphia and Pennsylvania, respectively. It should be understood that in examining the characteristics of one trust, the second trust corresponds, accordingly, unless specifically noted.
14. Franklin, *1788 Will and 1789 Codicil*, pp. 7–8.
15. The term 'artificer' was the more popular English term to describe a skilled craftsman or industrial handicraftsman during the sixteenth and seventeenth centuries. The Statute of Artificers of 1563 is considered one of the most significant labour laws in English and American history and firmly established the meaning of the term. (See also J. M. Winter (ed.), *R. W. Tawney: The American Labour Movement and Other Essays* (New York: St Martin's Press, 1979), pp. 133–55, and the *Oxford English Dictionary*).
16. Olton, *Aritsans for Independence*, ch. 1, and T. J. Schlereth, 'Artisans and Craftsmen: A Historical Perspective' in I. M. G. Quimby (ed.), *The Craftsman in Early America* (New York: W.W. Norton & Company, 1984), pp. 34–61. Franklin first used the term 'Leather Apron Man' on 2 April 1722 in the 'Silence Dogood Letter No. 1', *The Papers,* vol. 1, p. 9. Occasionally, the term artificer referred to certain types of clerks and shopkeepers.
17. G. B. Nash, *The Urban Crucible; Social Change, Political Consciousness, and the Origins of the American Revolution* (Cambridge, MA: Harvard University Press, 1979), ch. 5, pp. 390–1.
18. Franklin, *1788 Will and 1789 Codicil*, p. 8.
19. Ibid., p. 7.
20. Ibid., pp. 7–8.
21. For Franklin's thought about paper currency and inflation see Franklin, *Memoirs*, pp. 170–2 and B. Franklin, 'Essay on Paper-Currency, Proposing a New Method for Fixing its Value', *Writing*, pp. 286–90. For his advice to Congress, see B. Franklin, *Writings of Benjamin Franklin*, ed. A. H. Smyth, 10 vols (New York: Macmillan, 1905–07) vol. 7, pp. 293–4.
22. Franklin, *1788 Will and 1789 Codicil*, pp. 7–8.
23. Ibid., pp. 8–9.
24. These percentages are calculated from Franklin's estimate of the value of the principal and the exact divisions that he specified.
25. Franklin, *1788 Will and 1789 Codicil*, pp. 8–9. The codicil adds additional notes regarding Philadelphia and public works. Franklin expressed concern about the deteriorating quality of well water and recommended that the Corporation tap the water of Wissahickon Creek, building a dam, if necessary. See also *1788 Will and 1789 Codicil*, p. 9.
26. Franklin, 'Information to Those Who Would Remove to America', published as a pamphlet in 1784, *Writings of Benjamin Franklin*, vol. 8, pp. 603–6.
27. Franklin, *Memoirs*, p. 204 and B. Franklin, *The Life of Benjamin Franklin, Written by Himself*, ed. J. Bigelow, 4th edn (Philadelphia, PA: J. B. Lippincott & Co., 1899) vol. 2, p. 20.
28. Franklin, 'Reply to a Piece of Advice', appearing in *Pennsylvania Gazette*, 4 March 1734/5, in *The Papers*, vol. 2, pp. 23–4.

29. Franklin, 'Observations concerning the Increase of Mankind', *The Papers*, vol. 4, pp. 227–8.
30. A. O. Aldridge, 'Franklin as Demographer', *Journal of Economic History*, vol. 9 (1949–50), pp. 25–44.
31. Franklin, 'Letter to John Alleyne', 9 August 1768, *The Papers*, vol. 15, p. 184.
32. Ibid.
33. Franklin, *Memoirs*, pp. 180, 204–6. See also C. A. Lopez and E. W. Herbert, *The Private Franklin: The Man and His Family* (New York: W. W. Norton & Company, 1975), pp. 30–41.
34. Franklin, *Memoirs*, p. 204.
35. Lopez and Herbert, *The Private Franklin* , pp. 164–5.
36. Franklin, 'Letter to Jan Ingenhousz', 12 February 1777, from *The Papers*, vol. 23, p. 311.
37. Franklin, 'Information to Those Who Would Remove to America', *Writings of Benjamin Franklin* vol. 8, pp. 603–6.
38. Franklin, '*Poor Richard's Almanack*', 1733, from *The Papers*, vol. 1, p. 312.
39. Franklin, *1788 Will and 1789 Codicil*, pp. 8–9. The features of the codicil relate to Boston and Massachusetts coupled with Philadelphia and Pennsylvania.
40. Franklin, *1788 Will and 1789 Codicil*, p. 4.
41. E. G. Dexter, *A History of Education in the United States* (New York: Macmillan Company, 1904), pp. 25–7 and C. Bridenbaugh, *Cities in the Wilderness: The First Century of Urban Life in America 1625–1742* (New York: Alfred A. Knopf, 1955) pp. 442–3.
42. T. Jefferson, 'Letter to Mrs. Cosway dated 12 October 1786, Paris', in A. Koch and W. Peden (eds), *The Life and Selected Writings of Thomas Jefferson* (New York: Random House, 1944) p. 396.
43. Franklin, *1788 Will and 1789 Codicil*, pp. 4–5. Franklin wrote about the Schuylkill River in a letter to Samuel Rhodes dated 22 August 1772, from *The Papers*, vol. 19, pp. 278–9, comparing rivers to canals. See also Infra, pp. 25–6 for an explanation of Franklin's changes to this provision.
44. R. H. Tawney, *Religion and the Rise of Capitalism: A Historical Study* (Gloucester, MA: Peter Smith, 1926) pp. 240–1, 245, and W. Perkins, a selection from 'A Treatise of the Vocations or Callings of Men, with Sorts and Kinds of them, and the Right use Thereof', in I. Legatt, *The Workes of that Famous and Worthy Minister of Christ in the Universitie of Cambridge, Mr. William Perkins*, 3 vols (London, 1626–31), vol. 2, pp. 750–9, reprinted in E. S. Morgan (ed.), *Puritan Political Ideas* (Indianapolis, IN: Bobbs-Merrill Educational Publishing, 1965) pp. 35–58.
45. Franklin, 'Letter to Samuel Mather' dated 12 May 1784 from *Writings of Benjamin Franklin*, vol. 9, p. 208.
46. C. Mather, *Essays to Do Good, Addressed To All Christians, Whether in Public or Private Capacities*, ed. G. Burder (Johnstown, NY: Printed and Sold by Asa Child, 1815), p. 140.
47. Ketcham, *Benjamin Franklin*, p. 66. Franklin clearly recognized and articulated a faith in God. He certainly did not consider himself a Puritan, Congregationalist, Anglican, Quaker or any other kind of sectarian. See also Franklin's 'Articles of Belief and Acts of Religion, November 20, 1728', *The Papers*, vol. 1, pp. 101–9, and Franklin's letter to Ezra Stiles, dated 9 March 1790 in *Writings*, pp. 1178–80.
48. Franklin, *Memoirs*, pp. 44–6. Franklin does not identify the pseudonyms that he wrote under in the *Memoirs*, only that he started the practice in an effort to prevent his brother

from refusing to print them. See also C. Van Doren, *Benjamin Franklin* (New York: Viking Press, 1938), pp. 4, 15–33, 118, 150.

49. Franklin, 'Silence Dogood letter, No. 4', published on 14 May 1722 in *The New England Courant* from *The Papers*, vol. 1, pp. 14–18. See also Van Doren, *Benjamin Franklin*, p. 22.
50. Franklin, *Memoirs*, pp. 30–8.
51. Ibid., pp. 28, 30, 36, 40. It is presumed that Franklin read the texts of Plutarch and Xenophon in translation, although he does not specify.
52. Ibid., pp. 46–8.
53. A. B. Tourtellot, *Benjamin Franklin, The Shaping of Genius, The Boston Years* (Garden City, NY: Doubleday, 1977), p. 234.
54. Franklin, *Memoirs*, pp. 48–50.
55. Ibid., p. 48–50. See also R. W. Clark, *Benjamin Franklin: A Biography*, (New York: Random House, 1983), pp. 21–2 and Van Doren, *Benjamin Franklin*, pp. 31–2.
56. This episode became the basis for a landmark legal case regarding freedom of the press. James Franklin's conviction was later overturned as an illegal act of prior restraint.
57. Franklin, *Memoirs*, p. 50.
58. Ibid., p. 50.
59. Ibid., p. 50.
60. Franklin, 'James Franklin [Jr] : Indenture of Apprenticeship', 5 November 1740, *The Papers* vol. 2, pp. 261–3.
61. Franklin, *Memoirs*, pp. 172, 174 and Van Doren, *Benjamin Franklin*, pp. 117, 121.
62. Franklin, *1788 Will and 1789 Codicil*, p. 7.
63. Franklin, *Memoirs*, p. 50.
64. Ibid., p. 140.
65. Ibid., p. 172.
66. Franklin, *1788 Will and 1789 Codicil*, pp. 7–8.
67. Nash, *The Urban Crucible* , pp. 102–28.
68. Franklin , *Memoirs*, p. 30 and E. Wright, *Franklin of Philadelphia* (Cambridge, MA and London: the Belknap Press of Harvard University Press, 1986), pp. 25–6, 37–9.
69. Franklin, *1788 Will and 1789 Codicil*, pp. 7–8.
70. Franklin, *Memoirs*, pp. 152–4, 166–8.
71. Franklin, *The Papers*, vol. 1, p. 209 (Footnote).
72. Ibid., vol. 2, p. 406 (Footnote).
73. Franklin, 'Standing Queries for the Junto', especially Questions 14 and 15, 1751, *The Papers*, vol. 1, pp. 255–9 and Ketcham, *Presidents Above Parties*, pp. 176–81.
74. Wright, *Franklin of Philadelphia*, pp. 250–1.
75. Nash, *The Urban Crucible* , pp. 374–84.
76. Franklin, *Memoirs*, p. 18.
77. Franklin, *1788 Will and 1789 Codicil*, p. 7.
78. Nash, *The Urban Crucible*, pp. 120–2, 243. The prospects for artisans varied in Philadelphia, as in other cities with the shifts of trade, waves of immigration and factors influencing each distinctive urban economy. The overall success of artisans in Philadelphia was noteworthy.
79. Franklin required the participation of religious leaders in Boston only. He acknowledged in the codicil the incorporated status of the City of Philadelphia and designated the Corporation as the manager of the Philadelphia based trust. The gratis administration

was presumed to be binding on the Philadelphia trust was well as the Boston trust. See also Franklin, *1788 Will and 1789 Codicil*, p. 9.
80. Franklin, *1788 Will and 1789 Codicil*, pp. 7–8.
81. Franklin, *Writings of Benjamin Franklin*, vol. 7, pp. 603–6.
82. R. L. Ketcham, (ed.), *The Anti-Federalist Papers and the Constitutional Convention Debates* (New York: The New American Library, 1986) pp. 176–7.
83. A. O. Aldridge, *Franklin and His French Contemporaries* (New York: New York University Press, 1956), pp. 47–52.
84. Ibid., p. 49. Mathon de la Cour (1738–93) was a native of Lyons, resident of Paris, and a second generation mathematician. See also Franklin, *Writings of Benjamin Franklin*, vol. 9, p. 476 (Footnote). This subject will be treated in greater detail, Infra., Chapter 2.
85. Franklin, 'Letter to Charles Joseph Mathon de la Cour dated 18 November 1785', *Writings of Benjamin Franklin,* vol. 9, p. 477.
86. Franklin, *1788 Will and 1789 Codicil*, p. 9.
87. Ibid., pp. 9–10.
88. Ibid., p. 10.
89. M. R. Fremont-Smith, *Foundations and Government: State and Federal Law Supervision* (New York: Russell Sage Foundation, 1965), pp. 24–5 in discussion of the Statute of Charitable Uses of 1601 and on pp. 27–8 in discussion of conditions leading to the passage of the Gilbert's Act in 1786 and the creation of the Charities Commission by Parliament in 1819.
90. Fremont-Smith, *Foundations and Government* , pp. 31–43, 88–9, 129, 302–3. On p. 32 Fremont-Smith states: 'As developed by the English courts, the doctrine of *cy pres* was used where a clear charitable intention was expressed, but the mode or purpose specified by the donor was or became impossible to carry out'.
91. One of the most common problems for testamentary trusts is management malfeasance after the trust has outlived any interested stewards. Obscurity often leads to violations of the testator's intent.
92. J. Windsor (ed.), *The Memorial History of Boston including Suffolk County, Massachusetts: 1630–1880,* 4 vols (Boston, MA: James R. Osgood and Company 1882), vol. 4, p. 672.
93. Franklin, 'Letter to Jean-Baptiste Le Roy, 13 November 1789', *Writings of Benjamin Franklin,* vol. 10. pp. 68–9.

2 Franklin's Intent: the Sources of Political and Economic Concepts

1. For recent scholarship on Hamilton's financial revolution, see R. E. Wright and D. Cowen, *Financial Founding Fathers: The Men Who Made America Rich* (Chicago, IL: Chicago University Press 2006) and R. E. Wright, *One Nation Under Debt: Hamilton, Jefferson, and the History of What We Owe* (New York: McGraw-Hill, 2008).
2. A sinking fund is a device to pay off significant debt. A fund is established that has a continuing source of new capital which is lent out at interest. The interest returned on investment with new capital is added to the original principal to provide for the rapid compounding of the capital in the fund. The compounding aspect makes the fund ultimately capable of 'sinking' any size debt.
3. G. Stourzh, *Benjamin Franklin and American Foreign Policy*, 2nd edn (Chicago, IL and London, 1954 and 1969), p. 139.

4. Stourzh, *Benjamin Franklin and American Foreign Policy*, pp. 135–9, 155–7, 161, 167, 176–7.
5. Aldridge, *Franklin and His French Contemporaries*, p. 16. Turgot composed the famous Latin epigram in tribute to Franklin translated as '(He seized the lightning from the sky, and the scepter from tyrants.)' They had mutual friends and were guests of the same social salon. See also D. Schoenbrun, *Triumph in Paris: The Exploits of Benjamin Franklin* (New York: Harper & Row, Publishers, 1976), pp. 150, 195, 298.
6. D. Dakin, *Turgot and the Ancien Regime in France* (New York: Octagon Books, Inc., 1965), p. 265.
7. R. D. Harris, *Necker: Reform Statesman of the Ancien Régime* (Berkeley, CA: University of California Press, 1979), p. 119, Dakin, *Turgot*, p. 265, C. A. Lopez, *Mon Cher Papa: Franklin and the Ladies of France* (New Haven, CT: Yale University Press, 1966), p. 16 and Van Doren, *Benjamin Franklin*, p. 567.
8. Turgot, *Oeuvres de Turgot*, IV, Paris, 1923, p. 109, as translated by Dakin, *Turgot*, p. 131.
9. Dakin, *Turgot*, p. 265., Letter, Turgot to Price, 22 March 1778 in R. Price, *Richard Price and the Ethical Foundations of the American Revolution*, ed. B. Peach (Durham, NC: Duke University Press, 1979), p. 220.
10. B. Franklin to M. Veillard, 15 April 1787 in B. Franklin, *The Works of Benjamin Franklin*, 12 vols (New York and London: G. P. Putnam's Sons The Knickerbocker Press, 1904), Vol 11, p.306 and B. Franklin *The Works of Benjamin Franklin*. ed. J. Sparks 10 vols (Boston,MA: Tappan, Whittemore and Mason, 1840), vol. 10, p. 292.
11. B. Franklin to A. Chalut and Arnaud, 17 April 1787 in B. Franklin, *The Works of Benjamin Franklin*, vol. 10, p. 297.
12. B. Franklin to B. Vaughn 'Dr. Price's pamphlet ... will do good'. 26 July 1784, in B. Franklin, *The Works of Benjamin Franklin*,12 vols (New York and London: G. P. Putnam's Sons The Knickerbocker Press, 1904), Vol. 10, p.371. B. Franklin apparently received an advance copy of the work from Price.
13. R. Price, *Observations on the Importance of the American Revolution ...* (Dublin: Printed for L. White, W. Whitestone, P. Byrne, P. Wogan, J. Cash and R. Marchank, 1785). The exploration of Price and Franklin's fascination with the sinking fund follows beginning on page 21 of this chapter.
14. Albany Plan of Union, 1754, Franklin, *The Papers*, vol. 5, pp. 361–4 and Articles of Confederation for United Colonies in 1775, Franklin, *The Papers*, vol. 22, pp. 120–5.
15. This essay is famous for Franklin's articulation of the 'labour theory of value', commented upon by Karl Marx. Although the editors of the Papers of Franklin recognize that much of Franklin's thought in the pamphlet is derivative and in several places a direct lift from the work of Sir William Petty *Treatise of Taxes and Contributions (1662)*, they assign Franklin credit for taking complex economic issues and articulating them in a style accessible to a broad public audience.
16. Report of the Committee of Legacies and Trusts, made in Common Council of Philadelphia, 27 April 1837. See also Appendix to Boston City Document #89, 1866.
17. 'Statement of Devises, Bequests, & Grants to the Corporation of Philadelphia in Trust'. Published by Order of Councils, June 1832, Philadelphia: Printed by Lydia R. Bailey, p. 8.
18. Franklin, *The Papers*, vol. 12, p. 55.
19. Franklin, *Writings of Benjamin Franklin*, vol. 2, p. 353–4.
20. H. Phillips, Jr, *Historical Sketches of the Paper Currency of the American Colonies* (Roxbury, MA: Printed for W. Elliot Woodward, 1865), p. 17–18.

21. M. Zuckerman, 'Doing Good While Doing Well', *Reappraising Benjamin Franklin*, ed. L. Lemay (Cranbury, NJ: Associated University Presses, 1993), p. 445.
22. Franklin, 'Proposals Relating to the Education of Youth in Pennsylvania', 1749, *The Papers*, vol. 3, p. 419.
23. Franklin, *1788 Will and 1789 Codicil*, and 'Scheme for Supplying the Colonies with a Paper Currency', *The Papers*, vol. 12, pp. 51–60.
24. Franklin, 'The Nature and Necessity of a Paper Currency', 1729, *The Papers*, vol. 1, p. 149.
25. Franklin, *Writings*, p. 997.
26. Aldridge, *Franklin and His French Contemporaries*, p. 49.
27. Franklin, *The Papers*, vol. 9, p. 476 (Footnote).
28. Franklin, 'Letter to Charles Joseph Mathon de la Cour dated Philadelphia', 18 November 1765 from *Writings of Benjamin Franklin*, vol. 9, p. 477.
29. Ibid.
30. See also B. Franklin's 2 June 1787 speech on salaries for the Executive in the Constitutional Convention Debates from Ketcham, *The Anti-Federalist Papers*, pp. 43–7.
31. C. J. Mathon de la Cour, *Testament, de M. Fortune Ricard, maître d'arithemétique à D**. Lu & publié à l'audience du bailliage de cette cille, le 19 août 1784, [n.p., 1785]* in Price's *Observations*, p 133–49.
32. Price, *Observations*, p. 135.
33. Ibid., p. 136.
34. Ibid., p. 137.
35. Ibid., p. 140.
36. Franklin did make a token gesture of deference to the church when he designated the three clerics as additional managers of the Boston fund.
37. Ibid., p. 145.
38. Ibid., p. 147.
39. Ibid., p. 147.
40. Franklin, *1788 Will and 1789 Codicil*, p. 5.
41. Franklin, *1788 Will and 1789 Codicil*, p. 6.
42. See also the Franklin forecast in Appendix F of this monograph.
43. Franklin, 'Letter to Richard Price dated 1 February 1785', *Writings of Benjamin Franklin*, vol. 9, p. 286, and 'Letter to Benjamin Vaughan dated 21 April 1785', *Writings of Benjamin Franklin*, vol. 9, pp. 304–6. Price, *Observations*, p.131.
44. Price, *Observations*. p. 129
45. A. Hamilton, *Papers of Alexander Hamilton*, ed. H. C. Syrett, 26 vols (New York and London: Columbia University Press, 1966) vol. 6, p. 63, W. Blackstone, *Commentaries on the Laws of England, A Facsimile of the First Edition of 1765*–1769 (Chicago, IL: University of Chicago Press, 1979), vol. 1, pp. 315–26 and C. de Montesquieu, *The Spirit of the Laws*, translated and edited by A. M. Cohler, et al., (Cambridge: Cambridge University Press, 1989), pp. 418–19. Franklin purchased a copy of *Spirit of Laws* on 27 November 1750, from footnote found in *The Papers*, vol. 4, p. 76.
46. Letter from Benjamin Vaughan to Benjamin Franklin dated 22 March 1785.
47. Mathon de la Cour published a collection of French financial reports called '*Collection des comptes-rendus, pieces authentiques, écrit et tableaux concernant les finances de la France depuis 1758 jusqu'en 1789*', in Paris in1788. See also J. Hoefer, *Nouvelle Biographie Générale*, 46 vols (Paris: Firmin Didot 1861), vol. 34, pp. 261–3.
48. Letter from Benjamin Franklin to Richard Price dated 1 February 1785.

49. J. Necker, *A Treatise on the Administration of the Finances of France in three volumes*, trans. T. Mortimer, 3 vols (London: Logographic Press, 1786), vol. 3, p. 422–3.
50. Hamilton, *Papers of Hamilton*, vol. 2, p. 627.
51. Hamilton, *Papers of Hamilton*, vol. 2, p. 595, Hamilton, 'Letter to Colonel Timothy Pickering dated 20 April 1781 and notes', *Papers of Hamilton*, vol. 2, pp. 604–5n, 607n.
52. See also D. O. Thomas, *The Honest Mind: The Thought and Work of Richard Price* (Oxford: Oxford University Press, 1977) pp. 235–6.
53. Both Price and Alexander Hamilton have been criticized for their commonly held belief. Price was taken to task by economic historian, Robert Hamilton, in *An Inquiry Concerning the Rise and Progress, the Redemption and Present State and the Management of the National Debt of Great Britain*, written in 1813. R. Hamilton found fault in Price's contention that borrowed funds could sustain a Sinking Fund which would eventually extinguish all debt. The focus of Hamilton's argument was on Price's application of simple interest on funds borrowed while paying into a sinking fund that generated compounded interest. In 1895, in his book *Public Debts*, historian Henry C. Adams criticized Robert Hamilton for his acceptance of the theory that debt should be serviced by an inalienable stream of revenue. Adams decried the fixing of debt reduction expenditures, especially when the source of payment might be fresh loans. Hamilton won praise with Charles F. Dunbar in *Economic Essays* for making the redemption of the debt an irrevocable obligation of government. Dunbar defends William Pitt and Hamilton for their willingness to bind the nation to constant service on the debt even when it required new loans to supplement tax revenue. Despite the circularity of the debt, Dunbar argued, as did Hamilton, Price and Pitt, that the good credit of the present and the future depended less on the amount of debt at any given time, than on the loyal and reliable payment on past indebtedness.
54. Hamilton, *Papers of Hamilton*, vol. 5, p. 547.
55. Hamilton repeatedly praised Necker and in the 9 January 1790 *Report on Public Credit* copied Necker's description of the French Caisse d'amortisement (Sinking Fund) as proposed in Necker's speech to the States General in 1789. See Hamilton, '*Ouverture des États-Généraux*, 1789', *Papers of Hamilton*, vol. 6, pp. 52–3, editors' Introductory note.
56. T. Jefferson, 'Letter, Jefferson to James Madison, 6 September 1789', *Life and Selected Writings of Thomas Jefferson*, ed. A. Koch and W. Penden, (New York: Random House, 1944) pp. 488–9.

3 Boston: The First Century

1. *Records Relating to the Early History of Boston*, vol. 31, Registry Department of the City of Boston, Boston, Boston Town Records, 1790, p. 234.
2. *Franklin Foundation* v. *Attorney General*, 340 Mass. 197, p. 201 (1960).
3. City of Boston, *A Sketch of the Origin, Object and Character of the Franklin Fund for the Benefit of Young Married Mechanics of Boston*, City Document #89, (Boston, 1866), p. 26.
4. Ibid.
5. These accurate figures came from an audit of the accounts as described in the Franklin Fund's account books in Boston City Archives and Minot's private account books found in the collection of the Massachusetts Historical Society. While Minot's public accounting to the town and then city of Boston was scrupulously detailed and accurate,

his characterizations and generalizations misrepresented trends and overstated problems with the loan fund.

6. From the account books of the Franklin Fund, Boston City Archives and Minot's General Ledger for the year 1818, p. 56.
7. Windsor (ed.), *The Memorial History of Boston*, p. 236.
8. Letter, William Minot, Treasurer of the Franklin Fund in Boston, to Committee of Legacies and Trusts, made in Common Council of Philadelphia, 23 December 1836 as reprinted in a report, 27 April 1837, by Mr John Thomason, Chairman of the Committee.
9. J. Modell, F. F. Furstenburg, Jr, and D. Strong, 'The Timing of Marriage in the Transition to Adulthood: Continuity and Change, 1860–1975', *American Journal of Sociology*, 84: *Supplement: Turning Points: Historical and Sociological Essays on the Family* (1978), p. S123.
10. *Franklin Foundation* v. *Attorney General*, 340 Mass. 197, p. 201 (1960).
11. Ibid.
12. This explanation was reconstructed by the Franklin Fund board of managers in 1962 in its petition to the Massachusetts Supreme Judicial Court requesting permission to modify the terms of the loan programme. (The Franklin Foundation, Financial Statements and Statistics, 30 June 1989 audit report by Peat Marwick Main & Co. dated 31 August 1989).
13. Letter, Minot to Committee, 23 December 1836.
14. D. Montgomery, *The Fall of the House of Labor: The Workplace, the State and American Labor Activism, 1865–1925* (Cambridge, MA, Cambridge University Press, 1989), pp. 184–5.
15. City of Boston, *Report to the Committee of the City Council Appointed to Obtain the Census of Boston for the Year 1845, Embracing Collateral Facts and Statistical Researches, Illustrating the History and Condition of Population, and Their Means of Progress and Prosperity*, ed. L. Shattuck (Boston, 1846), p. 103.
16. C. W. Eliot, 'The New Education', in R. Hofstadter and W. Smith, *American Higher Education: A Documentary History*, 2 vols (Chicago, IL: The University of Chicago Press, 1961), vol. 2, pp. 624–41 and C. F. Thwing, *Higher Education in America* (New York: D. Appleton and Co., 1906), pp. 302–3.
17. P. R. Knights, *The Plain People of Boston, 1830–1860: A Study in City Growth* (New York: Oxford University Press, 1971), 'Table II-1, Population Growth of Boston, 1820–1860', p. 20. 'Table V-1 Estimated Numbers of Household Heads in Various Socio-economic Groups, and Per Cent Decadal Change in Size of those Groups, Boston, 1830–1860, p. 85' and pp. 152–4.
18. There is a problem of inconsistent use of terms, but the author has attempted to carefully apply Franklin's definitions when citing nineteenth-century sources.
19. A. B. Darling, *Political Changes in Massachusetts, 1824–1848* (New Haven, CT: Yale University Press, 1925) pp. 49–53, 85–129, 172.
20. R. P. Formisano, *The Transformation of Political Culture: Massachusetts Parties, 1790's–1840's* (New York and Oxford: Oxford University Press, 1983), pp. 181–7.
21. J. Tuckerman, 'An Essay on the Wages Paid to Females for their Labour in the Form of a Letter, From a Gentleman in Boston to his Friend in Philadelphia', as reprinted in D.J. Rothman and S.M. Rothman (eds), *Low Wages and Great Sins: Two Antebellum American Views on Prostitution and the Working Girl* (New York and London: Garland Publishing Inc., 1987), pp.25–26.

22. This type of modification was approved by decree of the Court of Common Pleas of Philadelphia regarding the Philadelphia-based Franklin Fund but not until 1970.
23. For example, Formisano, *The Transformation of Political Culture*, p. 229.
24. H. B. Rock, *Artisans of the New Republic: The Tradesmen of New York in the Age of Jefferson* (New York: New York University Press, 1979), p. 165.
25. Letter from William Minot dated 23 December 1836.
26. Trustee Records, p. 13, 2 May 1791.
27. City Document #89, p. 24.
28. Trustee Records, 19 July 1820, see also City Document, #89, p. 25.
29. Letter, Minot, 23 December 1836.
30. A. B. Hart, *Commonwealth History of Massachusetts* (New York: The States History Company, 1930), p. 431.
31. F. C. Jaher, 'The Boston Brahmins in the Age of Industrial Capitalism', *The Age of Industrialism in America: Essays in Social Structure and Cultural Values* (New York: The Free Press, 1968), p. 193, and Rock, *Artisans of the New Republic*, p. 165.
32. R. F. Dalzell, Jr, *Enterprising Elite: The Boston Associates and the World They Made* (Cambridge MA and London: Harvard University Press, 1987), pp. 8, 79–80.
33. Franklin, *1788 Will and 1789 Codicil*, p. 7–8.
34. Ibid., p. 7.
35. 'Letter from Richard Jackson to Benjamin Franklin dated 17 June 1755', *The Papers*, vol. 6, p. 81.
36. The interest rates were affected by the nationwide credit contraction. By May of 1834, banking in Boston had resumed its normal vitality. See also W. H. Pease and J. H. Pease, *The Web of Progress: Private Values and Public Styles in Boston and Charleston, 1828–1843* (New York: Oxford University Press, 1985), pp. 29–30.
37. William Minot, *Diary* from 16 March 1837 to 31 December 1850 entry dated 12 May 1837.
38. F. X. Blouin, Jr, *The Boston Region 1810–1850: A Study of Urbanization* (Ann Arbor, MI: UMI Research Press, 1878, 1980) p. 97, and Dalzell, *Enterprising Elite*, pp. 93–108.
39. Formisano, *The Transformation of Political Culture*, p. 234.
40. Franklin, 'Speech in the Convention on the Subject of Salaries', 2 June 1787, *Writings*, p. 1131.
41. The reference is to Poor Richard's aphorism 'Tis hard for an empty Bag to stand upright', from Franklin, 'Poor Richard Improved, 1758', *The Papers*, vol. 7, p. 348.
42. R. C. Winthrop, 'Tribute to William Minot', *Proceedings of the Massachusetts Historical Society*, vol. 13, (Boston, MA: Massachusetts Historical Society, 1873–5), pp. 255–63 and W. Minot, *William Minot* (Boston, MA: David Clapp & Sons, Printers, 1873–1900), pp. 3–6.
43. Minot, *Diary* entry dated 18 March 1837.
44. *Franklin Foundation* v. *Attorney General*, 340 Mass. 197, pp. 201–2, 276, 560 (1960).
45. Although the charter was granted in 1818, the company did not commence business until 1823 in light of the financial crisis of the intervening years. To the great good fortune of the hospital, the Directors extended the one third profit sharing plan to include all activities of the company. See also Dalzell, *Enterprising Elite*, p. 103.
46. G. T. White, *Massachusetts Hospital Life Insurance Company* (Cambridge, MA: Harvard University Press, 1955), Appendix 3, 'Resources and Liabilities of the Massachusetts Hospital Life Insurance Company, 1824–1900', pp. 190–4.

47. Letter, John Lowell to Samuel Appleton, 26 December 1834 as quoted in White, *Massachusetts Hospital Life*, Notes to Chapter 3, p. 200.
48. Dalzell, *Enterprising Elite*, p. 103.
49. H. Martineau, *Society in America*, (London, 1837), pp. 33–4.
50. Pease and Pease, *Web of Progress*, p. 21.
51. White, *Massachusetts Hospital Life*, pp. 52–3.
52. City of Boston, Committee of the Board of Mayor and Alderman appointed to examine the Accounts of the Treasurer of the Franklin Report dated 11 April 1853, identified as City Document #26, p. 6.
53. Windsor (ed.), *The Memorial History of Boston*, pp. 648–50 and Pease and Pease, *Web of Progress*, pp. 95–6.
54. J. Quincy, *A Municipal History of the Town of Boston during Two Centuries from September 17, 1630 to September 17, 1830* (Boston, MA: Charles C. Little and James Brown, 1852), p. 138.
55. In the Dartmouth College Case the Legislature of the State of New Hampshire attempted to alter the college's royal charter dating from 1769 and reshape the university according to public need and public will. The US Supreme Court ultimately protected the rights of Dartmouth College as a private, eleemosynary institution, by upholding the original charter, and denying the Legislature the right to legislate the affairs of private corporations. The Girard Case of 1843 reinforced the legal sanctity of the testamentary trusts, restricted them to the settler's intent and insulated them from public invasion or preemption.
56. P. D. Hall, *The Organization of American Culture, 1700–1900: Private Institutions, Elites, and the Origins of American Nationality* (New York: New York University Press, 1982), pp. 109–10.
57. This valuation was actually made on 1 July 1893.
58. *Higginson* v. *Turner*, 171 Mass. 586, pp. 589–90 (1898).

4 Philadelphia: The First Century

1. Since Yenawine wrote, much has been learned about Philadelphia's leading role in America's early financial development. For an overview, see Wright, *The First Wall Street*.
2. E. P. Link, *Democratic Republican Societies, 1790–1800* (New York: Octagon Books, 1973 and 1942), p. 72.
3. General Account Ledger, Dr Franklin's Legacy. 1791–18.
4. J. Mease, *The Picture of Philadelphia, etc.* (Philadelphia, PA: B. & T. Kite, 1811), p. 338.
5. General Account Ledger, Dr Franklin's Legacy. 1791–18 and J. T. Scharf and T. Westcott, *A History of Philadelphia, 1609–1884*, 3 vols (Philadelphia, 1884), pp. 564, 571.
6. General Account Ledger, Dr Franklin's Legacy. 1791–18.
7. Ibid., 1791–18.
8. Mease, *Picture of Philadelphia*, p. 130.
9. *Statement of Devises, Bequests, Grants to the Corporation of the City of Philadelphia, In Trust*, Published by Order of Councils, June, 1832 (Philadelphia, PA: Printed by Lydia R. Bailey, 1832), p. 8.
10. In review of the Franklin Legacy account books, very few instances of female sureties were found and there was no correlation between female sureties and loan default. The author postulates that the conservatism of the Committee came with contemporaneous changes in the legal status of women.

11. City of Philadelphia, Common Council, Committee on Legacies and Trusts, 27 April 1837.
12. Undated report (*c.* 1955) from the Board of Directors of City Trusts, Philadelphia, composed for the Court of Common Pleas entitled 'Benjamin Franklin Bequests to the City of Philadelphia for Loans to Artificers and for Public Improvements', p. 3.
13. City of Philadelphia, Common Council, Committee on Legacies and Trusts, 27 April, 1837, p. 7.
14. Ibid., p. 8.
15. Ibid., p. 7.
16. *Franklin's Administratrix* v. *City of Philadelphia*, 9 Pa. Court of Common Pleas 484, (1891) p. 485.
17. City of Philadelphia, Common Council, Committee on Legacies and Trusts, 27 April 1837, pp. 7–9.
18. E. P. Allinson and B. Penrose, *Philadelphia 1681–1887: A History of Municipal Development* (Philadelphia, PA: Allen, Lane & Scott, Publishers, 1887), p. 58.
19. 'Benjamin Franklin Bequest to the City of Philadelphia for Loans to Artificers and for Public Improvements', Undated Report, p. 5.
20. R. Fox, 'The John Scott Medal', *Proceedings of the American Philosophical Society*, 5.113:6 (1968), pp. 416–30.
21. Ibid., p. 418.
22. B. Laurie, *Working People of Philadelphia, 1800–1850* (Philadelphia, PA: Temple University Press 1980), p. 26.
23. *First Annual Report of the Directors of City Trusts*, 1871, Appendix C. p. 74. With the creation of the Board of Directors of City Trusts (BODCT) in 1869, formal annual reports were published.
24. E. P. Richardson, 'The Athens of America, 1800–1825', in R. F. Weighley (ed.), *Philadelphia: A 300 Year History* (New York and London: W. W. Norton & Company, 1982), pp. 208–57, pp. 241, 255–6.
25. R. A. Foulke, *The Sinews of American Commerce* (New York: Dun & Bradstreet, Inc., 1941), p. 154.
26. Richardson, 'The Athens of America, 1800–1825'. p. 241.
27. Franklin, *1788 Will and 1789 Codicil*, p. 10.
28. *Second Annual Report*, BODCT, p. 8.
29. J. Bristed, as quoted by M. V. Brewington, 'Maritime Philadelphia, 1609–1837', *Pennsylvania Magazine of History and Biography*, 63 (1939), p. 117.
30. J. R. Commons, *History of Labour in The United States*, 4 vols (New York: Macmillan, 1966), vol. 1, pp. 88–9.
31. Ibid., p. 89.
32. Ibid., p. 92.
33. 'Benjamin Franklin Bequest to the City of Philadelphia for Loans to Artificers and for Public Improvements', Undated Report, p. 5.
34. Allison and Penrose, *Philadelphia 1681–1887,* pp. 117–18, 240–1.
35. Ibid., p. 121.
36. Ibid., p. 121.
37. D. G. Beers, 'The Centennial City, 1865–1876', in Weighley (ed.), *Philadelphia*, p. 425–38, p. 438.
38. M. J. Schiesl, *The Politics of Efficiency: Municipal Administration and Reform in America, 1880–1920* (Berkeley, CA: University of California Press, 1977), p. 52.

39. *Second Annual Report*, BODCT, 1872, p. 511.
40. *First Annual Report*, BODCT, 1871, p. 18.
41. Modell, Furstenburg, Jr and Strong, 'The Timing of Marriage in the Transition to Adulthood', p. S123.
42. *Third Annual Report*, BODCT, 1873, p. 495.
43. *Commonwealth of PA* v. *Conrow*, 2 Pa. 402 (1845).
44. E. M. Fee, *The Origin and Growth of Vocational Industrial Education in Philadelphia to 1917* (Philadelphia, PA: Westbrook Publishing Company, 1938), p. 43.
45. Fee, *Vocational Industrial Education*, p. 52.
46. Commons, *History of Labour*, p. 190. The MUTA's chief interest was the establishment of the ten-hour day.
47. *Mechanics Free Press*, 24 January 1829, p. 2, also Fee, *Vocational Industrial Education,* p. 83.
48. J. P. Wickersham, *A History of Education in Pennsylvania* (Lancaster, PA: Inquirer Publishing Company, 1886) p. 312, see also S. B. Warner, Jr, *The Private City: Philadelphia in the Three Periods of Its Growth* (Philadelphia, PA: University of Pennsylvania Press, 1968) p. 116.
49. The city school system experienced exponential growth and, in 1843, there were 214 tax supported schools and 33,130 students. See Warner, *The Private City*, p. 116.
50. *Girard College*, Report of the Superintendent of Binding Out. (1855), p. 14, also Fee, *Vocational Industrial Education,* p. 50.
51. R. A. Ferguson, 'The Girard Will Case: Charity and Inheritance in the City of Brotherly Love', in J. Saltzman (ed.), *Philanthropy and American Society* (New York: Columbia University, 1987), pp. 1–16, pp. 6–10.
52. S. Girard, *Last Will and Testament*, signed and witnessed 16 February 1830, Section 20.
53. Ibid., Section 21, subsection 9.
54. Ibid., Section 21 (final paragraph).
55. Ferguson, 'The Girard Will Case', pp. 6–10.
56. Ibid.
57. Fremont-Smith, *Foundations and Government,* p. 32, Fremont-Smith states: 'As developed by the English courts, the doctrine of *cy pres* was used where a clear charitable intention was expressed, but the mode or purpose specified by the donor was or became impossible to carry out'.
58. Fee, *Vocational Industrial Education,* p. 48.

5 The Centennial in Boston and Philadelphia

1. W. Gladden, *Working People and Their Employers* (New York: Funk and Wagnalls Co., 1894), pp. 44–5.
2. G. L. Palmer, *Philadelphia Workers in a Changing Economy* (Philadelphia, PA: University of Pennsylvania Press, 1956), p. 14.
3. Franklin, *1788 Will and 1789 Codicil*, pp. 8–9.
4. This valuation is the most precise because it is the amount that actually was forwarded by the Franklin Fund to the City of Boston Treasurer as the 100/131 the portion of the total accumulated principal in 1 July 1893. See also *Daniel A. Madden* v. *City of Boston*, 177 Mass. 350 (1901), p. 352.
5. Franklin, *1788 Will and 1789 Codicil*, p. 8.

6. *Daniel A. Madden* v. *City of Boston*, p. 352.
7. *Annual Report of the City Auditors* dated 1 February 1892 to 31 January 1893 (Document #4) pp. 254–5.
8. S. F. McCleary, 'The Franklin Fund', *Proceedings of the Massachusetts Historical Society*, October, 1897, p. 24.
9. Franklin, *1788 Will and 1789 Codicil*, p. 8.
10. McCleary, 'The Franklin Fund', p. 25, and Dr H. S. Pritchett, 'The Story of the Franklin Fund' presented 17 January 1906 (Boston, MA: printed by the Members of the Franklin Foundation, 1956). Dr Pritchett was the Chairman of the Managers of the Fund.
11. City of Boston, 'Disposition of the Franklin Fund', *The City Record*, 45 (1893), p. 637. The date of action conflicts with the 9 November 1893 date reported in *The Franklin Institute: A Living Legacy*, published but undated (*c.* 1983) by the Franklin Foundation, unnumbered p. 2.
12. *Daniel A. Madden* v. *City of Boston*, p. 352.
13. McCleary, 'The Franklin Fund', p. 26.
14. City of Boston, 'Decision Regarding the Franklin Fund', *The City Record* 37 (1898), p. 526.
15. Ibid.
16. *Daniel A. Madden* v. *City of Boston*, p. 354 and *City of Boston* v. *James H. Doyle*, 184 Mass. 373 (1903), pp. 382–3.
17. *Henry L. Higginson* v. *Alfred T. Turner*, 171 Mass. 586 (1898), p. 594.
18. Ibid.
19. G. Blodgett, *The Gentle Reformers: Massachusetts Democrats in the Cleveland Era* (Cambridge, MA: Harvard University Press, 1966), pp. 244–54.
20. City of Boston, 'Disposition of the Franklin Fund', p. 638. Also City Document 138, 1898 p. 4.
21. 'Franklin Fund: A Hearing Before the Board of Managers of the Franklin Fund in the Aldermanic Chambers ... November 14, 1898', City of Boston, Document # 147–1898, p. 64. See also M. T. Williams, 'Urban Reform in the Gilded Age: The Public Baths of Boston', in J. Trager and J. W. Ifkovic (eds), *Massachusetts in the Gilded Age: selected essays* (Amherst, MA: University of Massachusetts Press, 1985), pp. 210–31 and Blodgett, 'Mayor Quincy's Boston' in *The Gentle Reformers*, pp. 244–54.
22. City of Boston, 'Disposition of the Franklin Fund', , p. 639.
23. C. M. Woodward, *The Manual Training School* (Boston, MA: D.C. Health & Co., 1887), p. 217.
24. Seaver as quoted by Woodward, ibid., p. 223–4.
25. City Document #147 (1898), p. 19.
26. Ibid., p. 30.
27. Ibid., p. 29.
28. Ibid., p. 28.
29. Ibid., p. 22–3.
30. Ibid., p. 60.
31. Ibid., p. 35–6.
32. Ibid., p. 36.
33. *The Will of Benjamin Franklin and Proceedings of Managers and Courts Relating Thereto.* (Boston, Municipal Printing Office, 1904), p. 43.
34. Ibid., p. 43.
35. Ibid., p. 44.

36. Ibid., p. 47.
37. Ibid.
38. *City of Boston* v. *James H. Doyle* (1903), p. 387.
39. R. P. Formisano and C. K. Burns, *Boston 1700–1980: The Evolution of Urban Politics* (Westport, CT and London: Greenwood Press, 1984), p. 125.
40. Pritchett, 'The Story of the Franklin Fund'.
41. This valuation is based on the amount that actually was forwarded by the Franklin Fund to the City of Boston Treasurer as the 100/131 the portion of the total accumulated principal in 1 July 1893 plus interest accruing since 1893.
42. For Pritchett biography see *The National Cyclopædia of American Biography*, 1930 vol. C (current) (New York, 1930); *The Franklin Foundation* v. *City of Boston*, 336 Mass. 39 (1957), pp. 41–4.
43. *The Franklin Foundation* v. *City of Boston*, p. 41–2.
44. Ibid., p. 41.
45. H. C. Livesay, *Andrew Carnegie and the Risk of Big Business* (Boston, MA and Toronto: Little Brown and Company, 1975), p. 16.
46. Ibid., p. 21.
47. *The Franklin Foundation* v. *City of Boston* (1957), 41.
48. Formisano and Burns, *Boston 1700–1980*, p. 142.
49. *The National Cyclopædia of American Biography*, vol. 33, (New York, 1947) pp. 198–9.
50. Formisano and Burns, *Boston 1700–1980*, p. 144.
51. Pritchett, 'The Story of the Franklin Fund'.
52. Minutes of the Franklin Foundation/Union/Institute, 12 October 1904, pp. 17–18.
53. Minutes of the Franklin Foundation/Untion/Institute, 16 December 1904, pp. 19–20.
54. Ibid., p. 20.
55. Ibid., pp. 25, 27.
56. Minutes of the Franklin Foundation/Union/Institute, 15 February 1905, pp. 30–1. It is difficult to discern how much influence Carnegie actually had on the Board of Managers. Clearly the Board was concerned with his need to approve of their plans witnessed by a letter reporting their progress dated 9 March 1905 from Secretary James Storrow to Mr Carnegie. Carnegie in a letter dated 28 October 1904 made an examination of both the Mechanics's and Tradesmen's School of New York and the Cooper Union a condition of his gift.
57. Minutes of the Franklin Foundation/Union/Institute, 31 March 1905, pp. 35–7.
58. Ibid., p. 38.
59. Minutes of the Franklin Foundation/Union/Institute, 20 March 1906, p. 54.
60. Franklin, *1788 Will and 1789 Codicil*, p. 9–10.
61. B. Franklin, 'Letter to George Washington, 5 March 1780', in *Mr. Franklin: A Selection from his Personal Letters* ed. L. W. Labaree and W. J. Bell Jr (New Haven, CT: Yale University Press, 1956) p. 53.
62. *21st Annual Report*, Board of Directors of City Trusts dated 31 December 1890.
63. This course is taken when the executors that were named by Franklin were deceased, and the heirs wished to establish standing with the Orphans' Court in order to pursue the dissolution of the Franklin Trust and recovery of the appreciated Franklin estate of which the city held custody.
64. Philadelphia Bar Association, contributions of Hon. Hampton L. Carson, *In Memoriam, Clement B. Penrose, 1832–1911* (Philadelphia, PA: Palmer-Goodman, 1911), pp. 24–5. Carson traced the development of the Orphan's Court citing provincial acts of

1701, 1705 and 1715 as well as the state constitutions of 1776 and 1790. He especially credited the Orphans' Court law of 1832 for establishing the jurisdiction of this court.
65. *In Memoriam, Clement B. Penrose*, p. 39.
66. Scharf and Wescott, *History of Philadelphia, 1609–1884*, p. 1700 and 'The Centennial City 1865–1876', in Weighley (ed.), *Philadelphia*, pp. 460–2.
67. *Paper Book of Petitioners*, March 1891 arguments by counsellors Russell Duane, George Wharton Pepper and A. Sydney Biddle on behalf of the petitioners Elizabeth Duane Gillespie and Albert D. Bache presented in the July Term (records for 1890, p. 6).
68. Ibid., p. 30.
69. Ibid., p. 56.
70. Ibid., p. 4.
71. *Franklin's Administratrix* v. *City of Philadelphia*, 9 Pa. Court of Common Pleas 484, (1891), p. 488.
72. Ibid., p. 489.
73. Ibid.
74. Ibid., p. 491.
75. *Franklin's Administratrix* v. *City of Philadelphia*, 9 Pa. Court of Common Pleas 484, (1891).
76. Legal summary of Judge Arnold's decision in *Franklin's Administratrix* v. *City of Philadelphia*, 13 Pa. Court of Common Pleas 241 (1893), p. 241.
77. Undated history of the Benjamin Franklin Bequest published by the Board of Directors of City Trusts, Philadelphia, Part II: Fund for Public Improvements, p. 15.
78. Scharf and Wescott, *History of Philadelphia, 1609–1884,* p. 1700.
79. N. Burt and W. E. Davies, 'The Iron Age, 1876–1905' in Weighley (ed.), *Philadelphia*, pp. 471–523, pp. 501–2, 595.
80. Undated history of the Benjamin Franklin Bequest published by the Board of Directors of City Trusts, Philadelphia, Part II: Fund for Public Improvements, pp. 15–16.
81. *26th Annual Report*, Board of Directors of City Trusts, 1895, p. 32 [224].
82. *36th Annual Report*, Board of Directors of City Trusts, 1905, p. 34 [806].
83. Undated history of the Benjamin Franklin Bequest published by the Board of Directors of City Trusts, Philadelphia, Part II: Fund for Public Improvements, pp. 16–17.
84. Original Application of Franklin Institute addressed to the Committee on Minor Trusts of the Board of City Trusts dated 4 May 1906, Philadelphia, p. 2.
85. 'Reasons why ground at 16th & Arch Streets should be set aside by the City of Philadelphia for the use of the Franklin Institute', document, undated from BODCT files, p. 1.
86. Ibid., p. 4.
87. S. L. Wright *The Story of the Franklin Institute* (Philadelphia, PA: The Franklin Institute, 1938), p. 74.
88. Franklin, *1788 Will and 1789 Codicil*, p. 8.
89. S. Bruchey, *The Roots of American Economic Growth, 1607–1861* (New York: Harper & Row Publishers, 1968), pp. 14–15.
90. Fremont-Smith, *Foundations and Government,* p. 32, Fremont-Smith states: 'As developed by the English courts, the doctrine of *cy pres* was used where a clear charitable intention was expressed, but the mode or purpose specified by the donor was or became impossible to carry out'.

6 Boston: The Second Century

1. Massachusetts Statute 1908, c. 569, and 276, p. 54.
2. Ibid., pp. 54–5.
3. Ibid.
4. Patrick Collins speaking on behalf of gubernatorial candidate, Charles Francis Adams, 1876 as quoted in J. Beatty, *The Rascal King: The Life and Times of James Michael Curley* (Reading, MA: Addison Wesley Publishing Company, 1992), p. 7.
5. A. Siegel, *Living Legacy: A History of the Franklin Institute of Boston* (Boston, MA: Franklin Foundation, 1993), ch. 4, p. 3.
6. *Records of the Executive Committee of the Franklin Foundation 1908–1918*, p. 316.
7. *Records of the Franklin Foundation* (hereafter referred to as *Records*), Report of the Director, 10 May 1920, p. 416.
8. Ibid., and see also Siegel, *Living Legacy*, ch. 4.
9. *Records*, 16th Annual Report of the Director, 12 May 1924, pp. 540–1.
10. *Boston* v. *Curley & others*., Massachusetts Supreme Judicial Court, Case 276 (1931) pp. 551–4.
11. Ibid., p. 560.
12. Ibid., p. 551–4 and *Records*, letter dated 21 January 1930 to Everett Morss from Frank S. Deland, p. 769.
13. Ibid.
14. *Records*, letter dated 31 July 1929 to Howard Stockton, Actuary for Massachusetts Hospital Life Insurance Company from Bentley W. Warren, independent counsel, pp. 771–3.
15. *Boston* v. *Curley*, p. 549.
16. Ibid., p. 557.
17. Ibid., p. 559.
18. Ibid., p. 549.
19. Ibid., p. 564.
20. *The Franklin Institute: A Living Legacy*, published but undated by the Franklin Foundation, (*c.* 1983), unnumbered p. 3, 6.
21. *Chapter 212 of the Acts of the Massachusetts Legislature of 1941*, and *The Franklin Institute: A Living Legacy*, p. 3, 6.
22. See Siegel, *Living Legacy*, ch. 4, p. 13.
23. *Records*, Minutes dated 16 May, 1957, p. 2128.
24. Ibid.
25. Ibid., p. 2101.
26. *Franklin Foundation* v. *Boston*, 36 Mass 39, 1957.
27. Massachusetts General Assembly, *Report of the Special Commission Established to Investigate and Study Certain Matters Relating to the Franklin Technical Institute* (Boston, MA Wright and Potter Printing Co., 1958), ch. 596, p. 4.
28. Chapter 111, Resolve of The Commonwealth of Massachusetts, 1957.
29. Franklin, *1788 Will and 1789 Codicil*, pp. 8–9.
30. Massachusetts General Assembly, *Report of the Special Commission*, Chapter 596, p. 4.
31. Ibid.
32. *Franklin Foundation* v. *Attorney General*, pp. 198–9.
33. Fremont-Smith, *Foundations and Government*, p. 32, Fremont-Smith states: 'As developed by the English courts, the doctrine of *cy pres* was used where a clear charitable

intention was expressed, but the mode or purpose specified by the donor was or became impossible to carry out', and *Franklin Foundation* v. *Attorney General*, p. 201.

34. *Franklin Foundation* v. *Attorney General*, p. 201.
35. Ibid., pp. 206–7.
36. Ibid., p. 207.
37. Ibid., p. 205.
38. *Records*, Report from President John Lunn and Counsel Noel Morss, dated 5 October 1960, p. 2379.
39. Ibid., pp. 2380–1.
40. *Records*, Final Decree dated 20 March 1962 of *Franklin Foundation* v. *McCormack*, Suffolk No. 6198, eq., pp. 2507–14, and *Records*, Report of Loan Committee dated 10 December 1974, p. 3622, and *Records*, report of the Loan Committee, p. 3696.
41. *Records*, Report of the Loan Committee, 12 June 1979, p. 3961.
42. *The Franklin Institute: A Living Legacy*, unnumbered p. 8.
43. Siegel, *Living Legacy*, ch. 5.
44. *Records*, Report of the Development Committee dated 25 April 1974, p. 3614 and *Records*, Annual Report of the Director, 8 October 1975, p. 3664.
45. *Records*, pp. 3614, 3621, 3651 and Siegel, *Living Legacy,* Chapter 5, p. 8.
46. *Records*, Annual Report of the Director, 8 October 1975, p. 3666.
47. *Records*, Report of the Treasurer, 4 June 1975, p. 3626.
48. Ibid.
49. Ibid., p. 3625.
50. *Records*, Annual Report of the Director, 8 October 1975, p. 3666, and Records, Minutes of the Annual Meeting, Mr R. I. Rossbacher's Report, 8 October 1975, p. 3653.
51. *Records*, Report of the Loan Committee, Report of Mr Rossbacher, 16 November 1976, p. 3744.
52. The Franklin Foundation, Financial Statements and Statistics, 30 June 1989 audit report by Peat Marwick Main & Co. dated 31 August 1989 and Franklin, *1788 Will and 1789 Codicil*, p. 7.
53. *Records*, Other Business, 8 June 1976, pp. 3711–12.
54. *Records*, Report of the Director, 16 June 1977, p. 3817.
55. Commonwealth of Massachusetts General Assembly, House Bill No 5503, entitled 'An Act to Authorize Transfer to Trustees of Boston University by the Franklin Foundation and the City of Boston of the ownership ad control of Franklin Institute of Boston and exercise by the city of the city's power to dispose of its share of the accumulating bequest of Benjamin Franklin, and to exercise in favour of the Trustees of Boston University of the Commonwealth's power to dispose of its share of said bequest', January, 1977 Section 1 (c).
56. Ibid., Section 1a.
57. *Records*, Report of the Director, 16 June 1977, p. 3817.
58. Ibid., p. 3818.
59. Ibid.
60. Massachusetts Supreme Judicial Court, Case 374, as reproduced in House Record No. 6935, December, 1977, p. 11.
61. Ibid., pp. 6–18.
62. *Records*, Directors Report Annual Meeting, 23 February 1984, p. 4277.
63. *Records*, dated 29 June 1978, in Volume # 8, unnumbered page.

7 Philadelphia: The Second Century

1. Fremont-Smith, *Foundations and Government*, p. 32, Fremont-Smith states: 'As developed by the English courts, the doctrine of *cy pres* was used where a clear charitable intention was expressed, but the mode or purpose specified by the donor was or became impossible to carry out'.
2. Board of Directors of City Trusts Petition before the Court of Common Pleas, No. 685, decree dated 11 June 1917, p. 4. While the BODCT records and historical sources sometimes refer to the Orphan's Court Division of the Court of Common Pleas, citation will only use the shorter reference 'Court of Common Pleas'.
3. Ibid.
4. Ibid., pp. 5–6.
5. *Forty-Fourth Annual Report of the Board of Directors of City Trusts*, 1917. With the creation of the Board of Directors of City Trusts (BODCT) in 1869, formal annual reports were published.
6. BODCT Petition, 1917, p. 5–6.
7. *Second Annual Report of the Commissioner of Labor and Industry of the Commonwealth of Pennsylvania*, 1914, Part I, (Harrisburg, PA: 1915), p. 62.
8. L. M. Abernathy, 'Progressivism 1905–1919', in R. F. Weighley (ed.), *Philadelphia,* pp. 526–54, pp. 526–8.
9. Ibid., p. 529.
10. R. H. Wiebe, *The Search for Order, 1877–1920* (New York: Hill and Wang, 1967), pp. 154–5.
11. US Commission of Labor, *Report of the Congressional Commission on Industrial Relations*, Testimony of William C. Ash, Superintendent of the Philadelphia Trade School, 26 June 1914 (Washington, DC: Government Printing Office, 1915), pp.2946–7.
12. Board of Directors of City Trusts Petition before the Court of Common Pleas, No. 685, decree dated 11 June 1917.
13. *Statement of Devises, Bequests, & Grants to the Corporation of the City of Philadelphia. In Trust.* Published by Order of Councils, June 1832, (Philadelphia, PA: Printed by Lydia R. Bailey) p. 8.
14. Benjamin Franklin Bequest to the City of Philadelphia for Loans to Artificers and for Public Improvements: Part I: Fund for Loans, an unpublished, undated (probably 1955) history issued by the Board of Directors of City Trusts (Hereafter referred to as BODCT history), Philadelphia, p. 9.
15. Ibid.
16. Ibid.
17. Ibid.
18. M. B. Tinkham, 'Depression and War 1929–1946', in R. F. Weighley (ed.), *Philadelphia*, pp. 601–48, pp. 608–9, 610–14.
19. Ibid., p. 614.
20. BODCT history, p. 10 and Testimony of Louis O. Heiland, secretary of the BODCT from 1911 before the Court of Common Pleas, 1939, p. 4.
21. Tinkham, 'Depression and War 1929–1946', p. 615.
22. Ibid., p. 637.
23. Ibid.
24. Orphans' Court Division, Court of Common Pleas, City of Philadelphia, 1939, Master's Discussion of Testimony, pp. 5–6.

25. Board of Directors of City Trusts Petition before the Court of Common Pleas, decree dated 17 August 1939.
26. J. A. Clark, Jr and D. J. Clark, 'Rally and Relapse 1946–1968', in Weighley (ed.), *Philadelphia*, p. 652.
27. BODCT history, pp. 11–12.
28. Tinkham, 'Depression and War 1929–1946', pp. 647–8.
29. Ibid.
30. Ibid.
31. BODCT history, pp. 10–11.
32. Ibid., p. 11.
33. Clark and Clark, 'Rally and Relapse 1946–1968', pp. 654–7.
34. BODCT history, p. 12.
35. Ibid., p. 12, The Board solicitor at the time was Joseph Gaffney.
36. R. W. Brown for the Plaintiff, US District Court for the Eastern District of Pennsylvania, Civil action #39404, p. 10, and Clark and Clark, 'Rally and Relapse 1946–1968', *Philadelphia,* p. 659.
37. Clark and Clark, 'Rally and Relapse 1946–1968', pp. 662, 680–1.
38. Ibid.
39. BODCT history, p. 15.
40. Board of Directors of City Trusts Petition before the Court of Common Pleas, decree dated 18 October 1966, Petition, pp. 13–14.
41. H. Husock, 'Ben's Bequest', *Boston Globe*, 7 May 1989, p. 37.
42. J. Enda, 'Franklin's Will Splits Legislature, House Plans Gift To Organizations', *Philadelphia Inquirer*, 2 October 1990, p. B01.
43. Interview with Kent Roberts, Philadelphia, Pennsylvania, 28 June 1993.
44. Husock, 'Ben's Bequest', p. 37 and Ferrick, 'Franklin's Gift: What Now?', , p. 22A.
45. Ferrick, 'Franklin's Gift', p. 22A.
46. Ibid.

8 Bicentennial: Boston and Philadelphia

1. *The Franklin Foundation* v. *Attorney General*, 416 Mass. 483 (1993), p. 488.
2. *Records of the Franklin Foundation* (hereafter referred to as *Records*), p. 4105.
3. Chapter 569 of the Acts of the Massachusetts Legislature of 1908 established the Franklin Foundation as a new charitable corporation with a board identical to the Franklin Fund appointed by the Supreme Judicial Court in 1904 whose purpose was to operate the Franklin Union (later Institute) as a department of city government on behalf of the city. The Franklin Foundation also completely controlled the management of the Franklin Fund (Second Part) until dissolution in 1991, although subject to the judgment and control of trusts by the Supreme Judicial Court. The City of Boston held title to all land, equipment and money that was part of the original Franklin Fund/Carnegie gift/state/city deal. The title to surplus funds from operations or other endowments for the benefit of the institute was fully vested in the private, charitable corporation - the Franklin Foundation.
4. *Records*, p. 4502.
5. *Records*, p. 4515.
6. Commonwealth of Massachusetts, Executive Order # 294 dated 31 December 1990.

7. Commonwealth of Massachusetts, Statute 1958, Chapter 596 and Boston City Council action 29 & 31December 1958. See also pp. 168–72 of Chapter 6 of this monograph.
8. *The Franklin Foundation* v. *Attorney General*, p. 490.
9. *Ibid.*, p. 491.
10. *Chapter 111, Resolve of The Commonwealth of Massachusetts, 1957.*
11. Ibid., p. 8.
12. *The Franklin Foundation* v. *Attorney General*, p. 493.
13. M. Resendes, 'Franklin's Largess Has Long Reach', *The Boston Globe*, 17 April 1990, p. 17.
14. Ibid.
15. Benjamin Franklin Bequest to the City of Philadelphia for Loans to Artificers and For Public Improvements: Part I: Fund for Loans, an unpublished, undated (probably 1955) history issued by the Board of Directors of City Trusts (Hereafter referred to as BODCT history), Philadelphia, p. 9.
16. Memorandum, Eric H. Auerbach, Deputy City Solicitor, City of Philadelphia, to Richard Gold, First Deputy Solicitor, City of Philadelphia, 20 March 1989.
17. Ibid. Footnote 2.
18. T. Ferrick Jr, 'Ben Franklin's Bequest has put Two Cities to the Test', *Philadelphia Inquirer*, 25 October 1987, p. 22A.
19. T. Ferrick, Jr, 'Some Fear Franklin's Fund Will be Philadelphia's Folly', *Philadelphia Enquirer*, 14 January 1990, p. 1A.
20. M. Duvoisin, 'Goode is Said to Enlist Academics on Franklin Fund Use', *Philadelphia Inquirer*, 26 January 1990, p. 4B.
21. Ferrick, 'Some Fear Franklin's Fund Will be Philadelphia's Folly', *Philadelphia Enquirer*, p. 18A.
22. Ibid.
23. T. Ferrick, Jr, *'City Rethinking its Use of $500,000 Franklin Fund'*, *Philadelphia Enquirer*, 18 January 1990, p. 3B.
24. Letter, Honorable W. Wilson Goode to Dr Whitfield Bell, 1 February 1990.
25. *Report of the Master*, Court of Common Pleas, 24 December 1992, p. 10.
26. Franklin, *1788 Will and 1789 Codicil*, pp. 8–9.
27. *Report of the Advisory Committee*, 17 April 1990.
28. Undated list of ten 'Proposals-Franklin Trust' from the papers of the Advisory Committee and another list with sixty-one proposed uses listed entitled 'Benjamin Franklin Trust Letters/Proposals, marked 12 March [1990] and hand written notes of Advisory Committee meeting.
29. Proposal submitted with two separate identical letters to Mayor W. Wilson Goode and Governor Robert P. Casey on 17 February 1989 from Constance Clayton, Superintendent of the School District of Philadelphia, on behalf of the Board of Education.
30. Proposal submitted with two separate identical letters to Mayor W. Wilson Goode and Governor Robert P. Casey on 17 February 1989 by Constance Clayton, Superintendent of the School District of Philadelphia, on behalf of the Board of Education.
31. *Report of the Advisory Committee*, 17 April 1990, and The Philadelphia Foundation, 'A Proposal For Use of the Benjamin Franklin Trust' submitted November 1989, p. 3.
32. Memorandum, Whitfield Bell to Advisory Committee on the Franklin Fund, 26 February 1990.
33. *Report of the Advisory Committee*, 17 April 1990, p. 2.
34. Ibid., p. 3.

35. Ibid., p. 6.
36. Ibid., p. 6.
37. J. Enda, 'Franklin's Will Splits Legislature', p. B01.
38. Senate Bill 1135, 17 December 1990 as quoted in *Report of the Master*, Final Account, p. 2.
39. Ibid.
40. *Fund Agreement*, Section 5, Subsection 1(f).
41. Ibid.

Conclusion

1. Franklin, *The Papers*, vol. 4, pp. 504–5.
2. B. Barber, *Strong Democracy: Participatory Politics for a New Age* (Berkeley, CA: University of California Press, 1984), p. 151.
3. *The Franklin Foundation* v. *Attorney General*, 416 Mass. 483 (1993) p. 488, and 'Benjamin Franklin Bequest to the City of Philadelphia for Loans to Artificers and For Public Improvements: Part I Fund for Loans', an unpublished, undated (probably 1955) history issued by the Board of Directors of City Trusts.
4. Franklin, 'Speech in the Convention on the Subject of Salaries', 2 June 1787, *Writings*, p. 1131.
5. Franklin, 'Poor Richard Improved', 7 July 1757, *Writings*, p. 1301–2.
6. Franklin *1788 Will and 1789 Codicil*, pp. 9–10.

WORKS CITED

Newspapers and Magazines

Boston Globe

Business Week

The New York Times

The Philadelphia Inquirer

The Seattle Times

Primary Sources

Anon. (A Mechanic), *'Common Sense', Especially Addressed to the Most Suffering Portion of our Fellow Citizens, the 'Bone and Sinew' of our Country - The Mechanics* (Philadelphia: Charles Bell, 1837).

American Society for the Encouragement of Domestic Manufactures, Committee of Correspondence, *Address of The American Society for the Encouragement of Domestic Manufactures, to the People of the United States* (New York: 1817).

Boston Mechanics' Institution, *The First Annual Report of the Board of Managers* (Boston: 1828).

—, *The Third Annual Report of the Board of Managers* (Boston: 1830).

Boston, Town (then City), 'Annual Report of the Treasurer of the Franklin Fund', in the *Annual Report of Expenditures and Revenues of the Town (then City) of Boston and the County of Suffolk issued by the City Auditor* (Boston: 1819–1919). Boston, City of, *Report to the Committee of the City Council Appointed to Obtain the Census of Boston for the Year 1845, Embracing Collateral Facts and Statistical Researches, Illustrating the History and Condition of Population, and Their Means of Progress and Prosperity*, ed. Lemuel Shattuck (Boston, MA: John H. Eastburn, City Printer, 1846).

—, City Council records of the Trustees of the Benjamin Franklin Trust Fund, *c.* 1791– 1902, including Minute Books 1791–1886, and 1893–1902, Account Books. 1791–1898, Copies of Bonds for Fund Borrowers, 1820–7.

—, Registry Department. Records Relating to the Early History of Boston – Document 101 (Boston:1903).

—, 'Franklin Fund', Document 147 (Boston: 1898).

—, 'Message of the Mayor Relative to the Disposition of the Franklin Fund', Document 138 (Boston: 1898).

—, 'Disposition of the Franklin Fund', *The City Record*, 45 (1893), pp. 637–40, 650.

—, 'Remarks of Mayor Quincy at the Opening of the Dover Bath-House', *The City Record*, 42 (1898), pp. 593–7.

—, 'Decision Regarding the Franklin Fund', *The City Record*, 37 (1898), pp. 525–6.

Defoe, D., *The Earlier Life and The Chief Earlier Works of Daniel Defoe*, ed. H. Morley (London: George Routledge and Sons, 1889).

Emerson, G. B., *An Address delivered at the Opening of the Boston Mechanics' Institution, February 7, 1827* (Boston: 1827).

Franklin, B., *My Last Will and Testament dated July 17, 1788 with a Codicil or Addition dated June 3, 1789* (Original in collection of the American Philosophical Society).

—, *The works of Benjamin Franklin,* ed. J. Sparks, 10 vols (Boston, MA: Tappan, Whittemore and Mason, 1840).

—, *The Life of Benjamin Franklin, Written by Himself,* ed. J. Bigelow, 4th edn (Philadelphia, PA: J. B. Lippincott & Co., 1899).

—, *The Works of Benjamin Franklin,*12 vols (New York and London: G.P. Putnam's Sons The Knickerbocker Press, 1904).

—, *The Writings of Benjamin Franklin*, ed. A. H. Smyth, 10 vols (New York: Macmillan, 1905–7).

—, *Benjamin Franklin's Memoirs*, 'Parallel Text Edition' trans. L. Guillaume le Veillard, ed. W. T. Franklin and M. Farrand (Berkeley, CA and Los Angeles, CA: University of California Press, 1949).

—, *Mr. Franklin: A Selection from his Personal Letter*, ed. L. W. Labaree and W. J. Bell Jr (New Haven, CT: Yale University Press, 1956).

—, *The Papers of Benjamin Franklin*, ed. L. W. Labaree and W. J. Bell, 39 vols (New Haven, CT: Yale University Press, 1959), vols 1–30.

—, *The Autobiography of Benjamin Franklin: A Genetic Text*, ed. J. A. Leo Lemay and P. M. Zall (Knoxville, TN: The University of Tennessee Press, 1981).

—, *Benjamin Franklin: Writings*, ed. J. A. Leo Lemay (New York: The Library of America, 1987).

Girard College, *Annual Reports – 1859–69* (Philadelphia, PA: 1859–69).

Hamilton, A., *Papers of Alexander Hamilton*, ed. H. C. Syrett, 26 vols (New York and London: Columbia University Press, 1966).

Jefferson, T., 'Letter to Mrs Cosway dated 12 October 1786, Paris', and 'Letter, Jefferson to James Madison, 6 September 1789' in A. Koch and W. Peden (eds), *The Life and Selected Writings of Thomas Jefferson* (New York: Random House, 1944).

Massachusetts Acts of 1905, Chapter 448.

Massachusetts Acts of 1908, Chapter 569.

Massachusetts Acts of 1927, Chapter 40.

Massachusetts Acts of 1958, Chapter 596.

Massachusetts General Assembly, *Report of the Special Commission Established to Investigate and Study Certain Matters Relating to the Franklin Technical Institute* (Boston, MA: Wright and Potter Printing Co., 1958).

Massachusetts House Bill 5503, 1977.

Massachusetts Supreme Judicial Court, Massachusetts Reports 171, April 1891–August 1898 (Boston, MA: Little, Brown and Company, 1899).

—, Massachusetts Reports 177, October 1900–February 1901 (Boston: Little, Brown and Company, 1901).

—, Massachusetts Reports 184, June 1903–January 1904 (Boston: Little, Brown and Company, 1904).

—, Massachusetts Reports 276, June 1931–January 1931 (Boston: Wright & Potter Printing Co., 1932).

—, Massachusetts Reports 336, May 1957–February 1958 (Boston: Wright & Potter Printing Co., 1958).

—, Massachusetts Reports 340 (Boston: 1960).

—, Massachusetts Reports 344, March 1962–July 1962 (Boston: University Press of Cambridge, Inc., 1963).

—, Massachusetts Reports 374 (Boston: University Press of Cambridge, Inc., 1978).

Mather, C., *Essays to Do Good, Addressed To All Christians, Whether in Public or Private Capacities*, ed. G. Burder (Johnstown, NY: Printed and Sold by Asa Child, 1815).

Mathon De La Cour, C. J., Misc. Correspondence.

Minot, W., *Cash Receipts and Disbursement Journals* (called Day Books), 1835–42, 1847–51, 1851–4, 1855–8, 1858–61, 1861–2, 1863–4 and 1864 (Uncatalogued manuscript, Massachusetts Historical Society).

—, *Diary* – 1837 (Uncategorized manuscript, Massachusetts Historical Society).

—, *General Ledgers*, May, 1811–March, 1837 (Uncatalogued manuscript, Massachusetts Historical Society).

Miscellaneous Pamphlets and Broadsides relating to the Mechanics Interest in Philadelphia.

Necker, J., *A Treatise on the Administration of the Finances of France in three volumes,* trans. T. Mortimer, 3 vols (London: Logographic Press, 1786).

Pennsylvania County Court Reports, 9 Pa. C. C. 484, 1891.

—, 13 Pa. C. C. 241, 1893.

Pennsylvania District Reports, 2 Pa. D. C., 1893.

Pennsylvania State Reports, Supreme Court of Pa. 150 Pa. 437, 1893.

Perkins, W., 'A Treatise of the Vocations or Callings of Men, with Sorts and Kinds of them, and the Right use Thereof', in I. Legatt, *The workes of that Famous and Worthy Minister of Christ in the Universitie of Cambridge, Mr. William Perkins*, 3 vols (London: 1626–31), reprinted in E. S. Morgan (ed.), *Puritan Political Ideas* (Indianapolis, IN: Bobbs-Merril Educational Publishing, 1965).

Philadelphia, City of, *Accounts Ledger, 1791–1868 – Franklin Legacy.*

—, *Bond Book, 1791–1825 – Franklin Legacy.*

—, *Journal, 1791–1870 – Franklin Legacy.*

—, Misc. Pamphlets relating to the Franklin Legacy/Trust.

—, *Report of the Committee on Legacies and Trusts Made in Common Council, Thursday April 27, 1837* (Philadelphia: Printed by L. R. Bailey, 1837).

Philadelphia, City of, Board of Directors of City Trusts, *Annual Reports* 1871–1992.

—, Misc, Correspondence with the Franklin Institute.

—, Petitions to and Final Decrees from Orphans Court Division, Court of Common Pleas of Philadelphia, 1874, 1917, 1939, 1949, 1963, 1966, 1970, 1979.

Price, R., *Observations on the Importance of the American Revolution and the Means of Making it a Benefit to the World. To which is Added, a Letter from M. Turgot ... with an Appendix, Containing a Translation of the will of M. Fortuné Ricard, lately Published in France* (Dublin: Printed for L. White, W. Whitestone, P. Byrne, P. Wogan, J. Cash and R. Marchbank, 1785) Microfilm.

—, Misc. Correspondence to Benjamin Franklin.

—, *Richard Price and the Ethical Foundations of the American Revolution*, ed. B. Peach (Durham, NC: Duke University Press, 1979).

US Commission of Labor, *The Final Report of the Commission on Industrial Relations* (Washington, DC: Government Printing Office, 1915).

—, *The First Annual Report of the Commissioner of Labor, March 1986 – Industrial Depressions* (Washington, DC: Government Printing Office, 1886).

US Department of Labor, *Apprenticeship Training in the 1970's: Report of a Conference*, Manpower Research Monograph No. 37 (Washington, DC: Government Printing Office, 1973).

US House of Representatives, 57th Congress, *Document No. 184, Reports of the Industrial Commission on Immigration ... and Education ...*, vol. 15 (Washington, DC: Government Printing Office, 1901).

US Senate, 64th Congress, *Document No. 415, Industrial Relations: Final Report and Testimony Submitted to Congress by the Commission on Industrial Relations, Vols. 2 and 3* (Washington, DC: Government Printing Office, 1916).

Vaughan, B., Misc. Correspondence to Benjamin Franklin.

Winthrop, J., 'A Model of Christian Charity' (1630), reprinted in E. Morgan (ed.) *Puritan Political Ideas* (Indianapolis, IN: Bobbs-Merrill, 1965), p.75–93

Young Man of Boston, *An Address to the People of Massachusetts on the Justice and Importance of a Law, for the Relief of Insolvent Debtors* (Boston, MA: Printed by Nathaniel Willis, 1813).

Secondary Sources

Abernathy, 'Progressivism 1905–1919', in R. F. Weighley (ed.), *Philadelphia: A 300 Year History* (New York and London: W. W. Norton & Company, 1982), pp. 526–54.

Abrams, R. M., *Conservatism in the Progressive Era: Massachusetts Politics, 1900–1912* (Cambridge, MA: Harvard University Press, 1964).

Adams, H. C., *Public Debts; an essay in the science of finance* (New York: D. Appleton & Co., 1887).

Aldridge, A. O. 'Franklin as Demographer', *Journal of Economic History*, vol. 9 (1949–50), pp. 25–44.

—, *Franklin and His French Contemporaries* (New York: New York University Press, 1957).

Allinson, E. P. and B. Penrose, *Philadelphia 1681–1887: A History of Municipal Development* (Philadelphia, PA: Allen, Lane & Scott, Publishers, 1887).

Armendariz, B., and J. Morduch, *The Economics of Microfinance* (Cambridge, MA: MIT Press, 2007).

Aronowitz, S., *False Promises: The Shaping of American Working Class Consciousness* (New York: McGraw-Hill Book Company, 1973).

Baer, M. F. and E. C. Boeber, *Occupational Information: Its Nature and Use* (Chicago, IL: Science Research Associates, Inc., 1951).

Bakke, E. W., *Citizens Without Work: A Study of the Effects of Unemployment upon the Workers' Social Relations and Practices* (New Haven, CT: Yale University Press,1940).

Baltzell, E. D., *The Protestant Establishment: Aristocracy and Caste in America* (New York: Random House, 1964).

Barber, B. , *Strong Democracy: Participatory Politics for a New Age* (Berkeley, CA: University of California Press, 1984).

Barth, G., *City People: The Rise of Modern City Culture in Nineteenth-Century America* (Oxford: Oxford University Press, 1980).

Beatty, J., *The Rascal King: The Life and Times of James Michael Curley* (Reading, MA: Addison Wesley Publishing Company, 1992).

Beers, D. G., 'The Centennial City, 1865–1876', in R. F., *Philadelphia: A 300 year History* (New York and London: W. W. Norton & Company, 1982), pp. 425–38.

Bemis, E. W., 'Relation of Trades-Unions to Apprentices', *Quarterly Journal of Economics*, 6:1 (1891), p. 76–93.

Berger, M. and L. Goldmark, T. M. Sanabria (eds), *An Inside View of Latin American Microfinance* (Washington, DC: Inter-American Development Bank, 2006).

Bjerkoe, E. H., *The Cabinetmakers of America* (Garden City, NY: Doubleday & Company, Inc., 1957).

Blackstone, W., *Commentaries on the Laws of England, A Facsimile of the First Edition of 1765–1769* (Chicago, IL: University of Chicago Press, 1979).

Blau, P. M. and O. D. Duncan, *The American Occupational Structure* (New York, London and Sydney: John Wiley & Sons, Inc., 1967).

Blodgett, G., *The Gentle Reformers: Massachusetts Democrats in the Cleveland Era* (Cambridge, MA: Harvard University Press, 1966).

Blouin, F. X. Jr, *The Boston Region, 1810–1850: A Study of Urbanization* (Ann Arbor, MI: UMI Research Press, 1978, 1980).

Bolland, S., *The Iron Founder: A Comprehensive Treatise on the Art of Moulding* (New York: John Wiley & Sons, 1906).

Boston, Town of, *Records Relating to the Early History of Boston* vol. 31, Registry Department of the city of Boston, Boston Town Records, 1790.

Bremner, R. H., *American Philanthropy* (Chicago, IL: The University of Chicago Press, 1960).

Bridenbaugh, C., *Cities in the Wilderness: The First Century of Urban Life in America 1625–1742* (New York: Alfred A. Knopf, 1955).

Bristed, J., as quoted by M. V. Brewington, 'Maritime Philadelphia, 1609–1837', *Pennsylvania Magazine of History and Biography*, 63 (1939).

Brown, R., *The Republic in Peril: 1812* (New York and London: W.W. Norton & Company, 1964, 1971).

Bruchey, S., *The Roots of American Economic Growth, 1607–1861* (New York: Harper & Row Publishers, 1968).

Burgess, P. , 'Is Microfinance the Answer to the Missing Middle?', *Microfinance Focus*, 2 January 2010, online posting (no pagination).

Burns, R., *Success in America: The Yeoman Dream and the Industrial Revolution* (Amherst, MA: University of Massachusetts Press, 1976).

Burt, N., and W. E. Davies, 'The Iron Age, 1876–1905', in R. F. Weighley (ed.), *Philadelphia: A 300 Year History* (New York and London: W. W. Norton & Company, 1982), pp. 471–523.

Butterfield, F., 'From Ben Franklin, a Gift that's worth Two Fights (Boston and Philadelphia become Beneficiaries of Benjamin Franklin's Will)', *New York Times*, 21 April 1990, p. 1.

Buxbaum, M. H., *Critical Essays on Benjamin Franklin* (Boston, MA: G. K. Hall & Co., 1987).

Chinoy, E., *Automobile Workers and the American Dream* (Garden City, NY: Doubleday & Company, Inc., 1955).

Christen, R. 'Commercialization and Mission Drift: The Transformation of Microfinance in Latin America', CGAP Occasional Paper Number 5 (2001).

Christie, R. A., *Empire in Wood: A History of the Carpenters' Union* (Ithaca, NY: Cornell University, 1956).

Clark, R. W., *Benjamin Franklin: A Biography* (New York: Random House, 1983).

Clark, V. S., *History of Manufactures in the United States*, 3 vols (New York: McGraw-Hill Book Company, Inc., 1929), vols 1–3.

Commons, J. R., et al. *History of Labour in the United States*, 4 vols (New York: Macmillan, 1918–1935), vol. 1.

Dakin, D., *Turgot and the* Ancien Regime *in France* (New York: Octagon Books, Inc., 1965).

Dalzell, R. F. Jr, *The Enterprising Elite: The Boston Associates and the World They Made* (Cambridge, MA and London: Harvard University Press, 1987).

Dawley, A., *Class and Community: The Industrial Revolution in Lynn* (Cambridge, MA: Harvard University Press, 1976).

Demos, J. and S. S. Boocock (eds), *Turning Points: Historical and Sociological Essays on the Family* (Chicago, IL and London: The University of Chicago Press, 1978). (Published as: Modell, J. Furstenburg, F.F. Jr, and Strong, D., 'The Timing of Marriage in the Transition to Adulthood: Continuity and Change, 1860–1975', *The American Journal of Sociology*, 84: *Supplement: Turning Points: Historical and Sociological Essays on the Family* (1978), pp. S120–S150.

Darling, A. B, *Political Changes in Massachusetts, 1824–1848* (New Haven, CT: Yale University Press, 1925).

Dexter, E. G., *A History of Education in the United States* (New York: Macmillan Company, 1904).

Douglas, P. H., *American Apprenticeship and Industrial Education* (New York: Columbia University, 1921).

Douglas, P. H., C. N. Hitchcock and W. E. Atkins, *The Worker in Modern Economic Society* (Chicago, IL: The University of Chicago Press, 1923).

Dubofsky, M., *Industrialization and the American Worker, 1865–1920* (Arlington Heights, IL: AHM Publishing Corporation, 1975).

Dubrow, E. and R. Dubrow, *American Furniture of the 19th Century 1840–1880* (Exton, PA: Schiffer Publishing, Ltd., 1983).

Dunlop, O. J. and R. D. Denman, *English Apprenticeship and Child Labour: A History* (New York: The Macmillan Company, 1912).

Duvoisin, M., 'Goode is Said to Enlist Academics on Franklin Fund Use', *Philadelphia Inquirer*, 26 January 1990, p. 4B.

Eisenmenger, R. W., *The Dynamics of Growth in New England's Economy, 1870–1964* (Middletown, CT: Wesleyan University Press, 1967).

Eliot, C. W., 'The New Education', in R. Hofstadter and W. Smith, *American Higher Education: A Documentary History*, 2 vols (Chicago, IL: The University of Chicago Press, 1961), vol. 2, pp. 624–41.

Enda, J., 'Franklin's Will Splits Legislature, House Plans Gift To Organizations', *Philadelphia Inquirer*, 2 October 1990, p. B01.

Epstein, K. and G. Smith, 'Compartamos: From Nonprofit to Profit', *Business Week*, 13 December 2007.

Faler, P. G., *Mechanics and Manufacturers in the Early Industrial Revolution: Lynn, Massachusetts, 1780–1860* (Albany, NY: State University of New York Press, 1981).

Fee, E. M., *The Origin and Growth of Vocational Industrial Education in Philadelphia to 1917* (Philadelphia, PA: Westbrook Publishing Company, 1938).

Ferguson, R. A., 'The Girard Will Case: Charity and Inheritance in the City of Brotherly Love', in J. Saltzman (ed.), *Philanthropy and American Society* (New York: Columbia University, 1987), pp. 1–16.

Ferrick, T. Jr, 'Ben Franklin's Bequest has put Two Cities to the Test', *Philadelphia Inquirer*, 25 October 1987, p. 22A.

—, 'Franklin's Gift: What Now?', *The Philadelphia Inquirer*, 10 November 1987, p. 22A.

—, 'Some Fear Franklin's Fund Will be Philadelphia's Folly', *Philadelphia Enquirer*, 14 January 1990, p. 1A.

—, 'City Rethinking its Use of $500,000 Franklin Fund', *The Philadelphia Enquirer*, 18 January 1990, p. 3B.

Foner, E., *Free Soil, Free Labor, Free Men: The Ideology of the Republican Party before the Civil War* (London: Oxford University Press, 1970).

—, *Tom Paine and Revolutionary America* (London: Oxford University Press, 1976).

Forbes, E., *Paul Revere & the World He Lived In* (Boston, MA: Houghton Mifflin Company, 1942).

Formisano, R. P., *The Transformation of Political Culture: Massachusetts Parties, 1790's–1840's* (New York: Oxford University Press, 1983).

Formisano, R. P., and C. K. Burns, *Boston 1700–1980: The Evolution of Urban Politics* (Westport, CT and London: Greenwood Press, 1984).

Foster, B.F., *The Clerk's Guide, etc.* (Boston, MA: Perkins and Marvin, 1837).

Foulke, R. A., *The Sinews of American Commerce* (New York: Dun & Bradstreet, Inc., 1941).

Fox, R., 'The John Scott Medal', *Proceedings of the American Philosophical Society*, 5.113: 6 (1968), pp. 416–30.

Franklin Foundation, *The Franklin Institute: A Living Legacy*, published but undated (c.1983).

—, *Financial Statements and Statistics, June 30, 1989*, audit report by Peat Marwick Main & Co., 31 August 1989.

Fremont-Smith, M. R., *Foundations and Government: State and Federal Law Supervision* (New York: Russell Sage Foundation, 1965).

Gladden, W., *Working People and Their Employers* (New York: Funk and Wagnalls Co., 1894).

Groenewegen, P. D., *The Economics of A. R. J. Turgot* (The Hauge: Martinus Nijhoff, 1977).

Guérard, A., *France: A Modern History* (Ann Arbor, MI: The University of Michigan Press, 1959).

Hale, E. E. and E. E. Hale, Jr, *Franklin in France* (Boston, MA: Roberts Brothers, 1887). Hall, P. D., *The Organization of American Culture, 1700–1900: Private Institutions, Elites, and the Origins of American Nationality* (New York: New York University Press, 1982).

Ham, C. H., *Manual Training: The Solution of Social and Industrial Problems* (New York: Harper & Brothers, 1886).

Hamilton, R., *An Inquiry Concerning the Rise and Progress, the Redemption and Present State and the Management of the National Debt of Great Britain* Microcard, Early American Imprints, Second Series No. 37786 (Philadelphia: Published and Sold by M. Carey, 1813).

Handlin, O., *Boston's Immigrants, 1790–1880* (Cambridge, MA and London: The Belknap Press, 1941, 1991).

Harris, R. D., *Necker: Reform Statesman of the* Ancien Regime (Berkeley, CA: University of California Press, 1979).

Hart, A. B., *Commonwealth History of Massachusetts* (New York: The States History Company, 1930).

Hazard, B. E., *The Organization of the Boot and Shoe Industry in Massachusetts before 1875* (Cambridge, MA: Harvard University Press, 1921).

Heim, K., 'Making a Profit while helping the Poor', *Seattle Times*, 29 April 2007.

Hoefer, J., *Nouvelle Biographie Générale*, 46 vols (Paris: Firmin Didot, 1861).

Hofstadter, R. and W. Smith, *American Higher Education: A Documentary History*, 2 vols (Chicago, IL: The University of Chicago Press, 1961), vol. 2.

Huber, R. M, *The American Idea of Success* (New York: McGraw-Hill Book Company, 1971).

Hulock, H., 'Ben's Bequest', 5 May 1987, *Boston Globe Magazine*, pp. 17, 36–8, 43–6, 52.

Husock, H. 'Ben's Bequest', *Boston Globe*, 7 May 1989, p. 37

Huthmacher, J. J., *Massachusetts People and Politics, 1919–1933* (New York: Atheneum, 1969).

Jaher, F. C. (ed.), *The Age of Industrialism in America: Essays in Social Structure and Cultural Values* (New York: The Free Press, 1968).

Kaelble, H., *Social Mobility in the 19th and 20th Centuries: Europe and America in Comparative Perspective* (New York: St Martin's Press, 1986). Kahler, A. and E. Hamburger, *Education for an Industrial Age* (Ithaca, NY and New York: Cornell University Press, 1948).

Ketcham, R. L., (ed.), *The Political Thought of Benjamin Franklin* (Indianapolis, IN: The Bobb-Merrill Company, Inc., 1965).

—, *Benjamin Franklin* (New York: Washington Square Press, 1966).

—, *Presidents Above Parties: The First American Presidency, 1789–1829* (Chapel Hill, NC: The University of North Carolina Press, 1984).

— (ed.), *The Anti-Federalist Papers and the Constitutional Convention Debates* (New York: The New American Library, 1986).

Kirker, H. and J. Kirker, *Bulfinch's Boston, 1787–1817* (New York: Oxford University Press, 1964).

Kirkland, E. C., *Industry Comes of Age: Business, Labor, and Public Policy 1860–1897* (Chicago, IL: Quadrangle Books, Inc., 1967).

Knights, P. R., *The Plain People of Boston, 1830–1860: A Study in city Growth* (New York: Oxford University Press, 1971).

—, *Yankee Destinies: The Lives of Ordinary Nineteenth-Century Bostonians* (Chapel Hill, NC and London: The University of North Carolina Press, 1991).

Krooss, H. E. and M. R. Blyn, *A History of Financial Intermediaries* (New York: Random House, 1971).

Kulikoff, A., 'The Progress of Inequality in Revolutionary Boston', *William and Mary Quarterly*, 28:3 (1971), pp. 375–412.

Kutner, L., *Legal Aspects of Charitable Trusts and Foundations: A Guide for Philanthropoids* (New York: Commerce Clearing House Inc., 1970).

Laurie, B., *Working People of Philadelphia, 1800–1850* (Philadelphia, PA: Temple University Press, 1980).

Ledgerwood, J., *Microfinance Handbook: An Institutional and Financial Perspective* (Washington, DC: The World Bank, 2001).

Lemay, L. (ed.), *Reappraising Benjamin Franklin* (Cranbury, NJ: Associated University Presses, 1993).

Link, E. P., *Democratic Republican Societies, 1790–1800* (New York: Octagon Books, 1973 and 1942).

Litwack, L., *The American Labor Movement* (Englewood Cliffs, NJ: Prentice-Hall, Inc., 1962).

Livesay, H. C., *Andrew Carnegie and the Risk of Big Business* (Boston, MA and Toronto: Little Brown and Company, 1975).

Lopez, C. A. and E. W. Herbert, *The Private Franklin: The Man and His Family* (New York: W. W. Norton & Company, 1975).

Lopez, C. A., *Mon Cher Papa: Franklin and the Ladies of France* (New Haven, CT: Yale University Press, 1966).

Mann, A., *Yankee Reformers in the Urban Age* (Cambridge, MA: The Belknap Press of Harvard University Press, 1954).

Martineau, H., *Society in America* (London: Saunders and Otley, Conduit Street, 1837; reprinted New York: AMS Press, Inc., 1966).

McCleary, S. F., 'The Franklin Fund', *Proceedings of the Massachusetts Historical Society*, October, 1897, p. 24.

McCoy, D. R., 'Benjamin Franklin's Vision of a Republican Political Economy for America', *The William and Mary Quarterly*, 35:4 (1978), pp. 605–28.

—, *The Elusive Republic: Political Economy in Jeffersonian America* (New York and London: W. W. Norton & Company, 1980).

McGrane, R. C., *The Panic of 1837: Some Financial Problems of the Jacksonian Era* (New York: Russell & Russell, 1965).

Mease, J., *The Picture of Philadelphia, etc.* (Philadelphia, PA: B. & T. Kite, 1811).

Minot, W., *William Minot* (Boston, MA: David Clapp & Sons, Printers, 1873–1900).

Montesquieu, C., *The Spirit of the Laws*, trans. and ed. A. M. Cohler, et. al., (Cambridge: Cambridge University Press, 1989).

Montgomery, D., *The Fall of the House of Labor: The Workplace, the State and American Labor Activism, 1865–1925* (Cambridge, MA: Cambridge University Press, 1989).

Motley, J. M., *Apprenticeship in American Trade Unions* , (Lancaster, PA: The Johns Hopkins Press, 1907).

Nash, G. B., *The Urban Crucible: Social Change, Political Consciousness, and the Origins of the American Revolution* (Cambridge, MA: Harvard University Press, 1979).

National Cyclopædia of American Biography, 33 (1947), pp. 198–9.

Norton, T. L., *Trade-Union Policies in the Massachusetts Shoe Industry 1919–1929* (New York: Columbia University Press, 1932).

—, *Education for Work* (New York and London: The McGraw Hill Book Company, Inc., 1938).

Olton, C. S., *Artisans for Independence: Philadelphia Mechanics and the American Revolution* (Syracuse, NY: Syracuse University Press, 1975).

Otto, C. J., *American Furniture of the Nineteenth Century* (New York: The Viking Press, 1965).

Palmer, G. L., *Philadelphia Workers in a Changing Economy* (Philadelphia, PA: University of Pennsylvania Press, 1956).

Panschar, W. G., *Baking in America, - Vol. I: Economic Development* (Evanston, IL: Northwestern University Press, 1956).

Pease, W. H. and J. H. Pease, *The Web of Progress: Private Values and Public Styles in Boston and Charleston, 1828–1843* (New York: Oxford University Press, 1985).

Philadelphia Bar Association, *In Memoriam, Clement B. Penrose, 1832–1911* (Philadelphia, PA: Palmer-Goodman, 1911).

Phillips, H. Jr, *Historical Sketches of the Paper Currency of The American Colonies Prior to the Adoption of the Federal Constitution* (Roxbury, MA: Printed for W. Elliot Woodward, 1865).

Porter, G. and H. C. Livesay, *Merchants and Manufacturers: Studies in the Changing Structure of Nineteenth-Century Marketing* (Baltimore, MD and London: The Johns Hopkins Press, 1971).

Pritchett, Dr H. S., 'The Story of the Franklin Fund' presented 17 January 1906 (Boston, MA: printed by the Members of the Franklin Foundation, 1956).

Quimby, I. M. G. (ed.), *The Craftsman in Early America* (New York: W. W. Norton & Company, 1984).

Quincy, J., *A Municipal History of the Town of Boston during Two Centuries from September 17, 1630, to September 17, 1830* (Boston, MA: Charles C. Little and James Brown, 1852).

Resendes, M., 'Franklin's Largess Has Long Reach', *The Boston Globe*, 17 April 1990, pp. 15, 17.

Retail Shoe Salesmen's Institute, Boston, *Shoemaking* (Boston: Retail Shoe Salesmen's Institute, 1920).

Rhyne, E., *Microfinance for Bankers and Investors* (New York: McGraw Hill, 2009).

Richardson, E. P., 'The Athens of America, 1800–1825', in R. F. Weighley (ed.), *Philadelphia: A 300 Year History* (New York and London: W. W. Norton & Company, 1982), pp. 208–57.

Rock, H. B., *Artisans of the New Republic: The Tradesmen of New York in The Age of Jefferson* (New York: New York University Press, 1979).

Robinson, M., *The Microfinance Revolution* (Washington, DC; The World Bank, 2001).

Rorabaugh, W. J., *The Craft Apprentice: From Franklin to the Machine Age in America* (New York and Oxford: Oxford University Press, 1986).

Row, R. K., *The Educational Meaning of Manual Arts and Industries* (Chicago, IL: Row, Peterson and Company, 1909).

Ryerson, R. A., *The Revolution is Now Begun: The Radical Committees of Philadelphia, 1765–1776* (Philadelphia, PA: University of Pennsylvania Press, 1978).

Salinger, S. V., 'Artisans, Journeymen, and the Transformation of Labor in Late Eighteenth-Century Philadelphia', *William and Mary Quarterly*, 40:1 (1983), pp. 62–84.

Saltzman, J. (ed.), *Philanthropy and American Society: selected papers* (New York: Columbia University, 1987).

Sanger, C. P., 'The Fair Number of Apprentices in a Trade', *The Economic Journal*, 5:20 (1895), pp. 616–36.

Schiesl, M. J., *The Politics of Efficiency: Municipal Administration and Reform in America: 1880–1920* (Berkeley, CA, Los Angeles, CA and London: University of California Press, 1977).

Scharf, J. T. and T. Wescott, *History of Philadelphia, 1609–1884*, 3 vols (Philadelphia, PA: L. H. Everts and Co., 1884).

Schoenbrun, D., *Triumph in Paris: The Exploits of Benjamin Franklin* (New York: Harper & Row, Publishers, 1976).

Siegel, A., *Living Legacy: A History of the Franklin Institute of Boston* (Boston, MA: Franklin Foundation, 1993).

Sikes, G. C., 'The Apprentice System in the Building Trades', *The Journal of Political Economy*, 2:3 (1894), pp.397–423.

Sinclair, B., *Philadelphia's Philosopher Mechanics: A History of the Franklin Institute 1824–1865* (Baltimore, MD: Johns Hopkins University Press, 1974).

Siracusa, C., *A Mechanical People: Perceptions of the Industrial Order in Massachusetts, 1815–1880* (Middletown, CT: Wesleyan University Press, 1979).

Smith, B. G., *The 'Lower Sort': Philadelphia's Laboring People, 1750–1800* (Ithaca, NY Cornell University Press, 1990).

Smith, P., and E. Thurman, *A Billion Bootstraps* (New York: McGraw Hill, 2007).

Steffen, C. G., *The Mechanics of Baltimore: Workers and Politics in the Age of Revolution 1763–1812* (Urbana, IL and London: University of Illinois Press, 1984).

Stourzh, G., *Benjamin Franklin and American Foreign Policy*, 2nd edn (Chicago, IL and London: The University of Chicago Press, 1954 and 1969).

Tager, J. and J. W. Ifkovic (eds), *Massachusetts in the Gilded Age: Selected Essays* (Amherst, MA: The University of Massachusetts Press, 1985).

Tawney, R. H., *Religion and the Rise of Capitalism: A Historical Study* (Gloucester, MA: Peter Smith, 1962).

Thernstrom, S., *Poverty and Progress: Social Mobility in a Nineteenth Century City* (Cambridge, MA: Harvard University Press, 1964).

—, *The Other Bostonians: Poverty and Progress in the American Metropolis, 1880–1970* (Cambridge, MA: Harvard University Press, 1973).

Thomas, D. O., *The Honest Mind: The Thought and Work of Richard Price* (Oxford: Oxford University Press, 1977).

Thwing, C. F., *Higher Education in America* (New York: D. Appleton and Co., 1906).

Tinkham, M. B., 'Depression and War 1929–1946', R. F. Weighley (ed.), *Philadelphia: A 300 Year History* (New York and London: W. W. Norton & Company, 1982), pp. 601–48.

Tourtellot, A. B., *Benjamin Franklin, The Shaping of Genius: The Boston Years* (Garden City, NY: Doubleday, 1977).

Tuckerman, J., 'An Essay on the Wages Paid to Females for Their Labour in the Form of a Letter, From a Gentleman in Boston to his Friend in Philadelphia', in D. J. Rothman and S. M. Rothman (eds), *Low Wages and Great Sins: Two Antebellum American Views on Prostitution and the Working Girl* (New York and London: Garland Publishing, Inc., 1987), pp.25–6.

Van Doren, C., *Benjamin Franklin* (New York: Viking Press, 1938).

Volkov, S., *The Rise of Popular Antimodernism in Germany: The Urban Master Artisans, 1873–1896* (Princeton, NJ: Princeton University Press, 1978).

Warner, S. B., Jr, *The Private City: Philadelphia in the Three Periods of Its Growth* (Philadelphia, PA: University of Pennsylvania Press, 1968).

Warner, W. L. and J. O. Low, *The Social System of the Modern Factory - The Strike: A Social Analysis* (New Haven, CT and London: Yale University Press, 1947).

Weighley, R. F. (ed.), *Philadelphia: A 300 year History* (New York and London: W. W. Norton & Company, 1982).

White, G. T., *Massachusetts Hospital Life Insurance Company* (Cambridge, MA: Harvard University Press, 1955).

Wickersham, J. P., *A History of Education in Pennsylvania* (Lancaster, PA: Inquirer Publishing Company, 1886).

Wiebe, R. H., *The Search for Order, 1877–1920* (New York: Hill and Wang, 1967).

Wilentz, S., *Chants Democratic: New York City & the Rise of the American Working Class, 1788–1850* (New York and Oxford: Oxford University Press, 1984).

Williams, M. T., 'Urban Reform in the Gilded Age: The Public Baths of Boston', in J. Trager and J. W. Ifkovic (eds), *Massachusetts in the Gilded Age: selected essays* (Amherst, MA: University of Massachusetts Press, 1985).

Windsor, J. (ed.), *The Memorial History of Boston, Including Suffolk County, Massachusetts, 1630–1880,* 4 vols (Boston, MA: James R. Osgood and Company, 1882),

Winter, J. M., (ed.). *R.H Tawney: The American Labour Movement and Other Essays* (New York: St Martin's Press, 1979).

Winthrop, R.C., *Proceedings of the Massachusetts Historical Society*, Vol. 13, (Boston, MA: Massachusetts Historical Society, 1873 - 1875).

Wood, G. S., *The Radicalism of the American Revolution: How a Revolution Transformed A Monarchial Society into a Democratic One Unlike Any That Had ever Existed* (New York: Alfred A. Knopf, 1992).

Woodward, C. M., *The Manual Training School* (Boston, MA: D. C. Health & Co., 1887).

Wright, C. D., *The Industrial Evolution of the United States* (New York: Flood and Vincent, Chautauqua Century Press, 1895).

Wright, C. E., *Massachusetts and the New Nation* (Boston, MA: Massachusetts Historical Society, 1992).

Wright, E., *Franklin of Philadelphia* (Cambridge, MA and London: The Belknap Press of Harvard University Press, 1986).

Wright, R. E., *The First Wall Street: Chestnut Street, Philadelphia, and the Birth of American Finance* (Chicago, IL: Chicago University Press 2005).

Wright, R. E., and D. Cowen, *Financial Founding Fathers: The Men Who Made America Rich* (Chicago, IL: Chicago University Press 2006).

—, *One Nation Under Debt: Hamilton, Jefferson, and the History of What We Owe* (New York: McGraw-Hill, 2008).

Wright, S. L., *The Story of the Franklin Institute* (Philadelphia, PA: The Franklin Institute, 1938).

Yunus, M., and K. Weber, *Creating a World Without Poverty* (New York: Public Affairs, 2007).

Zuckerman, M., 'Doing Good While Doing Well', *Reappraising Benjamin Franklin*, ed. L. Lemay (Cranbury, NJ: Associated University Presses, 1993)

INDEX

For Product Safety Concerns and Information please contact our EU representative GPSR@taylorandfrancis.com
Taylor & Francis Verlag GmbH, Kaufingerstraße 24, 80331 München, Germany

www.ingramcontent.com/pod-product-compliance
Ingram Content Group UK Ltd.
Pitfield, Milton Keynes, MK11 3LW, UK
UKHW020157260926
475702UK00047B/546

* 9 7 8 1 8 4 8 9 3 0 3 4 6 *